Leadership
and Change
in Special Education

Leadership
and Change
in Special Education

Leonard C. Burrello
INDIANA UNIVERSITY

Daniel D. Sage
SYRACUSE UNIVERSITY

Prentice-Hall, Inc., Englewood Cliffs, New Jersey 07632

Library of Congress Cataloging in Publication Data

BURRELLO, LEONARD C., 1942–
  Leadership and change in special education.

  (Prentice-Hall series in special education)
  Includes bibliographical references and index.
  1. Handicapped children—Education—United
States.   I. Sage, Daniel D., joint author.
II. Title.
LC4031.B84   371.9′0973   78-6792
ISBN   0-13-526921-0

PRENTICE-HALL SERIES IN SPECIAL EDUCATION
William M. Cruickshank, Series Editor

Printed in the United States of America

10   9   8   7   6   5   4   3   2

PRENTICE-HALL INTERNATIONAL, INC., *London*
PRENTICE-HALL OF AUSTRALIA PTY. LIMITED, *Sydney*
PRENTICE-HALL OF CANADA, LTD., *Toronto*
PRENTICE-HALL OF INDIA PRIVATE LIMITED,*New Delhi*
PRENTICE-HALL OF JAPAN, INC., *Tokyo*
PRENTICE-HALL OF SOUTHEAST ASIA PTE. LTD., *Singapore*
WHITEHALL BOOKS LIMITED, *Wellington, New Zealand*

To Doris and Sheila
who gave much of themselves
to allow us to give
to others.

Contents

Preface

The process of educating *all* children has become legitimate through the growing public awareness that a significant number of children have been denied the right to an education. The era of banishment to a life within institutions or within their parents' homes without access to a free, publicly supported educational program has ended. Numerous court decisions and an organized lobby of parents and professional practitioners concerned with the welfare of children with specialized learning needs have led to the securing of mandatory special education legislation that requires equal educational opportunities for all children for the first time in our history.

This new and pervasive impetus has caused leadership personnel in general and special education to assess the implications of these new mandates for human services. Some of the implications have resulted in requiring a new partnership between general and special educators. Program definition and identification for the large groups of mildly handicapped, mentally retarded, learning disabled, and emotionally disturbed children demand a renegotiation of responsibilities between general and special educators for planning, implementation, and evaluation. For the more severely handicapped, many are the responsibility of the public schools for the first time. New technologies, new measurement devices, new criteria, and some newly trained personnel are needed. Continued cooperation with other human service agencies outside the schools for serving the severely handicapped is necessary. This will be the confirming leadership challenge facing the special education leadership into the 1980s.

These changes and new programs will not occur without changing funding priorities or new monies appropriated to meet the identified needs. Many policy makers and leadership personnel administering these new programs will demand new information. Alternatives will be needed that attend to rising personnel costs and potential consequences of adding these new programs on to existing programs and services.

The need to know what should be done, how it should be accomplished, who should implement the programs, how and what criteria should be established for evaluation of programs, and many other important questions will have an impact upon professional educators. In this volume we will be addressing the role of and relationship between leadership personnel within general and special education at the local, regional, and state levels who will deal with these and related questions.

It is our intent to provide a historical backdrop to the special education role in the schools, especially for the general educator readers, so that they might follow the evolution of the changing contribution and development of this subsystem of education. For the special educator, this backdrop should provide both a baseline for change and a frame of reference for further changes. It should also provide some insights into which strategies and tactics should either be terminated, modified, or continued in the pursuit of equal educational opportunity for all handicapped persons.

Special education leadership personnel will be offered a conceptual framework and an organizational structure that can either be adopted, adapted, or integrated in part in their own district and building programs. Certainly a process for negotiating a relationship with general education leadership personnel will be described. Other special education personnel may gain perspective regarding how organizational change occurs and regarding alternative role expectations that they may want to incorporate in their own practice.

At this juncture in the evolution of special education, we hope to identify the forces facilitating and hindering the mandate for change. Within this context, we will provide a redefinition of special education's place within the larger system of education utilizing a conceptual framework that offers us guidance in choosing the direction. We will specify alternative organizational models complete with clear role definitions and functions that facilitate the creation of new mechanisms of collaborative goal-setting, problem-solving, and decision-making between general and special educators. Finally, we will generate what we consider desirable characteristics of programs directed toward the leadership training of pre-service and in-service personnel. We will also offer testable hypotheses to guide future researchers toward determining the validity and reliability of our assumptions contained with a suggested conceptual framework.

As we begin this exploration of our leadership history, we should begin by acknowledging the contribution of many state and local leaders who, with many parents and professionals in universities and colleges, have developed a comprehensive system of educational services for the handicapped. Their greatest contribution for tomorrow's leaders is probably their spirit and commitment to enhance the lives of children who differ.

Given the leadership challenges before us then, we have listed the assumptions that guide our work. First, a study of the role of special education within general education suggests that a theory of leadership and administration within a social system perspective will assist the reader in understanding the dynamic elements of human behavior within organizations. Second, we presently view special education as a subsystem of education that is fragmented while entering into a new phase of its development without a conceptual framework to guide its future. Third, we view special education's leadership role within a generic concept of leadership and administration, not as one restricted to a specialized, technical set of concepts and practices which justify separate disciplinary status. This status has been our enigma. While it has served us *well* in the short-term, we must begin to demonstrate how our models, strategies, and techniques can be used to serve the needs of all children and our professional colleagues in the larger system of education. Fourth, we must continue to seize the initiative to redefine our role within the larger system of education by generating new vehicles for collaborative involvement.

1

Leadership Challenge in a Changing Special Education Social System

INTRODUCTION

The leadership challenge in special education intensified with the enactment of Public Law 94-142. Guaranteeing equal educational opportunity for all, there still are great disparities between the statutory mandate to provide for the education of *all* children and the actual level of current service delivery. This federal legislative victory was acquired through the combined efforts of parents and professionals. They succeeded in establishing recognition and support for equal benefits under law for handicapped children.

Much has been learned from the struggle for recognition. During the state by state push for mandatory legislation and class action suits, special educators found themselves in a political coalition with other disenfranchised populations in the larger community. Ethnic and cultural minorities, women, and the poor were inextricably woven by a common bond—the need for equal opportunity under law. Each was excluded by subtle and more obvious means from equal participation in community life, employment, public facility accessibility, educational programs and services, housing, and medical care. Each had to employ unusual economic and social sanctions to gain attention and a place on the public agenda. The community sense of social justice and concern for all had to be confronted. The various groups had to deal with the slow assimilation process that follows major litigation and legislation. They found that the courts do not know

1

how to provide essential and appropriate program components. The courts shied away from spelling out assessment packages, weighting placement criteria, or determining the amount of integration versus separation necessary for educating handicapped children. They also found that the courts cannot monitor any but the most obvious violations of newly passed legislation or violations of the subsequent rules and regulations guiding the law's implementation. Finally, each group of petitioners found the public agenda filled with other requests for redress that were eventually ordered from available funds in terms of the amount of visibility and the sense of outrage the issue generated in the community. For special educators, the future agenda then will be to reduce the great discrepancies between statutory mandate and the actual level of current service delivery.

Now as parents and professionals continue to work for full implementation of the equal educational opportunity mandate, there appear to be two major divisions developing within the handicapped: the mildly handicapped and the severely handicapped. While the categorical emphasis is far from diminishing in professional and parent associations and on university campuses, the major leadership challenge in the future will be the organization of public school programs and services for these two major divisions of the handicapped. The nature of the programs and services will be distinguished by the amount of insulation versus integration that educators and parents believe is necessary. Public school leadership, as well as the community agencies of mental health, social services, vocational rehabilitation, and public health, will also be challenged to examine eligibility criteria, the type and level of services, costs, monitoring procedures, and their individual and collective advocacy activities in order to provide comprehensive services for handicapped persons. All public human service agencies will be forced to cooperate resources more efficiently. Both public accountability and limited fiscal resources will require a more interdependent attitude and commitment.

The major dilemma confronting special educators will be to redefine themselves as something other than disciplinary specialists, distinctive and separate from their regular education colleagues, in the management and instruction of the handicapped. In order to increase regular education's accountability for this group of children, special educators must share and, in many instances, give the responsibility for management and instruction of this group to their regular education counterparts. Special educators must support regular administrators and teachers in this new endeavor. It is incumbent upon special educators to demonstrate their value through the application of their accumulated research and practice in the regular classroom. By modeling the application of their learnings to the world of the teacher's classroom, increased credibility and utility of special education in schools will be attained.

Before moving to a detailed presentation of the forces that will shape the future agenda of special education leadership, the authors believe two major sets

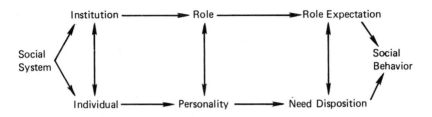

Figure 1-1. The Normative and Personal Dimensions of Social Behavior. *Reprinted with permission from J. W. Getzels and E. G. Guba,* School Review *(1957), 65, 429.*

of concepts about social systems and leadership will enhance the reader's application of leadership strategies to the future of special education.

A SOCIAL SYSTEM PERSPECTIVE

The original model describing educational administration as a social process was developed by Getzels and Guba[1], and was later expanded by Getzels, Lipham, and Campbell.[2] The original model is presented in Figure 1–1. The model is composed of two classes of phenomena, the normative and the personal. Each component interacts with the other to produce observed social behavior in a specific social system.

The first class of phenomena has been described as a normative or nomothetic dimension that considers the institution's goals, role, and role expectations; each term serves as the analytical unit to determine the preceding. Briefly, these three terms are described in the following fashion: the *institution* is composed of people who have been structurally organized into *roles* that are normative in nature and maintained within prescribed parameters. In order to insure the attainment of institutional goals and objectives, role incumbents are given specific *expectations* to fulfill.

The second class of phenomena, described as the personal or idiographic dimension, also contains analytical units, each term being defined by the previous one. The units are the individual, his/her personality, and his/her need dispositions. In the personal dimension, the *individual*, like the institution, consists

[1]Jacob W. Getzels and Egon G. Guba, "Social Behavior and the Administrative Process," *School Review* 65, (1957), pp. 423–44.

[2]Jacob W. Getzels, James M. Lipham, and Roald F. Campbell, *Educational Administration as Social Process* (New York: Harper & Row, 1968).

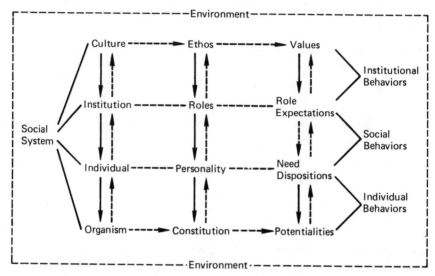

Figure 1-2. General Model of the Major Dimensions in Behavior in a Social System. *Reprinted with permission from J. W. Getzels, J. Lipham, and R. E. Campbell,* Educational Administration as a Social Process *(New York: Harper & Row, 1968), p. 105.*

of his/her component parts—in this case, personality and need dispositions. The *personality* is conceived in a dynamic fashion; the individual is not considered a passive actor but rather an active and stimulus-seeking person. *Need dispositions* are conceived as the forces within the individual.[3]

Getzels, Lipham and Campbell,[4] have adapted the basic model to include a series of generic factors on both the normative and personal dimensions to give a social system perspective. A model with all its dimensions is presented in Figure 1–2.

The generic factors which provide the basis for institutions and individuals are drawn from cultural anthropology, sociology, and biology. On the personal dimension, Getzels, Lipham and Campbell,[5] note the conspicuous need to acknowledge the biological nature of individuals. They contend that individual behavior can be viewed as separate and distinct from social behavior. Individual behavior is based on physical and psychological characteristics and dispositions. If the environment could be held constant, individual behavior would still vary in part due to inherent constitutional differences in individuals. In Figure 1–2 they depict this dimension in terms of organism, constitution, and potentialities which

---

[3]Leonard C. Burrello, "Research and Theory in Special Education Administration," in *The First Review of Special Education*, eds. L. Mann and D. Sabatino 2 (Philadelphia, Pa: Buttonwood Farms, 1973), pp. 229–60.

[4]Getzels, Lipham and Campbell, *Educational Administration*, p. 105.

[5]Getzels, Lipham and Campbell, *Educational Administration*, pp. 89–104.

are the corresponding forces tied to each of the individual dimensions in the general model. When these two strata interact, they represent observed individual behavior.

On the normative dimension of the model, the generic factors are represented by anthropological variables: culture, ethos, and values. These factors determine the context and focus of the institutional need, development, and support. Shifts in the culture and its ethos (or beliefs) occur very slowly. The values derived from the cultural context are more readily apparent and susceptible to change. The culture, represented by the values held by its constituents, sets the basic parameters of all institutions in a society. In the figure, this dimension is depicted in terms of culture, ethos, and values which are the corresponding forces tied to the institution, roles, and role expectations on the normative side. When these two strata interact, they represent observed institutional behavior in the general model.

Special Education as a Social System

The social system model was selected as the basis for conceptualizing special education as a distinctive subsystem within the larger social system of public school education. Both must be understood in the context of the larger society and its many social, economic, legal, and human service systems. For our purposes, the authors of the expanded model contend that it is legitimate to study administrative behavior within the context of a social system since it is, "in the analysis of administrative behavior, applicable regardless of the level or magnitude of the system under consideration."[6]

The nomothetic or normative dimension, for example, shows the cultural representatives (federal and state legislators) as having an ethos of a fundamental right to educate all citizens. The ethos is translated into values such as the maximum normalization of educational experiences for even the most deviant child. Ethos and value have been transformed into legal mandates that are shaping institutional expectations.

The leadership challenge in special education is twofold: (1) to define the parameters of the handicapped population and the types of programs and services available to them, and (2) to develop the capacity of the larger social system of education to provide equal and appropriate educational opportunity in the least restrictive environment for all handicapped children.

With the first challenge, special educators and their constituencies will continue to serve as the designated representatives of the larger social educational system in order to negotiate the parameters of public services to the handicapped. Any new milestones and fiscal gains achieved by education's professional and

---

[6]Getzels, Lipham and Campbell, *Educational Administration*, p. 55.

parent coalition may affect other public service agency development and support. Public, mental health, and vocational rehabilitation agencies also have responsibilities to provide for the handicapped. While they have not been actively seeking to expand their responsibilities for the handicapped, they nonetheless have mandates to participate in the development and training of the handicapped. Comprehensive services demand a cooperative attitude and commitment, rather than continuing competition in a time of scarcity. Special educators and their supporters must foster the integration of comprehensive programs and services rather than their fragmentation. An interagency coalition will be needed to adequately serve the severely handicapped and, to a lesser degree, to serve the more mildly disabled child.

While negotiating with external agencies, special educators must also continue to work within decision-making bodies in the public schools so that the schools may reaffirm their commitment to the most severely handicapped. This commitment must be demonstrated with financial support and guaranteed access to the most normalized environments in the schools. The support of the entire district or consortium of districts should be called upon to endorse equal educational opportunity for this newly acquired group of constituents.

With the second major challenge, special educators face the fundamental organization and definition of special education in the schools. In order to effectively provide for the least restrictive environment for all handicapped children, from the most handicapped to the least, special educators must demonstrate how *all children* will benefit and can be managed within schools. This demands new goals and targets for intervention. The individual class teacher, the teacher's union, building administrators, supervisors, superintendents, and board members must actively share in the education of all handicapped children. Increasing the accountability of all those engaged in education will be necessary before any significant movement will occur in the status of special education (now a subsystem operating in a dependent fashion within the larger social system of schools).

The prevailing institutional norm of a separate and distinct special education structure is slowly changing under the influence of the new legal mandates. New institutional expectations will be reflected in policy statements that the leaders in education will be expected to implement. Role incumbents in leadership positions will be expected to help other members of the public school organization to design and develop alternatives to the current separate categorical programs for the handicapped child.

On the idiographic or individual dimension of the general model, different classes of people, such as special education administrators and principals, each socialized into different roles, retain their unique personalities based upon their inherent constitution (biological and psychological aspects) and needs. Their individual differences are expressed in different professional aspirations, competencies, and needs for recognition, status, and affiliation. These differences cause a reaction to new roles and expectations derived from new institutional imperatives such as mainstreaming and case conferences.

In spite of these individual differences, organizational members are also conditioned by the same general environmental forces that shape institutional norms. Given the conflicting forces of a changing special education social system, many special educators will now confront their personal behavior in light of the conflicts within the changing cultural and institutional dimensions of the public schools.

Social System Perspective:
Implications for Special Education Leadership

The social system perspective was selected as a guide to assist special education administrators in determining the place of special education in the larger educational system. Potential and current leaders can determine a system's readiness for a proactive or a reactive thrust in the development of special education programs and services by collecting and analyzing information in each of the key elements of a general system model.[7] The key elements are:

1. *Values*, *goals*, and *objectives* represented by the education philosophy of significant others; the values or outcomes they subscribe to for *all* children; the translation of these values into specific objectives, activities and resources for previous and current operating programs and services.
2. *Organization and structures, distribution of power, influence and authority* as established by the board of education and top leadership personnel who formally identify responsibility and authority of individual administrators and specify articulation throughout the hierarchy. Different role incumbents, however, occupying superordinate, subordinate positions gain influence through informal, as well as formal, arrangements.
3. *Problem-solving* and *communication patterns* of leadership personnel with teachers, their unions, and the larger community, illustrating their commitment to participatory planning and decision-making.
4. *Initiation of change* and *response to organizational conflict*, as evidenced by the leader's tendency to initiate or react to change and conflict by planned avoidance until crisis proportions are reached, versus planned confrontation in an adverse contact, versus planned utilization of change and conflict as a means of energizing the system into action and development.

Leadership in the Social System

Leadership and administration are key concepts which deserve definition and discussion in this opening chapter. Getzels, Lipham and Campbell define these terms:

> . . . to lead is to engage in an act which initiates a structure in interaction with others, and (to administer) is to follow or to engage in an act which maintains a structure initiated by another.[8]

[7]Gordon, Lippitt, *Visualizing Change: Model Building and the Change Process* (Fairfax Va.: National Training Laboratories Learning Resources, 1973), p. 45.

[8]Getzels, Lipham and Campbell, *Educational Administration,* p. 145.

It is important to stress that the terms "leader" and "administrator" are relative, for the administrator is not altogether passive in maintaining the status quo, nor is the leader necessarily dominant in initiating radical changes in the existing order. The leader, however, is clearly distinguished from the administrator since he/she is establishing new goals, structures, processes and procedures rather than implementing the current set of goals and activities within the existing structure. We will now trace the evolution of leadership study to its current stage of development.

Most discussions of leadership note the early summary research of Stogdill[9] who analyzed leadership research up to the late forties. He concluded that leadership studies were primarily focused on the personality traits of the leader. Since 1950 a notable trend has been identified: there has been a switch from a "search for personality traits to a search for leadership behavior that makes a difference in the performance or satisfaction of the follower."[10]

Two new dimensions grew out of Stogdill's studies. They are the concepts of (1) initiating structure (or task emphasis), and, (2) consideration for others (or relationship emphasis). An *initiating structure* includes leadership behavior characterized by the individual authority setting specific objectives to be accomplished, determining expected levels of performances, determining time lines, and monitoring and controlling the staff's work schedules. A *consideration for others* includes leadership behaviors characterized by the individual authority's concern for the staff's needs for recognition, status, and affiliation, concern for work group member's interaction and cohesion, and ability to handle conflict.

Getzels and Guba[11] translate the initiating structure to the normative dimension and the consideration for others to the personal dimension. They depict leadership-follower styles in terms of three distinct types: (1) a normative style that emphasizes the institutional demands made on the chief executives and middle managers, (2) a personal style that emphasizes the individual needs of personnel within the social system, and (3) an emerging transactional style of leadership that alternates pattern of emphasis between the normative and personal dimensions.

The authors emphasize that each style is a different conception of attaining the same goal within the social system. Getzels, Lipham, and Campbell describe characteristics that provide some insight into the observed differences in role incumbents within each of the distinct styles of leadership-follower relationships.

---

[9]Ralph M. Stogdill, "Personal Factors Associated with Leadership: A Survey of the Literature," *Journal of Psychology*, XXV (1948), pp. 35–71.

[10]David Bowers and Stanley Seashore, "Predicting Organizational Effectiveness with a Four-factor Theory of Leadership," *Administration Science Quarterly*, Vol. 2 (1966), p. 239.

[11]Getzels and Guba, p. 436.

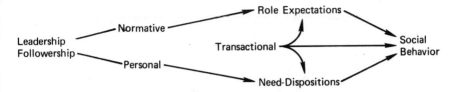

Figure 1-3. Three Leadership-Follower Styles. *Reprinted with permission from J. W. Getzels and E. G. Guba, "Social Behavior and the Administrative Process," School Review, 65, p. 436.*

They selected:

> . . . (1) the proportion of role and personality factors in the behavior; (2) the differences with respect to authority, scope, affectivity, and sanction dimensions; (3) the relative weight given to effectiveness, efficiency, and satisfaction; (4) the nature of the predominant conflicts dealt with; and (5) the nature of the major mechanisms of institutional-individual integration.[12]

A visual illustration is presented in Figure 1–3

Halpin[13] further examined the relationship between initiating structure (task focus behavior) and consideration for others (a focus on building relationships between staff personnel). The important aspect of Halpin's studies was the need to find a criterion level to determine leadership effectiveness. Within the social system perspective, effective leadership involves both dimensions of initiating structure and consideration for others.

The desire to illustrate the ideal type of leadership style, however, goes beyond bringing the initiating structure and consideration for others together within a social system. Effectiveness versus ineffectiveness is more than congruence between expectations held by both superordinates and subordinates. The context of the situation in which the leader may find himself may dictate a range of behavior along the two continuums suggested above. Hersey and Blanchard suggest that their review of empirical studies shows no normative or "best style of leadership":

> . . . successful leaders do adapt their leader behavior to meet the needs of the group and of the particular situation. Effectiveness (E) depends upon the leader, (l) the follower (f), and other situational variables (s) - E = f (l,f.s). E stands for effectiveness in the formula.[14]

[12]Getzels, Lipham and Campbell, *Educational Administration,* p. 87.

[13]Andrew W. Halpin, *Theory and Research in Administration* (New York: MacMillan, 1966).

[14]Paul Hersey and Kenneth N. Blanchard, *Management of Organizational Behavior: Utilizing Human Resources,* 2nd ed. (Englewood Cliffs, N.J.: Prentice-Hall, Inc., 1977), p. 87.

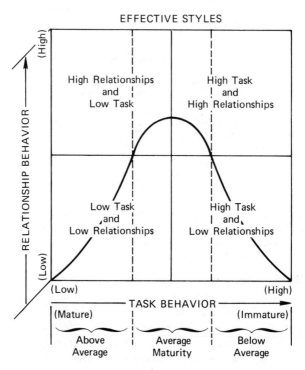

Figure 1-4. The Life Cycle Leadership Theory with Maturity Levels. *From P. Hersey and K. Blanchard.* Management of Organizational Behavior: Utilizing Human Resources, *Third Edition (Englewood Cliffs, N.J.: Prentice-Hall, Inc., 1977, P. 164. © (1977) Reprinted by permission of Prentice-Hall, Inc.*

This concept of group maturity and its variability adds an important dimension to discussions of leadership theory. Group maturity refers to behaviors amplified by sharing leadership; setting up mutual trust; assuming responsibility; making commitments and establishing accountability; actively listening to, giving and receiving performance feedback; and remaining open to evaluation. The leader's ability to assess staff behavior using these dimensions helps to determine the level of individual or group maturity. This assessment serves as a prerequisite to the leader's initiation of structure or consideration for others within the work group.

The leader and his/her followers must then determine those situational variables, such as power distribution, timing, and fiscal capability, which affect their group problem-solving and decision-making. In Figure 1–4, Hersey and Blanchard have depicted their leadership theory of three dimensions: effective styles, leadership behavior (concern for relationship and task), and group maturity.

Table 1-1. How the Basic Leader Behavior Styles Are Seen by Others When They Are Effective or Ineffective.

Basic Styles	Effective	Ineffective
High Task and Low Relationships	Often seen as knowing what he wants and imposing his methods for accomplishing this without creating resentment.	Often seen as having no confidence in others, unpleasant, and interested only in short-run output.
High Task and High Relationships	Often seen as satisfying the needs of the group for setting goals and organizing work, but also providing high levels of socioemotional support.	Often seen as initiating more structure than is needed by the group and spends more time on socioemotional support than necessary.
High Relationships and Low Task	Often seen as having implicit trust in people and as being primarily concerned with developing their talents.	Often seen as primarily interested in harmony and being seen as "a good person," and being unwilling to risk disruption of a relationship to accomplish a task.
Low Task and Low Relationships	Often seen as appropriately permitting his subordinates to decide how the work should be done and playing only a minor part in their social interaction.	Often seen as uninvolved and passive, as a "paper shuffler," who cares little about the task at hand or the people involved.

To conclude this discussion of leadership and effectiveness, Hersey and Blanchard[15] offer a tabular summary of the effective-ineffective continuum which clearly describes the four basic styles that evolve from their theory.

Leadership and Change: Implications for Special Educators

In order to meet leadership challenges, the authors believe that the situational leadership theory of Hersey and Blanchard provides a framework that will help special educators in their actual practice. Special educators will continue to work with a diverse set of professionals, staff, and lay groups. Determining

[15]Hersey and Blanchard, *Management of Organizational Behavior*, p. 85.

group maturity and capacity to perform will largely dictate the leadership style that the designated leader must adopt. The special educator must lead diverse groups through four stages of development: (1) identifying and sanctioning a reason and common purpose for group membership, (2) dealing with differences in the group's perception of the task and the process of reaching resolution, (3) establishing a set of group working conditions and standards of conducting the group task, and (4) allowing individual group members to assume responsibility freely, making and keeping commitments and publicly giving their support to the group's mission.

The special educator, working with general and special educators as well as interagency personnel, must develop a common purpose and need for group membership. Surfacing agendas, individual contributions, and needs for participation are major outcomes the leader must achieve in order to establish a group identity. Besides developing a group identity, a group commitment to implement and follow through leadership skills demands that the special educator identify the source and extent of the group members' power and influence and their capacity to negotiate and make decisions within their individual spheres of influence. Knowledge of the organization's goals, resources, and constituency are also important to the shaping and the adherence to a set of common group outcomes.

SUMMARY

This chapter serves as a framework for the presentation of the past, present and future, of the special education leadership role. The two major conceptual bases chosen for this framework are the Getzels–Guba Social Systems Model and the Hersey–Blanchard Life Cycle Leadership Theory. Both theories draw meaningful insights into the changing role of special education. They show that the study of education can only be accomplished within the context of the larger environment of the culture, the society, and the institutions which are designed to preserve that society. The authors will attempt, throughout the recording of the past, the description of the present, and the forecasting of the future of special education leadership roles, to place their observations into these frameworks.

We suggest that theories and conceptual frameworks are selected explanations and representations of reality. They offer a context by which the observer-participant enters into a dynamic spiraling process of growth. The infinite cycling and recycling process includes assessing needs and conditions, planning and implementing interventions, and evaluating effectiveness and outcomes. This process is empirical and continuous—one that simply cannot be reduced to linear relationships between variables. The feedback from evaluations determines the next level of growth of individuals and social systems and continually initiates the next growth cycle.

2

A Historical View
of Special Education
Administration

The leadership process in special education has generally been viewed as providing either administrative direction or supervisory/consultative expertise for the somewhat esoteric practices that have taken place within the special subsystem of education reserved for handicapped or otherwise exceptional students. An historical perspective will be presented in this chapter that deals with the role and function of special education administrators up to the beginning of the 1970s (which we see as the beginning of the acceleration of change).

In the earliest stages of this history, the special education programs tended to be limited to students whose exceptional conditions were obvious and whose needs for extraordinary instructional approaches and/or physical facilities were undeniable. Given such client characteristics, the programs tended to encourage organizational structures separate and distinct from the mainstream of public education. Instructional programs for sensory impaired students (the blind, the deaf) were predominently carried out in residential settings where the isolation from other regular schools, whether on grounds of complex instructional method or the need to concentrate a sparsely distributed population, was a natural and logical response to a patently obvious problem.

Even in instances (primarily the large cities) where special education services were made available under the legal auspices of the local public schools, the assumptions regarding placement, curriculum, and instructional methods tended to promote a separate, parallel organizational structure for the special schools, classes, and personnel provided. An early reference to the development of the leadership role in this field[1] cited data regarding forty-four cities with populations over one hundred thousand which offered public school special classes. It was reported that in 1923, sixteen of these cities employed twenty-nine supervisors and six directors of special instruction. Where special schools were established (for example, schools for the deaf) their administration was understandably perceived as best placed in the hands of a person whose expertise was in the technical aspects of education for that particular exceptional condition. The assumption that technical expertise, as a requirement for instructional practice, has dictated similar expertise as a requirement for administration has generated and reinforced a mystique of specialness which has further encouraged the segregated system concept. This was stated by Ayer and Barr[2] who justified the existence of the specialist role, "owing to the special nature of instruction offered in connection with the classes . . . it was necessary from the beginning to place them in charge of special teachers . . . special subjects . . . soon led to special supervision . . ."

The quantity and variety of personnel in leadership positions increased as the parameters of special education gradually expanded to include students with less apparent exceptionalities, functional as well as organic disabilities, and relatively less severe degrees of deviance from normalcy. However, the expectation persisted that such personnel would best function as a special department, somewhat divorced from the mainstream of the regular school system. In terms of the social system perspective presented in the previous chapter, the institutional role expectations generating from the cultural values of the time dictated the upholding of such a view of appropriate institutional and individual behavior.

Further reinforcing segregation is the propensity of the public school, as representative of society at large, for sorting, classifying, and labeling its individual clients at an early stage. With such classification, delivery of educational services on the basis of labeled categories has fostered the belief that "normal" children are the responsibility of the schools and that certain "other" children are not, and therefore belong to the special education system.

As general educators have assumed an inability to deal with certain children, the specialists have willingly stepped in. The temptation to come to the rescue when presented with such an opportunity is difficult to resist. A sincere desire to serve the needy, coupled with ambition to achieve professional prominence, has encouraged leaders to promote not only the cause, but at the same time their own departmental domain.

[1]F. C. Ayer and A. S. Barr, *The Organization of Supervision* (New York: Appleton, 1928), pp. 30–31.

[2]Ayer and Barr, *The Organization of Supervision,* p. 31.

PROFESSIONAL IDENTITY

In the development of any new field, the establishment and legitimation of a role identity becomes a critical concern. This concern has been seen among the growing group of persons finding themselves in special education leadership positions. This self-consciousness has been manifested in a number of events that are of historical interest.

Professional Organizations

One manifestation of role identity is the creation of professional organizations, two of which are especially worthy of note: (1) the Council of Administrators of Special Education, and (2) the National Association of State Directors of Special Education.

The Council of Administrators of Special Education (CASE) first convened in 1951 as an unofficial special interest group of twenty-four persons within the International Council for Exceptional Children; members held administrative positions in medium to large school systems. For the first few years the official name was the Council of Administrators, Supervisors, and Coordinators of Special Education in Local School Systems. This initial title of the organization reflects the interest of its membership, which until recently was restricted to personnel in local systems. The group specifically excluded state agency, residential and private school, and university personnel. The membership of the organization grew steadily to 172 in 1960, 387 in 1965, 649 in 1970, and, with a broadening of membership eligibility, to 2500 in 1974, and over 3600 in 1978.

A review of the proceedings of annual meetings during the early years suggests that the membership has placed great emphasis on getting together with others of similar status for the sharing of problems and attempts at solutions. This has persisted even as membership has accelerated, with one of the chief arguments for retaining narrow membership criteria being the understandable nostalgia for the social benefits of the small group of closely identified colleagues.

CASE has maintained committees concerned with the development of professional standards, and has designated members to serve on the Policy Commission of the larger Council for Exceptional Children (CEC), with which it is affiliated. Of particular note has been the policy statement on "Organization and Administration of Special Education" approved by the Delegate Assembly of CEC in 1973. This policy statement, which addresses a number of major issues regarding delivery of services according to most current principles, will be discussed at length in a later chapter.

The National Association of State Directors of Special Education records a similar history, dating from 1938 when a group of fifteen special education workers from thirteen state education departments convened under the chairmanship of Elise H. Martens, at the call of the U.S. Office of Education. Originally meeting under the title of Conference of State Directors and Supervisors of Special Education, the group met irregularly, usually with less than twenty-five participants, until 1950 when a constitution was adopted, the name changed to its present form, and the title of the chief officer changed from chairman to president. J. E. Wallace Wallin served as the chairman and secretary during the 1941 to 1947 period, and Ray Graham was the leader when the organization came of age in 1950. Meetings were held in conjunction with annual conventions of the (International) Council for Exceptional Children until 1962 when the organization took an additional step to establish its own place and time of meetings. Articles of incorporation were executed in 1972, when an Executive Director was engaged and a National Office established. The latest constitution describes unit (voting) membership for the education departments of each state, territory, protectorate, the District of Columbia, and Bureau of Indian Affairs, as well as individual membership for any person employed as a special education director, coordinator, supervisor or consultant in the offices of any of the membership units.

These two organizations constitute the primary expression of group identity for special education administrators. Since these organizations have relatively narrow membership status and do not invite nor have any attraction for persons outside that domain, they tend to have an internally oriented focus. It should be acknowledged, however, that organizational activity of special education administrators has also been evident, to a lesser extent, in outward looking contexts such as the American Association of School Administrators (AASA). Efforts to gain visibility within that much larger, mainstream organization have been particularly notable in recent years when, through the vigorous activity of certain special educators, prominent program offerings were included within the general convention schedule of AASA. While the purported aim of such offerings has been to inform the mainstream administrators of current special education issues, an additional anticipated outcome has been the extension of professional identity. However, there would seem to be a qualitative difference between the type of "identity building" which is associated with the establishment of an exclusive organization, and that associated with the enhancement of visibility within a larger, more inclusive one. It may be that the former is a necessary stage that must take place in the evolution of group identity before the latter can easily occur. On the other hand, the related forces within society—the education community specifically—could be expected to influence the degree of exclusivity/inclusivity of identity desired by the majority of the group at any time. This concept will be discussed fully in a later chapter.

Professional Roles and Functions: Specific Studies

Another reflection of professional self-consciousness has been the research studies conducted for the purpose of describing the roles and functions of special education leadership.

The U.S. Office of Education Studies. This effort was supported and conducted by the U.S. Office of Education in 1952–54 as part of a broad scale nationwide study of *Qualification and Preparation of Teachers of Exceptional Children*, which focused on personnel of all types (teachers, therapists, administrators) identified with a large variety of clients, (mentally retarded, speech impaired, deaf, blind, crippled, gifted, hard of hearing, partially seeing, socially and emotionally disturbed, and so on).

This study recognized a number of distinct leadership roles. One distinction was based on place of employment, which resulted in publication of a study by Mackie and Snyder[3], focusing on administrative roles in state departments of education; another report[4] examined local school systems. Within each of these components a second distinction was drawn between the role of director as opposed to that of supervisor or specialist.

The data for each of these reports were generated by two separate procedures. The first involved a committee of ten to twelve experts who identified and described the competencies believed to be needed by persons in each role. The second was a series of inquiry forms sent to 102 special educators (40 directors, 62 specialists) in state departments, 153 administrators (103 directors, 50 supervisors) in local school systems, 279 instructors in colleges and universities, and 1079 teachers distributed across ten areas of exceptionality.

Information derived by these procedures resulted in statements of functions typically performed by persons in each role, in terms of percentage of time allocated to each activity, statements of competencies perceived to be important, and training and experience deemed essential to the acquisition of such competencies.

The case of state department personnel showed considerable contrast between the time spent on various functions by the directors and the supervisors. Directors spent over half their time on duties described as administrative and supervisory at the state office and about one-fifth of their time in supervisory and

---

[3]Romaine P. Mackie and Walter E. Snyder, *Special Education Personnel in State Departments of Education*, U.S. Office of Education Bulletin 1956, No. 6 (Washington, D.C.: USGPO, 1957).

[4]Romaine P. Mackie and Anna M. Engel, *Directors and Supervisors of Special Education in Local School Systems*, U.S. Office of Education Bulletin 1955, No. 13 (Washington, D.C.: USGPO, 1956).

consulting activities in local communities. The major emphasis within the administrative category was on planning, approving, and giving leadership for the development of new programs and extending existing programs for education of exceptional children (19 percent); investigating, evaluating, and preparing budgets, legislation, standards of certification, and fund distributions (19 percent); and consulting with parents, local school, college and university educators, and personnel from private agencies and organizations (9 percent). Activities within the supervisory category included consulting with general educators (6 percent); observing teachers of exceptional children (5 percent); consulting with such teachers (5 percent); and consulting with parents, lay persons, and local special education administrators. By contrast, supervisors spent less time (37 percent) in administrative activity at the state office (although in certain duties, such as consultation with parents, educators, and personnel from private agencies, the emphasis equalled that of the directors) and relatively more time (33 percent) in supervisory/consultative work in local communities with the special education teachers and administrators.

Note that less than 10 percent of the time of either professional role was concerned with in-service education, and that professional study and research accounted for even less time. It was a reflection of the primitive state of services at the time of this study that the specialists were involved (12 percent) with direct services to children such as testing, counseling and even teaching.

Competencies considered essential for these roles focused on financial matters (preparing budgets and distributing state funds), evaluating legislation, fostering and improving local programs, establishing standards, recruiting teachers and cooperating in teacher education, encouraging in-service growth of teachers, supervising education in residential schools, maintaining interagency relationships, preparing publications, selecting and directing personnel, and sponsoring and directing research. These competencies were relevant to the director role, although also relevant for specialists, with the chief differentiation being the latter role's greater emphasis on technical supervision.

In the case of administrators in local school systems, an analysis of working time spent on various functions also showed considerable overlap between the director and supervisor roles, with differences being the emphasis on certain activities. Again, the largest single block of time (37 percent) was devoted to administrative duties such as preparing and reviewing reports and budgets; interviewing applicants for positions; setting criteria for membership in special classes and services; placing children; and consulting with parents, general administrators, and state department, college, and private agency representatives. Table 2-1 displays the distribution of time for directors and supervisors.

It should be noted that these data were generated from seventy-six directors and forty supervisors, and that the variance within each group was very large. For example, the percentage of time devoted to direct service to children by directors ranged from 0 to 60 percent and the time devoted to administrative duties

Table 2-1. Distribution of Time Devoted to Leadership Functions in Local
School Systems.

| *Functions* | *Average Percentage by* | | |
	Total	*Directors*	*Supervisors*
Administrative Duties	37	40	31
Supervisory and Consultative Duties	28	23	36
In-service Education	7	6	9
Self-directed Study and Research	6	6	6
Public Relations	9	11	7
Direct Services to Children	13	14	11

by supervisors ranged from 2 to 85 percent. Quite possibly representative of the field at that time, the population of professional leadership personnel from which this sample was drawn included a wide variety of roles within a single title, with a considerable number of titled administrators actually devoting more time to non-administrative activity. Given the primitive state of the field in 1952–54, this should not be suprising.

Competencies deemed to be important for professional leadership were developed by a committee of twelve experts. The resulting thirty-six competency statements (expressed as knowledges and abilities) were then placed in priority order for directors and supervisors by the 153 respondents who held such titles in the field. There was a rather clear distinction drawn between the directors' highest ranked competencies versus the supervisors'; the emphasis on broad management and community leadership competencies ranked high for directors, and more technical aspects of teaching methods, materials, curriculum and pupil characteristics accorded relatively greater importance for supervisors. It appeared that people in the field had a better idea of how the roles *should* be performed than they were able to perform in their own situations.

In drawing up the committee report on competencies, it was acknowledged that the role descriptions, particularly the distinction between the two roles, would apply mostly to larger school systems. In smaller systems a single person would probably fill both roles and might even function in a direct service capacity as well.

Policy Statements.   In translating competency recommendations into practice, the realities of school district organizational structures became most evident. The wide variation between leadership roles in the few large systems versus those in the multitude of small systems required an approach to role description that could accommodate such breadth. One of the more accepted and widely quoted statements regarding the functions of the director of special education was developed and promulgated by the State of Illinois, Superintendent of Public Instruction in 1956 under the leadership of Ray Graham[5]. The document, designed to serve as a guide for directing special education in local districts of all sizes, emphasized the breadth of functions that were applicable regardless of whether they were exercised by a single person or by many. Three general categories of functions, (1) administrative, (2) supervisory and (3) coordinating, were identified and elaborated upon.

The administrative domain placed emphasis on the special educator's contribution to the development of total school philosophy and his responsibility of consulting with generalists in determining policy for general and special school programs. Other administrative responsibilities included the establishment of special programs, the placement of children, the scheduling and accounting for staff and pupils, the management of transportation, the establishment of channels of communication, the evaluation of personnel, the procurement of equipment and supplies, and the planning and appraisal of programs. Each of these functions pointed toward the integration of the special program with the total system.

Supervisory functions were also described, with major emphasis on fostering professional growth through meetings, case conferences, workshops and development projects; evaluating personnel; serving as a resource person; and building staff morale.

Coordinating functions were distinguished from the other two categories by the concern for the articulation of the special programs with other aspects of the local system, and by the community agencies and the state level context within which the system operated. In that respect the importance of organizational and professional relationships with multiple agencies and disciplines was emphasized.

Graham's treatment of the important functions to be handled, his emphasis on the coordinative-relationship factors, and his recognition of the difficulty in assigning such functions on a role specific basis, made that document stand out as a landmark in the history of special education leadership development.

The CEC Professional Standards Project.   One decade after publication of the U.S. Office of Education study and the Illinois guide, a major statement regarding leadership functions was generated by the Council for Exceptional Children in 1966 as a part of a larger project on *Professional Standards for Per-*

---

[5]Superintendent of Public Instruction, "Functions of the Director of Special Education," *A Guide–Directing the Education for Exceptional Children in a Local School District* (State of Illinois, 1956).

sonnel in the Education of Exceptional Children.[6] Using input from approximately seven hundred persons, the committee prepared statements regarding areas of professional preparation and competence for a variety of educator specialties. In approaching the leadership roles, the report concluded that although the administrative and supervisory functions were clearly different, though complementary, the possibility of useful differentiation in preparation programs at that time was doubtful. Therefore, in the statement of major areas of professional competence which the project generated, the two types of functions were grouped together resulting in fifteen general areas of knowledge, from which seventy-nine more specific functions dependent upon those knowledges were listed.

The areas of knowledge which reflect the mixture of technical, human relations, and general conceptual competencies seen as basic for professional practice in the field, were:

1. Understanding of total educational process
2. Knowledge of school organization and administrative practices
3. Knowledge of various administrative provisions
4. Knowledge of fiscal procedures
5. Knowledge of curriculum development and methodology
6. Knowledge of supervisory practices and theory and techniques of staff development
7. Knowledge of psychoeducational and other diagnostic procedures
8. Knowledge of personnel practices
9. Knowledge and utilization of community organizations and resources
10. Ability to identify, define and influence the power structure both within and outside education
11. Knowledge of public relations
12. Knowledge of school law and legislative processes and their implementation
13. Knowledge of school plant planning and utilization
14. Knowledge of research techniques and procedures
15. Knowledge of professional responsibilities to the field

Normative Studies.   The information which has been discussed thus far has generated largely from the opinion of experts (however designated and defined) regarding functions performed by leadership personnel in the field. Although USOE studies (Mackie and Snyder, Mackie and Engel) solicited responses from a representative sample of practitioners in the field, the nature of the data was limited to classification reactions and competency statements provided by the experts.

---

[6]Council for Exceptional Children, *Professional Standards for Personnel in the Education of Exceptional Children*, Professional Standards Project Report 1966 (Washington, D.C.: CEC, NEA, 1966).

Using a different approach, Kohl's and Marro's study [7] was designed to gather normative data directly from practicing local administrators; the study's criteria discriminated administrators from persons who performed only in supervisory or coordinative capacities. On the basis of data supplied by state special education offices, with direct confirmation by individuals identified, a population of 1756 special education administrators fit the criteria, that is, "were in charge of more than two categories of exceptionality and spent at least 50% of their time in direct administration and supervision." [8]

Questionnaire data were collected that concerned personal characteristics, experience and preparatory background, supervision and administration role of the special education program, a description of the job and conditions of employment, organizational characteristics, programming elements, and perceptions on selected current issues and practices. Usable data were obtained from 1066 respondents, constituting about two-thirds of the estimated number of public school special education administrators. Analysis of data was primarily handled by tabulation of means and percentages using variables dealing with characteristics of administrators and their school systems.

Much of the information dealt with demographic factors of role incumbents, that is, relationship between sex, age, and experience. Men outnumbered women three to one, tended to have higher degrees and more experience as administrators, and attained an administrative job at an earlier age than did women.

Data dealing with titles showed that the title Director of Special Education was used most frequently (28.9 percent), followed by Coordinator (14 percent), Supervisor (12.8 percent), and Director of Pupil Personnel Services (10.3 percent). There was a tendency for men to be called Director more often than women, and for the Pupil Personnel Services title to be used more often in smaller systems where the role was likely to include the dual functions of special education and pupil personnel.

It was clear that the most promising avenue for career advancement to the special education administrator role was through school psychology. Although special education teaching roles of various types totaled a greater percentage of positions held just prior to administrative appointment, the relatively small proportion of school psychologists in the field (as compared to teachers) dramatizes the finding that 16.9 percent of the respondents had been advanced from a psychologist position.

The recent establishment of the role in systems across the nation has been reflected in the finding that over 40 percent had been in such positions less than four years, and another 37 percent from four to nine years. Mobility was corres-

[7]John W. Kohl, and Thomas D. Marro, *A Normative Study of the Administrative Position in Special Education*, (Grant No. OEG-0-70-2467 [607], U.S. Office of Education, The Pennsylvania State University, 1971).

[8]Kohl and Marro, *A Normative Study*, pp. 1–2.

pondingly low, with nearly 85 percent having held administrative positions in only one or two systems.

In viewing their professional development, it appeared that respondents tended to emphasize their specialist identity. College courses in child growth and development and in special education were seen as much more important than the more generic administrative preparation. The experiences valued most highly were self-directed study and research and direct work with children in classroom or therapy settings. Administrative experience was not accorded a high value (although in this sample there had been little experience from which to judge) and the administrative internship (that four out of ten had experienced) was ranked as most contributory to success by only 6 percent of the respondents. A further reflection of the emphasis on the specialist aspect of the role may be induced from the finding that while 69 percent of the sample held membership in the Council for Exceptional Children, only 38 percent were also members of the Council of Administrators of Special Education. This self-perceived emphasis on the specialist aspect of the role takes on greater significance when it is observed that the most common undergraduate major was found in generalist fields such as elementary education or content areas such as social sciences or psychology, and further, that a graduate major in educational administration was indicated just as frequently as a graduate major in special education. These two majors (representing about 23 percent of the sample each) far outstripped any other major except psychology (11 percent).

Analysis of the proportion of time administrators spent on various duties, contrasted with expressions of preferred distribution of time, showed a similarity with what had been reported by Mackie and Engel 15 years earlier. Respondents spent most of their time on administrative tasks (32 percent) and would have preferred less of that type of activity; the second greatest segment of time was spent on supervision and coordination of instruction (20 percent), and respondents would have preferred more time for this. Direct services to children and clerical work each accounted for approximately 12 percent of the time, but respondents would have preferred more of the former, less of the latter. They also would have preferred to devote more time than the 10.5 percent they spent for curriculum development.

The nature of an administrator's role in the system is much more difficult to put into discrete quantitative terms, and is highly subject to personal perceptions. Most (57.6 percent) believed that they were recognized as "in charge" and responsible for control of the special education program. Nearly two-thirds felt they were encouraged to participate in the development of educational policy directly with the board or superintendent. However, in certain personnel practices their role was diminished since other persons played the major role in staff selections (30 percent of the sample) and staff evaluations (37 percent). Budget preparation was a major responsibility for over half the administrators, and input on budget matters was requested for all but about 13 percent. Most felt they had an important role in shaping curriculum and in influencing teaching methods.

The majority of the respondents were employed by local school districts of over eight thousand enrollment, although county units, intermediate units, and cooperatives together employed nearly 40 percent of the group. The most frequently reported program of special education was for the educable mentally retarded, followed by programs for speech handicapped, trainable mentally retarded, emotionally disturbed, learning disabilities, visually handicapped, aurally handicapped and orthopedically handicapped. Programs for gifted were reported much less frequently.

Respondents tended to see their major obstacles to successful program operation in terms of shortages, primarily shortages of staff assistance, time for consultation, and financial resources. To a lesser degree they saw a need for more knowledge and more authority.

These views are in contrast to an earlier study by Wisland and Vaughan[9] which had focused on perceived administrative problems facing 180 special education directors and supervisors in the thirteen western states. In that analysis, although a major general problem area was time for self directed study and research, specific programmatic issues such as obtaining adequately prepared personnel, programming for multiple handicapped, and counseling of parents had also presented problems to the administrator, regardless of size or type of program or experience of the respondent.

In summary, the Kohl-Marro study has supplied the most comprehensive view thus far of the administrative role in special education up to 1970. While remaining limited to the public school field, the descriptive profile provided is one that aptly represents the total field; it can be useful in understanding the point of departure from which leadership might hopefully emerge. It would appear that the administrators of 1970 possessed some ideas about the kind of leadership they should and would like to provide, but considering the factors that stood in the way of exercising such leadership they were reacting primarily in terms of traditional models of organizational structure and behavior. The remedies sought tended to be equatable with power and money, rather than concerned with the conception of different roles or new functional relationships.

In view of the variety of titles used for the one role described by the Kohl-Marro study, an attempt at delineation of titles and roles by Wyatt[10] may help to clarify the status of the administrative field at that time. Wyatt's study was concerned with current (in 1967) and projected needs for leadership personnel in special education nationally. In order to set clear parameters, the definitions of five role titles were arbitrarily established for personnel employed in five

[9]Milton V. Wisland, and Tony D. Vaughan, "Administrative Problems in Special Education," *Exceptional Children*, 31 (1964), p. 87.

[10]Kenneth E. Wyatt, *Current Employment and Possible Future Needs for Leadership Personnel in Special Education*, Doctoral Dissertation, University of Illinois (Ann Arbor, Mich.: University Microfilms, 1968, No. 68–12), p. 226.

types of organizational settings. In using the titles in certain data collection instruments, respondents were instructed to classify leadership persons according to the established definition, regardless of the title that any individual might happen to hold.

Definitions for each role title were:

Directors—An individual who has administrative responsibility for a total special education program. This would imply that the greatest part of his time is spent with matters directly related to special education rather than to other duties such as guidance, pupil personnel, or general administration. His responsibilities would include such things as (1) budget development; (2) transportation arrangements; (3) personnel recruitment, assignment and evaluation; (4) interdistrict agreements; (5) policy formation, etc. Such a person may report only to an assistant superintendent in general education, or directly to the state, county, or district superintendent.

Principals—This category is primarily designed to include administrators in charge of day schools which are expressly devoted to some form of special education. He would be responsible not only for the educational program, teacher evaluation, etc., but also for the operation and maintenance of the physical plant as well. In this capacity, the principal may have dual responsibility to the program director, as well as to the superintendent or to an assistant superintendent in general education.

Coordinators—A person at this administrative level would be responsible for two or more areas of special education. Presumably these would be areas that are *not* closely related, as are the areas of the blind and partially sighted, or the deaf and hard of hearing. The coordinator's primary range of services would revolve around such things as (1) inservice training; (2) curriculum development; (3) pupil placement; (4) instructional materials, etc. This person could be responsible to a director of special education, or in the absence of this position, to some other person who may be even higher in the administrative chain.

Supervisors—In many ways this individual may function in a manner similar to a coordinator, the distinction being that a supervisor will be involved with a single area, or two closely related areas of exceptionality. In certain large programs a supervisor may be subordinate to a coordinator, but, in most instances, would report to a program director.

Consultants—This individual operates in only one area of special education and provides direct, immediate services to the classroom teacher, and in some instances to children. The consultant may report to a supervisor, coordinator, or director depending upon the administrative organization.[11]

The five types of settings employing personnel holding positions classified according to these definitions were (1) local public school districts, (2) intermediate districts or cooperative programs, (3) residential state schools, (4) state offices of public instruction, and (5) private schools.

Wyatt's data indicated that in 1967 the largest proportion (46 percent) of the 3,828 persons employed were in local public school districts; each of the other types of organizations accounted for a much smaller number. The title of director accounted for 32 percent of the total persons employed, approximately

[11]Wyatt, *Current Employment and Possible Future Needs* pp. 48–49.

twice the number of principals, supervisors, consultants and coordinators. Table 2–2 (adapted from Wyatt, 1968) summarizes the findings.

The major purpose of Wyatt's study was to project an estimate of leadership personnel needs for the five years from 1968 to 1972. Projections were generated from opinions of state education agency personnel who were presumed to have a data base regarding new program development, new legislation, and funding. Findings indicated an anticipated increase of 157 percent over the five year period with the largest growth area being in intermediate district and cooperative programs, and in the supervisor, rather than director role. The fact that directors constituted the predominant role at the time of the study was attributed to the small size of most programs, a situation in which only one administrator per organization unit was warranted. Therefore, that one person functioned in a capacity most nearly defined as the director role. The projected increase in other roles was interpreted as an anticipation of increase in size of programs rather than number of programs. In comparing Wyatt's data with that of Mackie and Engel, the distribution of personnel according to function had remained relatively constant, despite great growth in total program enrollment over the twelve year period.

An analysis of special education administrator functions was reported by Sage[12] in which a conceptual scheme developed by Hemphill, Griffiths, and Fredericksen[13] was employed to classify the problems facing various types of administrators. The scheme utilized a two dimensional grid in which one dimension was constituted by four categories of administrative tasks: (1) improving educational opportunities; (2) obtaining and developing personnel; (3) maintaining effective interrelationships with the community; and (4) providing and maintaining funds and facilities. Superimposed across these categories were three types of skills required for administrative functioning, that is, (1) technical skills, (2) human skills, and (3) conceptual skills, as discussed by Katz[14].

The functions of special education administrators were applied to this classification scheme, using data from two sources: (1) self perceptions of incumbents, and (2) statements of knowledges and functions listed in the Professional Standards Report[15].

Questionnaire returns from 37 of 150 randomly selected members of CASE, who were asked to estimate time and skill devoted to each cell on the grid, resulted in a distribution with heaviest emphasis (39 percent) in the first task

---

[12]Daniel D. Sage, "Functional Emphasis in Special Education Administration," *Exceptional Children*, 35 (1968) p. 69.

[13]J. K. Hemphill, D. E. Griffiths, and N. Fredericksen, *Administrative Performance and Personality* (New York: Bureau of Publications, Teachers College, Columbia University, 1962).

[14]R.L. Katz, "Skills of an Effective Administrator," *Harvard Business Review*, 33, (1955). pp. 33–42.

[15]Council for Exceptional Children, 1966.

Table 2-2. Roles and Locale of Employment of Leadership Personnel in Special Education, 1967.

Role	Number	Percent	Locale	Number	Percent
Directors	1243	32.47	Local Public School	1775	46.37
Principals	653	17.06	Intermediate/Cooperative Program	503	13.14
Coordinators	491	12.83	Residental State School	637	16.64
Supervisors	624	16.30	State Office	355	9.27
Consultants	644	16.82	Private School	558	14.58
Others	173	4.52			
Totals	3828	100.00		3828	100.00

category (improving educational program) and in the human skill category (41 percent). Table 2–3 illustrates the percentage distribution among the twelve cells.

Comparing this distribution to that employed by Hemphill, Griffiths, and Fredericksen in describing the role of the elementary principal, indicates much more emphasis on program development, correspondingly less emphasis on developing personnel and on community relationships, and slightly more emphasis on funds and facilities. On the other hand, the distribution across the three skill areas—technical, human, and conceptual—showed very nearly the same pattern as that suggested for principals.

To contrast this information with the view of special education administration as seen from the Professional Standards Report, an analysis was handled by having twelve doctoral students independently classify the seventy-nine func-

Table 2-3. Percentage of Emphasis from Practicing Special Education Administrators.

	Technical	Human	Conceptual	Total
	(T)	*(H)*	*(C)*	
Educational Program (E)	13	15	11	39
Developing Personnel (P)	7	14	6	27
Community Relationships (R)	4	8	4	16
Maintaining Funds and Facilities (F)	7	4	6	17
Totals	31	41	27	

tions listed in that report into the grid scheme. The resulting distribution was strikingly similar to the data collected from the practicing field, in terms of the task categories, but, compared to the principalship, it placed much greater emphasis on the technical skill area and correspondingly less on human skills. As Table 2-4 suggests, the major factor differentiating the special education administration role from that of the principal, when evaluated both by subjective impressions from the field and by a professional standards statement, appears in the cell of the grid concerned with the exercise of technical skills in developing educational programs.

This suggests that, compared to the generalist, the specialist administrator is concerned with securing services that are new or have not been sufficiently well established to be operating on their own momentum. The lack of standard objectives, curriculum, or procedure, together with the basic philosophy of relatively individualized programming, may cause the special administrator to spend a greater proportion of time in program development. Furthermore, as the specialist attempts to dissect his behavior, the technical aspects stand out. Even as an administrator, he does not get away from the demand for specialized skills that are normally associated with direct service personnel.

In his presentation of the three types of skill areas, Katz had postulated that as administrators move farther away from the actual physical operations of the organization, the need for technical skills diminishes and the need for conceptual skills increases. Confirming evidence was brought forth in Sage's study when the sample of practicing administrators was dichotomized on the basis of large organizations (those over fifty thousand average daily attendance [ADA]), and small organizations (those under ten thousand ADA). The results from this breakdown clearly showed that special education administrators in the larger systems viewed their job as requiring more conceptual skills and less technical skills as compared to their small system counterparts.

Table 2-4. Percentage of Emphasis from Analysis of Professional Standards Statement.

	Technical	Human	Conceptual	Total
	(T)	(H)	(C)	
Educational Program (E)	24	8	7	39
Developing Personnel (P)	8	14	6	28
Community Relationships (R)	6	7	3	16
Maintaining Funds and Facilities (F)	9	2	5	16
Total	47	31	21	—

Sloat[16] extended a similar concept in his study of the perceptions of general and special education administrative and supervisory personnel by showing the importance of task and skill areas. His model, developed through the use of judges' weightings, classified tasks on the basis of a six cell matrix consisting of administrative versus supervisory tasks on one dimension, and on the basis of human, technical, and conceptual skills required to accomplish the tasks on the other dimension. Sloat sought to address the question of whether the special education leader's role is unique and, if so, whether it is due to an emphasis on administrative, supervisory, or combined responsibilities, or if it is due to particular skills utilized. Further, he asked the question of whether there is more than one type of special education leader.

His findings indicated the more eclectic nature of the position, with emphasis placed on a broader variety of tasks than either the general administrator or supervisor. The specialist apparently perceived his role as similar to the general supervisor rather than similar to the general administrator. He perceived all tasks as being important, and therefore he might be labeled a *supervisory generalist*. Factor analysis suggested two distinct types of special education administrator. The "unique" type perceived their roles in ways which were distinctly different from either general administrators or general supervisors. The "combination" type perceived their roles as more closely aligned to other general administrators and supervisors. The unique individuals tended to be from smaller systems, were older, had less training, accumulated more teaching experience in special education, and had more frequent contact with higher level administrators and other outside representatives. A differentiation of the combination type into two subgroups was also possible, depending on how they rated the importance of their tasks.

Newman[17] reported a survey of 100 randomly selected public school districts of medium size (ADA 13,000 to 30,000) in which the functions of the special education administrator were studied with an instrument utilizing the classic Urwick "POSDCORB" theory of administration (planning, organizing, staffing, directing, coordinating, reporting, and budgeting). Importance of these functions, as viewed by respondents, suggested no significant differences between what they actually performed and what they felt they should ideally perform; the exceptions were research and publication functions which, even to clients in their systems, were being unduly neglected. High priority tasks included developing policies (a planning function), establishing channels of communication (an organizing function), and integrating special education with the entire school program (a coordinating function).

[16]Robert S. Sloat, *Identification of Special Education and Other Public School Leadership Personnel Through Task and Skill Area Delineation* (Doctoral Dissertation, University of Texas, 1969).

[17]Karen S. Newman, "Administrative Tasks in Special Education," *Exceptional Children*, 36 (1970), p. 521.

There was a direct relationship between the training of an administrator and the degree to which he was involved with planning and directing in-service training. A similar relationship was noted between experience in special education teaching and involvement with curriculum planning and evaluation of staff. These observations may have implications for the kind of behaviors that can be anticipated when the selection of special education leadership personnel becomes influenced by the availability of more highly trained and more extensively experienced personnel.

SUMMARY

One cannot state clear conclusions from the mixture of reported opinions, self perceptions, and crude attempts at job analysis which have been reviewed here. At best, some broad general impressions may be suggested.

One impression is that the circumstances under which the field of special education developed have predestined the leadership roles of the field to begin with and retain over time an emphasis on the technical, the clinical, the personal involvement with particular client service needs. Administrators identified with the field have retained their specialist identity more than they have developed the management identity which might have generic applications to broad system influence and leadership.

A related impression is that systems within which service delivery operate have also retained an expectation that the subsystem concerned with special education will be, to a considerable degree, a separate unit, distinct if not isolated from the system as a whole.

The relationship between these two impressions may be causal, without certainty as to which would precede the other. Or they may be coincident manifestations generating from still another common cause. In either case, the place of special education in the larger system and the place of its leadership personnel among other administrators appears to be constrained by the degree to which the "special" image is maintained. Whether this constraint should be interpreted as largely a positive or a negative factor, is a question for more extensive exploration. It is enough, at this point, to indicate what we believe to be an accurate description of the leadership role in the field, up to beginning of the 1970s.

3

Driving Forces for Change

As the title of this book indicates, we are interested in the process of change and its relationship to the process of leadership. We believe that leadership requires first a recognition of and accurate sensitivity to the elements of change that determine, at any point in time, the social system in which the actor (leader-administrator) must operate. Although this is essential, it is also necessary for leadership to be seen as facilitating and, more appropriately, promoting change. While a combination of reactive and proactive behavior typically constitutes the administrative role, the degree to which the proactive behavior is maximized is generally accepted as an important indicator of leadership.

The status of past special education administration does not particularly reflect a proactive posture. Nor does it show the special education leader as being outstandingly affected by change, any more than any other administrator within the public sector of society. Such a description, however, does not hold true beyond the early 1970s. At that point the special education administrator became a participant in the process of significant change, whether willing it or not. Whether that participation has been largely passive or largely active has varied according to a multitude of situational and personal factors, but the fact of accelerating change involving the whole society and the special educator's domain within it cannot be ignored. The implications for leadership constitute our major interest.

The forces that generate the changes that are of significance to the special education leader, both as a reactor and a proactor, can best be classified into two major categories: (a) those forces external to the school systems, and (b) those forces within the educational establishment. It is our view that the greater of these two is the external force; the nature of those forces will be discussed first, leaving the internal forces for change to the latter part of this chapter.

EXTERNAL FORCES FOR CHANGE

Within the context of external forces, we will classify the sources of change into three somewhat overlapping, but distinguishable elements: (a) the general social climate, (b) actions of the courts, and (c) specific legislation. We will discuss how each element has constituted a source of change for the special education leader's role.

Change Source #1: General Social Climate

It might be argued that schools have always been everybody's business, and, unlike other professions, the educator has had to accept the fact that every client could claim expertise. However, to a large extent, educators have until recent years been able to get away with promoting the image (whether based in fact or not) that they knew best what was good for each child. The conventional wisdom of school administration reinforced the idea that, public relations notwithstanding, the good administrator was one who retained firm control, not only of the system but of the clientele it served. While good public relations demanded at least token investment in parent advisory groups, the clear image of such input (the typical P.T.A., for instance) was one of fairly trivial consequence. The normative status of such groups took on a posture somewhat akin to the company union in which the clients were unquestionably "tamed" by the educational administration. While adversarial relationships might exist between labor and management elements within the system, the concept of consumerism as a significant force on educators was, until recently, given little attention. Lay boards of education have been judged, in the typical view of educational administrators, by the degree to which they allowed the professionals to make the decisions.

This status of relationships between bureaucracies and clients, and between the professionals within service agencies and the lay persons comprising policy governing boards is not confined to educational organizations. It has been the very essence of professionalism to maintain an aura of distance, if not mysticism regarding the processes by which services are provided. Decisions regarding the best course of legal action, medical treatment, mental health care, or any other service have traditionally been made with little, if any, participation of the client. Likewise, the prerogatives of the professional to function unfettered by interference from governing boards, have been carefully guarded.

Small but notable inroads on the traditional relationship status have developed in a variety of contexts, dating from the late 1960s. Some of the most obvious sources of an attitudinal shift can be cited, but to a large extent the changes that are evident must be attributed to a diffuse but pervasive climate of acknowledgment of human rights.

One of the more outstanding examples of this type of change is seen, in officially codified form, in the adoption of the principle of "maximum feasible participation." The federal poverty programs implemented under the provisions of the Economic Opportunity Act of 1964 (which touched on a wide variety of social needs and services) included the concept that the recipient of services should participate, either personally or through representation, in the decision-making process regarding such service delivery. The concept was extended into educational services more directly through provisions of the Elementary and Secondary Education Act of 1965, which also called for advisory boards containing persons who would presumably be affected by the programs.

The generally liberal posture of the courts during that period of time, the recognition that due process, customarily overlooked in the past, could be demanded, and encouragement of the exercise of civil rights in such areas as voting, criminal justice, social welfare, and education, further contributed to the atmosphere of active participation and self determination. The attention to civil liberties and the resulting success of activist movements also played a part in opening up significant portions of society. In the schools, the idea of participation by students in decisions concerning their own affairs gained acceptance. In most universities, and to a considerable extent in secondary schools as well, the headlong rush to embrace participatory decision-making was so pronounced as to leave some participants, including administrators, disoriented. The focus of activism has shifted from one issue to another, and the level has diminished from the peaks of student takeovers in 1970. However, the breakthrough that came with the activism—establishing the concept of client participation in all of society's institutions—continues to have effect.

The overall climate of the decade from 1965 to 1975 became one in which the unilateral control and monolithic strength of many basic social service institutions were, for the first time, seriously questioned. An antiestablishment and antiprofessionalism trend of thinking, coming together in the case of health, education and welfare agencies, created a changing setting for the practice of leadership in the entire domain of social services.

The nature of some of these changes has been delineated by Rhodes[1] in his projection of the future developments in human services, particularly as they relate to child variance. He points out that the public, the professionals, and the care receivers are all in revolt against the existing set of social/cultural/political

---

[1]William C. Rhodes, *A Study of Child Variance, Volume 4: The Future* (Ann Arbor: The University of Michigan, 1975), pp. 92–99.

arrangements for providing human services. He predicts a change in the basic relationship between caretaker (those professionals who are responsible for human service delivery) and recipient. The unidimensional role which has characterized the teacher-student, counselor-client, therapist-patient relationship would evolve into a more bilateral exchange, in which the recipient exercises greater voice. There is a developing realization that in spite of increased funding, facilities, and training, the encounter between caretaker and care receiver fails to solve anything. Rhodes suggests that a questioning of the conventional caretaking enterprise may lead to sweeping demands for reform. If the process comes to be seen as a social ritual, a vehicle for social control rather than for problem solution, a number of major

> . . . incompatibilities (e.g., between concepts of a melting pot and a pluralistic society, between rugged individualism and egalitarianism, between the Protestant ethic and the four freedoms, etc.) will be unveiled as variables in the care giving process. Individual differences and individual variance will emerge as antithetical to much of the labeling and treatment process.[2]

It is therefore predicted that major changes will be in the direction of a departure from the belief in "normality" as a concept in dealing with child variance, and an acceleration of the declassification effort, deinstitutionalization, and the debureaucratization of care giving. While the specific focus of Rhodes' predictions is on deviations in children, the social climate that he describes as possibly leading to major changes in service systems is much broader, encompassing the totality of relationships between individuals and society.

The liberalization of attitudes toward human variance is evidenced in a wide variety of contexts. The most striking examples are to be found in racial relationships, sexual behaviors, and general social mores. An increasing tolerance for deviance, including an honoring of the ideal of each individual being permitted, if not encouraged to "do his own thing" as expressed by the "Greening of America,"[3] has been pervasive since the late 1960s. It has had its effect on public education generally, and on services for the handicapped specifically. The types of cases taken on by the American Civil Liberties Union, the activism in such areas as Black Power, Women's Liberation, Gay Liberation, and the changes in laws regarding divorce, abortion, and drug use, are all indicators of a general social climate having implications for social service leadership. The normalization ideology, which provides the philosophic base for the deinstitutionalization and mainstreaming practices in public schools, is the specific manifestation of this force in the context of services for the handicapped.

The impact of action groups, citizens committees, advisory task forces, and the like on social service organizations has been increasing during recent

[2]Rhodes, *Child Variance*, pp. 93–94.
[3]Charles A. Reich, *The Greening of America* (New York: Random House, 1970).

years, as a result of the conditions cited above. However, in the area of special education, a somewhat different situation has existed, predating the influences of such groups on social institutions.

The significant impact of the National Association for Retarded Citizens (originally *Children*), from the early 1950s to the present time has been an outstanding example of a consumer group with a success story. Composed primarily of parents of mentally retarded persons, with minimal participation by professionals, the national, state, and local groups with various degrees of strength across the country have launched and maintained crusades for the betterment of their children. The thrust of such efforts has taken different forms among the various localities, and between state and national levels. Some chapters and state organizations have worked primarily on development and operation of direct services which might have been delivered by governmental agencies, but which have been lacking in the locales concerned. The national thrust, as well as that of some states, has avoided involvement in direct program operation and has focused on legislative advocacy, the exercise of public relations, and general political influence to enhance the development of public programs. This effort has had a positive impact on each of the major pieces of federal legislation.

While consumer organizational activity in legislative and public relations areas was evident as early as 1880 by the formation of the National Association of the Deaf, and in 1895 by the American Association of Workers for the Blind, the magnitude of the movement became dramatically greater with the growth of the NARC and its concern for the much larger population of mentally retarded. A great many other organizations, such as the National Easter Seal Society for Crippled Children and Adults, and the United Cerebral Palsy Association, Inc., which represent various handicapping conditions (and predate NARC), have engaged in activities promoting public policy development as well as direct service programs. However, the numbers of persons potentially represented has been much less than in the case of NARC.

The success of NARC, nationally and locally, in promoting its causes probably has served as an impetus to the organization and growth of other special interest consumer groups. The 1950s and 1960s saw the establishment of a number of national, state and locally based organizations of parents of mentally ill or emotionally disturbed children who had never before established a recognized identity. The establishment of the Association for Children with Learning Disabilities in 1963 was marked by activity which would appear to have been based on much the same type of action planning utilized successfully by NARC. The ACLD and its affiliates successfully promoted federal and state legislation, influenced local school system developments, and initiated their own direct service programs outside the public sector, in a surprisingly short period of time. Much of this success must be attributable to the ground breaking actions and organization for advocacy gained by the older NARC. The potency of ACLD is demonstrated by the successful fight to add categorical coverage for the particular, rather narrowly conceived interest in children with specific learning disabilities to existing federal laws in 1969, and to maintaining an earmarked status in subsequent amendments of the law.

The predominance of such consumer groups in promoting services for the handicapped, therefore constitutes a special case as compared to social services in general. Special educators tend to have experienced a longer history of such involvement and should therefore be accustomed to the practice. But by the same token the intensity of the intervention is greater and will probably continue to be so in the future. This has often been manifested in a form of "friendly agitation" that school administrators depend on from organizations representing the handicapped. Furthermore, the shrewd administrator can covertly utilize such a group to gain fiscal and conceptual support from other less interested segments of the influential (executives, policy boards, or legislators) in the public education establishment. When a special educator is unable to secure support for a needed program, a vocal group of parents can be manipulated to provide the necessary pressure on the superintendent and/or board. As long as the manipulator is not too obvious about the process, it has usually been tolerated as a peculiarity of the function of special education leadership. It is questionable whether such a relationship between the special interest agent of the school system and the client group of that system will continue as client organizations become more sophisticated in their activism, assume a larger role in influencing policy on their own, leaving the administrator within the system in a largely defensive stance, and rendering the relationship largely adversarial.

Change Source #2: The Impact of the Courts

As a part of the social climate of the times, and as a reflection of adversarial relations, the increasing intervention of the courts into the determination of specifics of social change constitutes a force of such significance as to warrant consideration in its own right.

Issues directly related to education have frequently been debated and decided in courts at all levels—state trial courts, appeals courts, federal district courts, and the U.S. Supreme Court—throughout the history of the country. The 1960s and 1970s have seen an increasing involvement of the U.S. Supreme Court in educational matters, with questions narrowing from basic human rights to a specific focus on education. Specific aspects of the right to education issue have involved such varied major social concerns as racial desegregation, methods of financing schools, discriminatory classification and exclusion. Related cases have dealt with specifics of students' rights, such as details of dress codes, corporal punishment, personal and familial privacy, religion, as well as with the teachers' and administrators' rights to act professionally and privately without unreasonable infringement.

It appears that the schools have increasingly become an arena in which major societal issues are confronted and the conflict between individual human rights and societal imperatives is thrashed out. The expectation that the courts will provide a means of settling complex problems has led to use of appeal procedures that have brought more and more cases to the U.S. Supreme Court while maintaining at each lower court an overflow of litigation on schools.

The involvement of the courts in actions concerning education of the handicapped and other exceptional pupils invariably must start with the assertion of a basic right to education for *all* children. The particulars of litigation may take many different paths, but the central tenet of *equal right* is understood, and usually stated. While courts have not always ruled negatively on specific issues concerning handicapped pupils at earlier points in our history, the words of the Supreme Court of the United States in the landmark decision of *Brown v. Board of Education* in 1954 stand as the foundation on which subsequent litigation rests:

> In these days, it is doubtful that any child may reasonably be expected to succeed in life if he is denied the opportunity of an education. Such an opportunity, where the state has undertaken to provide it, is a right which must be made available to all on equal terms. [4]

The utilization of the concept of equal rights for the particular minority group toward which that decision was directed, a segregated racial population, has appeared eminently relevant to courts concerned with another segregated minority group, the handicapped. Reviews of litigation concerning education of the handicapped usually cite, as a contrast to the impressive breakthroughs of the 1970s, the rulings of the early courts. Noteworthy is the case of *Watson v. City of Cambridge* (1893) in which a state court supported the school committee in expelling children who persisted in disorderly conduct "either voluntarily or by reason of imbecility." [5] Also cited is the case of *Beattie v. Board of Education* (1919) in which a Wisconsin Superior Court ruled that although a physically handicapped child constituted no threat, and was academically capable, his presence produced a "depressing and nauseating effect on the teachers and school children" and took up an undue portion of the teacher's time. Therefore "the rights of a child of school age to attend the public schools of the state cannot be insisted upon, when its presence therein is harmful to the best interests of the school." [6]

The principle in *Brown v. Board of Education*, while enunciated in 1954, lay dormant in its implications for further litigation (just as it had in its implementation of racial desegregation) for some time. Finally, in the case of *Wolfe v. Utah*

[4]*Brown v. Board of Education*, 347 U.S. 483, 493 (1954).
[5]*Watson v. City of Cambridge*, 157 Mass., 561, 32 N.E. 864, 865 (1893).
[6]*Beattie v. Board of Education*, 169 Wis. 231, 232, 172 N.W. 153, 154 (1919).

in 1969, a state court used the language of Brown in rendering a decision concerning the rights of mentally retarded children to regular public school admission. Affirming that no "child may reasonably be expected to succeed in life if he is denied the right and opportunity of an education" the court further ruled that "segregation of the plaintiff children from the public school system has a detrimental effect upon the children as well as their parents," that such segregation is "usually interpreted as denoting their inferiority, unusualness, uselessness and incompetency," and that "even though perhaps well intentioned, under the apparent sanction of law and state authority has a tendency to retard the educational, emotional and mental development of the children."[7] The recognition of the problem of governmentally sanctioned policies which leads to stigmatization beyond the point of minimum necessity marks the Wolfe decision as the first of many cases that have forced much special education reform.

In discussing the rapid upsurge of litigation, beginning in 1970, Gilhool[8] defines three distinct lines of cases bearing on the broad subject. The first line starts with the case of *Wyatt v. Stickney* (1971)[9] and deals with the issue of right to treatment. Such cases are concerned with the rights of institutionalized retarded persons to treatment—including habilitation, care, education in the least restrictive environment—with due regard for privacy and other basic attributes of human living. While the specific issues in that case, concerning the residents of a number of Alabama institutions, go beyond those that public school administrators usually have been concerned with, many of the basic principles of legal rights involved have universal applicability. The final ruling of the court, which set detailed standards for the administration of Bryce and Searcy Hospitals and for the Partlow State School and Hospital, stands as a stark example of judicial intervention into executive branches of government.

A second line of cases is more centrally involved with access to public school education, and goes beyond *Wolfe v. Utah*, mentioned earlier; the action brought by the Pennsylvania Association for Retarded Children against the Commonwealth of Pennsylvania (*PARC v. Pennsylvania*)[10] is described as the first case to recognize the particular learning needs of the retarded. In the Consent Agreement reached by the parties as a resolution of the case in 1972, a three-judge federal district court permanently prevented Pennsylvania officials from denying or postponing a free public program of education and training to any of the state's mentally retarded children. The case stands as a landmark by virtue of the expert testimony brought forth by its participants, the court's acknowledge-

[7]*Fred G. Wolfe v. The Legislature of the State of Utah*, No. 182546 (3rd Dist. Ct., Salt Lak. Co. 1969).

[8]Thomas K. Gilhool, *The Right of Access to Free Public Schooling for All Children: Special Education in Court.* Vol. 2 in the Leadership Series in Special Education, eds. R. A. Johnson, J. C. Gross, and R. F. Weatherman (Minneapolis, Minn.:University of Minnesota, 1973).

[9]*Wyatt v. Stickney*, 344 F. Supp. 387, 392 (M.D. Ala. 1972).

[10]*PARC v. Commonwealth of Pennsylvania*, 343 F. Supp. 279, 302 (E.D. Pa. 1972).

ment that every retarded child is capable of deriving benefit from education, and for the specific stipulations set forth regarding the manner by which the delivery of services to such children would be handled. Most prominent was the focus on procedural safeguards in decision processes and guarantees of right to service.

The action of the courts in spelling out detailed procedures for administrators of schools to follow, is commonly viewed as a dramatic change in the traditional relationship between the judicial and executive branches of government, and has been received by a significant proportion of the populace as totally improper. This has been seen in the cases of racial desegregation of schools and bussing. Among school administrators, the court-required management of programs for the handicapped has also been viewed with mixed reactions and apprehension.

Such specification rests on the particular legal and constitutional theory on which judicial rulings in favor of handicapped children are based. Despite the wording in some of the cases, a fundamental right to education is not mentioned and therefore not guaranteed under the United States Constitution in the same manner as are those guarantees of the Bill of Rights. Education is thereby remanded to the states. However, it is under the Fourteenth Amendment of the United States Constitution, in which the guaranteed equal protection of the laws prohibits discrimination against a class of persons for an arbitrary or unjustifiable reason, that rulings can be advanced providing a service (such as education) to everyone, not just a select few.

Equal protection was the principle upon which the Brown decision was based, applying to black children. The same principle was invoked in a way that involved race, but extended beyond a purely racial context in the case of *Hobson v. Hansen*[11] in 1967. That ruling abolished the discriminatory tracking system in the Washington, D.C. schools, finding that the procedure adversely affected the educational opportunities of disadvantaged minorities. The system that had been practiced was found to irreversibly assign students to tracks on the basis of behaviors which tended to be racially and culturally discriminatory, and which resulted in inequal quality of services. It was a short and logical step to the class of pupils represented by the plaintiffs in *PARC v. Pennsylvania*

In addition to the equal protection concept, the Fourteenth Amendment includes the "due process" clause, which holds that a state may interfere with one's fundamental rights only if that interference conforms with due process of law. The due process guarantee is the prime basis for the kind of procedural stipulations that generated from the PARC case. The requirements of prior notification, a hearing, the right to counsel, the right to present evidence and witnesses, and the right to cross examine first became a part of special education administrators' routine as a result of PARC.

Closely following the PARC case was the case of *Mills v. Board of Educa-*

---

[11]*Hobson v. Hanson*, 269 F. Supp. 401, 507–08 (D.D.C. 1967).

tion (in the District of Columbia), in which Judge Waddy's final ruling was issued in August 1972 finding that the school system had failed to provide a public education for all types of handicapped, disturbed, and retarded children. He ordered that such children be offered such services within 30 days. The order also directed the system to establish hearing procedures to guard against the indiscriminate suspension, exclusion, or placement of pupils in special education programs. Waddy went further in ruling that economic excuses for not implementing the programs could not be used:

> If sufficient funds are not available to finance all of the services and programs that are needed in the system then the available funds must be expended equitably in such a manner that no child is entirely excluded from a publicly supported education consistent with his needs and ability to benefit therefrom.[12]

Following the Mills case litigation was introduced in a large number of other states dealing with the provision of open access to education, with no rejection, regardless of handicap. Also dealt with was the proposition that parents and children are entitled to be heard regarding the appropriateness of the educational assignment.

Still a third line of litigation is cited by Gilhool[13], relating closely to those discussed above but focusing more particularly on the standards and practices used in classifying children. The case of *Diana v. State Board of Education*[14] appears to have established the beginning of this line, followed by *Larry P. v. Riles*[15], and *Ruiz v. State Board of Education*[16]. While the other cases were concerned with securing a desired and presumably appropriate and justified educational service, this latter line of litigation concerned the practices of placing children into special education programs who did not belong there. In each of these cases, the state school system in California was charged with using procedures which resulted in a disproportionate number of minority group children being certified for special education and placed in programs which were of questionable value and negative stigma.

In the Diana case, it was pointed out that classes for educable mentally retarded contained approximately double the number of Chicano pupils than should be expected by the proportion of such children in the general school population. It was clear that school personnel had been faced with children whose language background and culture was significantly different from the average Anglo child; the school personnel turned to the EMR program as the only available alternative to regular classroom programs. The plaintiff children had been certified as eligi-

---

[12]*Mills v. Board of Education*, C.A. No. 1939–71 (D.D.C. 1971).

[13]Gilhool, *Right of Access*.

[14]*Diana v. State Board of Education*, C–70, 37 RFP (N.D.CAL. 1970).

[15]*Larry P. v. Riles*, 343 F. Supp. 1306 (N. D. CAL. 1972).

[16]*Ruiz v. State Board of Education*, C.A. No. 218294 (Super. Ct. Sacramento, Cal. 1972).

ble for such placement on the basis of English intelligence tests which, as the court found obvious, were totally inappropriate for making a decision regarding the status of mental retardation. The universality of such practice, wherever populations of non-English speaking persons were found, led California to the mandate for developing test instruments and testing procedures that would be appropriate for children of other than English language and culture. The case also called for the state to develop interim programs for the many Chicano pupils who would be removed from EMR programs as a result of the retesting.

The foothold gained in the Diana case undoubtedly was influential in extending the principle to black children in *Larry P. v. Riles*. Data presented indicated that blacks constituted 9 percent of the school population, but 27 percent of the placement in classes for the educable mentally retarded. The class action suit alleged that the San Francisco Unified School district had improperly classified black children as educable mentally retarded and had placed them in classes which carried a stigma and "life sentence of illiteracy." It was argued that the children were not mentally retarded, but the victims of a testing procedure that failed to account for their different cultural background.

The relief sought in this case against the state and local school boards was a moratorium on the use of individual intelligence tests for the placement of black children, and a ceiling on placement of black children based on the percentage of Anglo children in the total school population who are placed in such EMR classes. Specifically the case called for a number of reforms: evaluation only with tests that properly account for the cultural background and experiences of such black children, the return of the plaintiff children to regular classes with intensive and supplemental individual training enabling them to rapidly equal their peers' level, the removal from school records any indication that the pupils are mentally retarded, and the recruitment of black and other minority group personnel as psychologists and consultants in local school districts so that the cultural background of children would be considered in admission and planning committees.

In a June 1972 ruling, Judge Robert F. Peckman issued a temporary injunction stopping the use of I.Q. tests as the main criteria for placing black students in classes for the mentally retarded. He ordered that yearly reevaluations of pupils currently in such classes be conducted in the future by means that do not deprive them of equal protection of the law. The other items of requested relief were not granted, allowing pupils currently placed to remain until reevaluation, but such evaluation could take place without waiting for the court ordered development of unbiased tests.

The case of *Ruiz v. State Board of Education* also dealt with testing and classification, and sought to eliminate the use of group intelligence tests from the schools, since the result of such tests, according to the argument advanced, was that the scores tended to create a self-fulfilling prophecy when given to teachers. Of particular note in the issue of group testing, was the fact that the membership of special programs for the gifted, where placement eligibility was determined by group tests, appeared to be sharply biased against other than Anglo children. Legislation in California ultimately accomplished part of the same purpose as the Ruiz case, abolishing mandatory group I.Q. testing, but it allowed for testing on local district option.

Much of the strength of the arguments regarding biased testing generated from the widely disseminated and popularized findings of Jane Mercer in her eight-year study of public school and agency classification of minority children in California school systems. Her data demonstrated that, of all agencies, the public school system was the primary labeler of individuals as mentally retarded, and suggested that "any major change in the labeling policies of this single system would have a significant impact on the labeling processes in the community as a whole."[17] In elaborating on the conclusions regarding the classification of black and Chicano children, Mercer stated:

> We believe that psychological assessment procedures have become a civil rights issue because present assessment and educational practices violate at least five rights of children: a) their right to be evaluated within a culturally appropriate normative framework; b) their right to be assessed as multi-dimensional, many faceted human beings; c) their right to be fully educated; d) their right to be free of stigmatizing labels; and e) their right to cultural identity and respect.[18]

A thorough discussion of the relationship between student classification and the courts is put forth by Kirp. In citing the U.S. Supreme Court's involvement in a number of decisions which had traditionally been made solely by school administrators, he points out that most of the issues had addressed school policy on a grand scale, and that this was appropriate in those cases where a state-wide or nation-wide question having broad generality was at stake. However, in matters which directly impinge on quality of the child's experiences in school, it is more likely that more crucial decisions are made in the individual school or classroom unit. Therefore, because of the minute detail of questions concerning quality within a classroom, there is an understandable reluctance of the courts to perceive the issues as legally manageable.

Within the domain of student classification, the courts have found intervention feasible. On the issue of overt exclusion from school, tracking, and special education placement, Kirp points out that the constitutional standards upon which such cases can be argued may be any of three distinct and identifiable approaches.

[17]Jane R. Mercer, "A Policy Statement on Assessment Procedures and the Rights of Children," *Harvard Educational Review*, 44 (1974), pp. 127–41.

[18]Mercer, "Assessment Procedures," p. 132.

1. the educational harm attributable to either exclusion of or assignment to slow ability groups, or special education programs that are not only inferior, but carry psychic injury in addition to deprivation.
2. the disproportionate assignment of minority group children, that creates racially or ethnically based isolation.
3. the school's procedure for determining how a particular student or class of students should be treated, irrespective of the legitimacy of the classifications themselves.[19]

Educators may fear that the courts' adherence to these legal arguments could lead to the requirement of substantially uniform treatment for all, thus drastically limiting the capability of the school to tailor programs to individual needs. On the other hand, if special education programs can be developed to provide an advantage to those assigned to them, and if assignment can be limited to short-term, flexible, goal specific programs, the relative vulnerability of minority group children to such assignment will not constitute the noxious condition that it has in the past. Adherence to the regularity of due process can encourage better placements and can serve to continually refocus attention on the assumptions regarding those classifications which are deemed necessary; it need not "convert the school into a courtroom."[20]

One major impact of the courts' actions has been the effects on the nature of legislation introduced and passed at both the state and federal levels. The pervasive themes in litigation activity have in many cases been translated quickly and directly into legislation within and across state lines.

Change Source #3: Specific Legislation

The turning point of 1970 also marks, to a considerable degree, the rapid upsurge in major legislative changes. While almost every state legislature had periodically added and modified existing statutes with some degree of regularity during the 1940s, 1950s, and 1960s, the focus of that period's legislation tended to be on incremental expansion and addition of services, the securing of somewhat more favorable fiscal provisions, and the development of standards for the delivery of quality instruction to the handicapped. Statutory provisions and the regulatory administrative provisions (developed under the authority of law for the implementation of statutes during the earlier period) contained much desirable encouragement and, in many cases, incentives for local educational systems to improve their service offerings. However, strongly worded mandates for com-

---

[19]David L. Kirp, "Student Classification, Public Policy and the Courts," *Harvard Educational Review*, 44 (1974), pp. 7–52.

[20]Kirp, "Student Classification," p. 52.

prehensive service for all conditions and degrees of handicaps were rare. Qualitative differences between legislation of the 1950s and 1960s, from that of the 1970s, can be discerned at the state level. At the federal level, legislation directly affecting local school system programs for the handicapped was negligible until 1967, and even then appropriations to give force to new laws were insufficient to constitute a signficiant impact. To appreciate the changing nature of the legislative influence over this period of years, a review of the content of some of the representative enactments may be in order.

State Legislation.   The Handicapped Children's Education Project (HACHE), a federally funded activity of the Education Commission of the States, has maintained a monitoring system on new legislation introduced and passed in the states. In recording and analyzing this legislative history, the project staff classified the basic data according to seven types of issue content:

1. rights to an education
2. mandatory legislation for the handicapped
3. statewide planning and advisory councils
4. state responsibility and advocacy
5. finance and funding patterns
6. minimum and maximum age ranges
7. manpower preparation[21]

Legislation regarding rights to education was passed in 1972 in the states of Arkansas, Idaho, Maine, New Mexico, and Oregon. In the same year, ten states (Colorado, Idaho, Maryland, Massachusetts, Michigan, New Mexico, South Carolina, South Dakota, Tennessee, and Virginia) enacted new or amended bills concerned with mandatory provisions. By the close of the 1975 legislative sessions, forty-six states had some form of mandatory legislation.[22] Abeson[23] points out that whereas almost all states now have some type of mandatory legislation for at least a portion of their handicapped population, exemption provisions and such loopholes prevent the realization of full service.

The newer legislation has tended to emphasize the policy of guaranteeing service for *all*, with no child excluded from services or education for any reason whatsoever. Another characteristic of the more recent legislation, according to Abeson, is the establishment of dates by which compliance must be achieved. Kansas, West Virginia, and Arkansas were cited as particular examples of states utilizing the "date of compliance" approach.

---

[21]HACHE, *A Summary of Issues and State Legislation Related to the Education of Handicapped Children in 1972* (A Report of the Education Commission of the States, March 1973).

[22]HACHE, *Questions and Answers: The Education of Exceptional Children* (Report No. 73, Education Commission of the States, September 1975).

[23]Alan Abeson, "Law Review: Movement and Momentum: Government and the Education of Handicapped Children," *Exceptional Children,* 41 (1974), pp. 109–15.

Due process protections, growing out of the upsurge of court actions, is another frequently found provision in the most recent legislative changes. Abeson cites a 1973 Missouri statute as being representative in requiring that:

1. Parents must be provided with the results of diagnostic, evaluation, or reevaluation procedures.
2. Written notice of recommended assignment, change in assignment, or denial of assignment must be sent to the child's family via certified mail.
3. The notice must also advise the parents of their right to examine all school records relating to their child.
4. The notice must also indicate the right of the parents to request a review of the action taken by the local or state boards of education.
5. Local education agencies must adhere to preestablished timelines governing the filing and handling of appeals.
6. Local education agencies must conform to procedures requiring that after an appeal an informal hearing must be held before an appeal body. Chairperson of this body must be the chief administrative officer of the school to which the child has been assigned. At that hearing both the parents and school may present information. It is likely that the intent of the informal hearing is to bring the parties together for careful consideration of the recommended placement of the child. It is not a substitute for a formal hearing.
7. Procedures and timelines governing a second formal hearing before the local or state board of education are also specified. Local boards are given the legal prerogative to designate as chairperson of such hearings individuals not involved in the original decision. The hearings must permit parents and their counsel to examine and cross-examine witnesses and introduce evidence. Also, a complete record of the hearing must be made.[24]

Another significant trend in more recent legislative enactments has been the focus on maximum feasible normalization, made possible by ensuring that placements for children with handicaps utilize the least restrictive alternative, of whatever continuum of service options is available. Wisconsin and Florida statutes were among the first to contain this emphasis, which was not seen in other states before 1970.

State legislation concerned with fiscal support also has shown significant change since 1970. While the typical practice has been to pass more authorizing legislation than is ever supported by fund appropriation (this will probably continue as a fact of political life), dramatic increases in state level financial provisions have been noted. The Education Commission of the States has reported an average of 60 percent increase in appropriations across all states in 1974.

Legislation concerned with statewide planning was passed in nine states in 1972, while advisory councils were authorized in legislation in seven states, bringing such provisions to a total of twenty-three states.

The provision of preschool educational services for handicapped children has been an increasingly common feature of later legislation, with more than 70 percent of the states now having permissive legislation and about 45 percent having mandatory provisions for such age levels. Of the twenty-three states providing for services below five years of age, the authorizing laws in eighteen of the states were passed after 1971.[25]

In summarizing the overall effect of new legislative enactments at the state level, the HACHE[26] report indicates that major changes in education statutes relative to the education of children with handicaps have occurred in almost all states since 1970. Those states which have not made major revisions in the past few years tend to be those which have adopted relatively comprehensive and mandatory services at an earlier time, primarily in the late 1960s.

Federal Legislation. Prior to 1965, federal legislation relating to local public school services, for any type of student, was limited to rather indirect intervention. Combination federal-state programs in vocational education had long been a source of program support to the schools, but they had been highly categorical and were not accompanied by direct cash grants. The implementation of the Elementary and Secondary Education Act (Public Law 89-10) in 1965 marked the beginning of a new era in broad scale federal involvement in local school systems. With the focus of Title I of ESEA on assistance for school systems to better provide for pupils who were economically disadvantaged, a debate immediately arose over the Congress' intent in passing the bill. Some insisted that Congress had intended that handicapped children be considered disadvantaged in the same sense as those whose disadvantage was economically based. Equally insistent were those who had become somewhat resentful of the successful efforts of special interest groups pressing for handicapped individuals' rights at the state level. While the attitudes and resulting decisions on the matter varied from state to state and locality to locality, a significant point of view held that ESEA was the long awaited chance for noncategorical public school programs to secure a share of money from Washington, and that the special interest pleaders were to be kept at a distance.

Edwin Martin[27] has vividly recounted the history of this debate and the interchanges that finally led to the amendments that in 1967 added a new Title VI to ESEA. This amendment dealt specifically with services for children with handicaps and authorized direct grants to LEA's for the development and improvement of programs at that level. Other significant provisions of the amendment were establishing a bureau level structure for education of the handicapped within the United States Office of Education, permitting considerably more influence and status in the federal organizational hierarchy, and organizing a National Advisory Committee to be an expert source of guidance to the Congress in matters of further federal involvement.

[25]HACHE, *Questions and Answers,* p. 47.

[26]HACHE, *Questions and Answers,* pp. 10–11.

[27]Edwin W. Martin, Jr., "Breakthrough for the Handicapped: Legislative History," *Exceptional Children,* 34 (1968) pp. 493–503.

At the local school system level, the grand promise of Title VI was over-shadowed only by the magnitude of dissolutionment over the large gap between funds authorized and those actually appropriated during the first years. However, with the "foot in the door" that the law provided, consistent pressure by in-terested groups gradually brought about increased appropriations so that by 1970, when many of the separate federal laws concerning the education of the hand-icapped were brought together under P.L. 91-230, the amount of federal funds finding their way through each state agency to local schools systems for program development were sufficient to begin to have an influence. In addition to the influentially significant funding leverage, Title VI, Part B of the law, that was concerned with Assistance to States for Education of Handicapped Children, es-tablished in some detail a requirement for state plans. These provisions set forth that any state desiring to receive grants under that part of the law shall submit to the Commissioner (U.S. Office of Education) a plan which would assure that federal funds distributed to the states would be expended solely to initiate, ex-pand, or improve programs or projects designed to meet the special eduation needs of handicapped children throughout the state; these funds were focused on programs of sufficient size, scope, and quality as to give reasonable promise of meeting those needs. Further requirements of the plan dealt with inclusion of children in private schools; the administration and control of funds; the guaran-teed supplementation of existing state, local, and private funds rather than the supplanting of such funds; the evaluation of effectiveness; and the filing of official reports. Provisions for administration of the program, the approvals between the federal and state levels, and the handling of questions regarding compliance by judicial review established an increasingly interdependent rela-tionship between local, state and federal education agencies. The details of the requirements and the magnitude of the money at stake were becoming sufficient to force the local special education administrator to be constantly aware of the status of federal legislation.

This phenomenon was only enhanced by the Education Amendments of 1974 (P. L. 93-380) that, under Part B (Education of the Handicapped), not only increased the funding authorizations, but established even more stringent and specific requirements of both the state and local agencies as a precondition of participation in any of the funded projects. The most significant of the new re-quirements dealt with the establishment of a goal providing full educational op-portunities to all handicapped children, with guarantees of procedural safeguards regarding identification, evaluation, and educational placement, including such things as prior notice to parents, impartial due process hearings, and the protec-tion of the children's rights when the parents are not available. The greatest im-pact on local administrative practices was the further requirement that to the maximum appropriate extent, handicapped children would be served with chil-dren who are not handicapped, that separate schooling would be utilized only when absolutely necessary, and that procedures would be implemented to ensure that testing and evaluation be carried out in ways that would not be racially or culturally discriminatory.

With each amendment of federal legislation in this field, the effects of the action of the courts have been brought into basic statutory law, and the role of the state level agencies in monitoring the local level and guaranteeing compliance has become more evident. The impact of federal legislation on local programming has become most pronounced by the passage of Public Law 94-142 (1975), which authorizes even more funds and even more detailed local and state administrative requirements.

Given the title The Education for *All* Handicapped Children Act, P. L. 94-142 adds to the previous acts' full services goal by specifying a "free appropriate public education" for all children ages three to eighteen by September 1, 1978 and for ages three to twenty-one by September 1, 1980, unless the extension of services to these younger and older age groups is contrary to individual state law. The law also mandates that the states place a priority in the use of federal funds on two groups of children: 1) handicapped children who are *not* receiving an education, and 2) those with the most severe handicaps, within each disability, who are receiving an inadequate education. While the intent of the legislation seems rather clear, and constitutes a considerable intervention of federal influence into state and local educational decision making, early discussions regarding the development of regulations for the enforcement of the law reveal that the definitions of some of the law's terms, such as "appropriate," "unserved," and "inadequately served," will require much interpretation. In a series of meetings convened by the Bureau of Education for the Handicapped in the spring of 1976, with representatives of professional and advocate organizations and school administrators gathering to discuss matters prior to the writing of the rules and regulations, rumors were reported that some states were considering opting out of qualifying for the federal money, due to the administrative complexities in meeting all requirements.[28]

The subsequent action in the Florida state legislature, resolving to refuse compliance with the provisions and the funding of P.L. 94–142, was a further demonstration of state level objection to the developing impact of federal intervention. Note that, to a large extent, the states expressing strongest resistance to the federal role were those claiming (and generally recognized as demonstrating) a high level of service quality on their own.

In addition to the full services goal, the contingencies for qualifying included annual state plans which would specify how the state and local school districts would conform to major administrative requirements such as:

1. Due Process Safeguards
    a. prior notice to parents of any change in their child's program, written in their primary language;

[28]*Education Daily*, March 30, 1976.

    b. access to relevant school records;

    c. opportunity for independent evaluation of child;

    d. impartial hearing, with parent accompanied by counsel, with the right to present evidence to confront, compel, and cross-examine witnesses; the right to obtain a transcript of the hearing, and a written decision by the hearing officer; the right to appeal decisions to state or federal court;

    e. the right to remain in the placement desired by the parent until proceedings are complete;

    f. the designation of a "surrogate parent" on behalf of children who are wards of the state or whose parents or guardians are unknown or unavailable.

2. Least Restrictive Alternative

Provides that handicapped children, including those in public and private institutions, must be educated as much as possible with children who are not handicapped.

3. Nondiscriminatory Testing and Evaluation

Tests and procedures used must be racially and culturally nondiscriminatory in both selection and administration, in the primary language or mode of communication of the child.

4. Individualized Educational Programs

Written plans, individualized for the child, must be developed and reviewed annually, with involvement of the child's parent and teacher; they must include statements of present levels of performance, short and long term goals, the specific services to be provided, and criteria to measure success.

5. Personnel Development

A comprehensive system must be developed to train both general and special education teachers and administrators to carry out requirements of the law.

6. Participation of Children in Private Schools

Free special education and related services must be provided for handicapped children in private schools when they are placed or referred to such schools by the local or state agencies to meet the requirements of the law.

In spelling out procedures for administration of the law, additional functions of the state and federal special education agencies are evident. While the local agency must ensure that funds received will not be used to supplant existing state and local service expenditures, and that the new funds be used to provide only for excess costs (those above the regular per pupil expenditures), the state education agency is designated as the responsible party for ensuring that all provisions of the law are carried out. This tends to place state personnel in a much more "policing" role than has been traditional, monitoring the local's compliance to all federal mandates. In turn, the staff of the Bureau is placed in a similar position regarding the possible sanctions for noncompliance on the part of the state. Due to the need for establishing rules and regulations on aspects of eligibility, the federal offices are further required to deal with the difficult task of defining criteria for such elusive concepts as specific learning diabilities. In this respect, the problems inherent in arriving at a workable answer to satisfy the broad and diverse national community are immense.

The scope and complexity of P.L. 94-142 is therefore sufficient to raise the question of whether its enforcement can or should be executed to the degree that the wording of the law seems to demand. Whether it is implemented in detail will undoubtedly depend on the degree to which the appropriations of funds in succeeding years approach those originally authorized, since the costs of fulfilling all requirements are fully expected to outstrip the additional funds to be earned. This has been discussed by Cronin[29] who cites a great number of instances in which the federal investment in local education since 1965 has been accompanied by regulation in ways disproportionate for the dollars received. Although the federal funds in local education still are under 10 percent of the local budget, major influence is cited by such examples as:

1 Many title programs require a comprehensive written proposal to secure the money, and most programs and grants require considerable documentation and formal evaluation.
2. The Congress in the 1970's required more than two dozen additional reports and studies to which states and local schools must respond (for example, in violence in the schools or on the impact of title programs).
3. The Buckley Amendment added new procedures regulating the keeping of student records and prescribing access to student information.
4. Other federal acts, such as the Environmental Protection Act, added new requirements for school safety and sewage and heating systems.
5. School districts in states using federal revenue-sharing funds for education must document compliance with the Civil Rights Act of 1964 upon request.[30]

In noting the implementation of P.L. 94-142, Cronin has pointed out that U.S. Commissioner of Education Terrel Bell publicly conceded that the new handicapped children bill "will be difficult to administer." The law is full of new and progressive entitlements, appeal procedures, specified treatment options, student and parental rights, and required state activities in the realms of monitoring and program evaluation. The new law stipulates that each child classified as handicapped must have a written prescription for education and treatment, and regulations governing these have been issued. Experience with equally complex mandated programs in Massachusetts, Pennsylvania, and Illinois indicates that millions of person-hours and dollars will be required just to develop the procedures, personnel systems, and forms to implement the law. By 1980 the phenomenon of "federal takeover" may appear to be an understatement of the problem.[31]

The increasing centralization of a national education policy provides the special educator with a promise of programming more nearly approximating the long sought ideal. But it clearly indicates a diminishing of the traditional options of local and state governments. This could be interpreted as reducing (or at

[29]Joseph M. Cronin, "The Federal Takeover: Should the Junior Partner Run the Firm?" *Phi Delta Kappan*, 57 (1976), p. 499.

[30]Cronin, "The Federal Takeover," p. 500.

[31]Cronin, "The Federal Takeover," p. 500.

least changing) the administrator's role from one of creative leadership to one of compliance enforcement. While the impact of the federal legislation on administrative behavior must be observed over a longer period to adequately evaluate it, the influence on the special educator can certainly be assumed as major.

INTERNAL FORCES FOR CHANGE

With the preponderance of activity from sources outside the conventional educational establishment, the initiation of change from within may appear comparatively insignificant. To some extent it may be that the societal and legal factors discussed previously came about, in part, because of the evolving attitudes and beliefs of persons within the system who, whether openly or covertly, promoted external change-inducing phenomena. This is seen in participation in liberal social causes, legislative lobbying, and even subtle encouragement of litigation calling attention to needed system reform. However, there appears to be evidence of more professional special educators acting as maintainers of the status quo than as change agents.

Some highly notable exceptions can be cited. Individual persons and groups have come out strongly for special education reform, and have promoted models for at least gradual (and sometimes radical) change. Many proposals have been advanced to modify and improve curriculum, instructional approaches, service delivery organization, and other management aspects of special education. In a few cases, major philosophic and policy revolutions have been proposed and pursued. A review of the major displays of change forces from within the system can be organized around a few topics of pressing concern, and by citing a few persons and /or groups who have most forcefully articulated the call for change in the critical years of the late 1960s and early 1970s.

Specific Catalysts

Efficacy. Discontent over the lack of clear evidence for successful results of existing special education programs and practices, though acknowledged by professionals such as Johnson[32] since the earliest attempts at measurement, had been discussed in somewhat subdued tones until the appearance of a landmark statement by Dunn in 1968.[33] In calling to question many of the standard practices affecting the largest proportion of the clientele served by special education organizations, those classified as educable retarded, and in suggesting some dif-

[32]G. Orville Johnson, "Special Education for Mentally Handicapped—A Paradox," *Exceptional Children*, 29 (1962), pp. 62–69.

[33]Lloyd M. Dunn, "Special Education for the Mildly Retarded: Is Much of It Justified?" *Exceptional Children*, 35 (1968), pp. 5–22.

ferent models for personnel development and service delivery, Dunn touched off the open consideration of a wide variety of issues, including instructional technology, the stigmatizing effects of labels, and alternative models of organization.

In a similar way, dissatisfaction with the way conventional practices tended to emphasize the pupil's faults, rather than the possible inadequacies in regular educational systems, sparked the development of a policy statement by the Council for Children with Behavior Disorders (1969). They charged professional special educators with complicity in allowing schools to cover up failure by branding as retarded or disturbed, children (particularly minority group members) whose characteristics did not conform with the middle class values of typical public school personnel. The call for a reconceptualization of special education put forth by the CCBD group was met with disdain and /or hostility by many of the established community of special educators (as the Dunn statement of the previous year had been). Nevertheless, the controversy brought to light the issues of biased identification of the handicapped and the need for a more open system of flexible alternatives under which pupils could receive appropriate services. Johnson's statement[34] of the misuse of special education for black children served as a conceptual rallying point for those who were willing to consider a major shift in practice.

Mainstreaming.   Although the concept of a continuum of services to fit a wide variety of special needs had been presented much earlier by Reynolds[35], the full development of the idea as a major professional issue occurred after the dissatisfactions cited above had come to the surface and stimulated the search for alternatives. The further development of the model by Deno[36] provided the link between conventional practices and the expression from sources both inside and outside the educational system for the use of the least restrictive alternative in prescribing services for handicapped pupils. In developing the idea of a "Cascade of Services" to meet all gradations of needs, Deno went on to propose special education as the research and development arm of regular education, and therefore, closely linked to it. She proposed that such a concept "facilitates tailoring of treatment to individual needs rather than a system for sorting out children so they will fit conditions designed according to group standards not necessarily suitable for the particular case".[37] The focus of the Leadership Training Institute for Special Education at University of Minnesota, directed primarily

---

[34]John L. Johnson, "Special Education in the Inner City: A Challenge for the Future or Another Means for Cooling the Mark Out?" *Journal of Special Education*, 3 (1969), pp. 241–51.

[35]Maynard Reynolds, "A Framework for Considering Some Issues in Special Education," *Exceptional Children*, 28 (1962), p. 368.

[36]Evelyn N. Deno, "Special Education as Developmental Capital," *Exceptional Children*, 37 (1970), pp. 229–40.

[37]Deno, "Special Education as Developmental Capital," p. 235.

at maximizing mainstream educational possibilities, has constituted a major concentration of inside professional force for change in organization and service delivery in the field.

New Models for Change.   In presenting a brief historical overview of the development of the mainstreaming concept and the debates surrounding it, Chaffin[38] cites four models or proposals for alternative delivery systems. In addition to the Deno model, a Training Based Model suggested by Lilly[39] emphasizes the failures of the regular school system rather than the child's failures and sets as the major goal of special education the development of skills for regular classroom teachers so that they will not have to refer children elsewhere. In Lilly's conceptualization, an instructional specialist would work with the regular teacher in the classroom to diagnose and cope more effectively with the instructional and behavioral interventions needed to help the child.

The Special Education Contract Model proposed by Gallagher[40] deals primarily with the problem of the "dead end" placement in classes for the educable mentally retarded and the problem of disproportionate assignment of minority group children to special education. In a similar way the Fail-Save Model proposed by Adamson and Van Etten[41] calls for a mandatory cycling of pupils through an evaluation and treatment program that assures periodic rechecking of and assignment to the most appropriate educational program.

In response to the need for service delivery models that might enhance the probability of a least restrictive environment for children with special education needs, the 1970s witnessed the evolution of the resource room from a limited approach for a few visually handicapped pupils to a major service model for almost all mildly handicapped. While no one person can properly be credited with responsibility for developing the resource room and resource teacher concept, an exhaustive articulation of characteristics of the model has been presented by Sabatino.[42] Reger and Koppman[43] have also provided enlightenment on the concept's application; this has undoubtedly had a strong influence on school administrators, and has led to a rapid increase in the use of the model. An extensive shift from self-contained classrooms to resource models for mildly handicapped has

[38]Jerry D. Chaffin, "Will the Real Mainstreaming Program Please Stand Up! Or Should Dunn Have Done It?" *Focus on Exceptional Children*, 6 (1974) No. 5, pp. 1–18.

[39]M. Stephen Lilly, "A Training Based Model for Special Education," *Exceptional Children*, 37 (1971), pp. 745–49.

[40]James J. Gallagher, "The Special Education Contract for Mildly Handicapped Children," *Exceptional Children*, 38 (1972), pp. 527–35.

[41]Gary Adamson and Glen Van Etten, "Zero Reject Model Revisited: A Workable Alternative," *Exceptional Children*, 38 (1972), pp. 735–38.

[42]David A. Sabatino, "Resource Rooms: The Renaissance in Special Education," *Journal of Special Education*, 6 (1972), pp. 335–46.

[43]Roger Reger and Marion Koppmann, "The Child Oriented Resource Room," *Exceptional Children,* 37 (1971), pp. 460–62.

been evident in many major school systems, calling for changes in some of the leadership functions of special education administrators.

In a similar vein, the promotion of the Diagnostic-Prescriptive Teacher model by Prouty and McGarry[44] and the Consulting Teacher model by McKenzie and his colleagues at University of Vermont[45] has had a significant impact on service delivery possibilities and therefore on the administrators of schools that might consider departing from the conventional self-contained classroom approach.

In each of the aforementioned cases, the need for a revised set of assumptions about the teacher's role, both in special education and in the general program, is called for. In turn, selection, development, and evaluation of personnel takes on new dimensions. The administrative organization of the school and the entire support system for which administrators are responsible are modified by the shift to these "less restrictive" mechanisms. Thus, while the original stimulus for organizational changes of this sort may come from outside the educational profession, the "model builders" internal to the sytem have constituted the direct force to which special education administrators have had to respond.

Labeling.   The major concern about the effects of labeling, brought on by the need for classification and categorization of pupils in order to identify and establish the need for service, has come from sources outside the system. However, many of the same proponents of a mainstream, or doctrine of least restrictive alternative, have emphasized the labeling issue—the stigmatizing effects of classification—as a central thrust of the argument for change. The position enunciated by Trippe[46] pointing out the stigma of being "special" was somewhat ahead of its time and little noticed until the notion of the self-fulfilling prophecy was advanced by Rosenthal and Jacobson.[47] The relationship between testing, classification, placement, and stigma became the center of much debate and some research, as reported by Jones.[48] The effects of labels on self-concept and peer relations in educable mentally retarded pupils have been reported by Jones (1974)[49] as being highly equivocal. However, this does not discourage the con-

[44]R. W. Prouty and F. M. McGarry, "The Diagnostic Prescriptive Teacher," in *Instructional Alternatives for Exceptional Children*, ed. E. N. Deno (Arlington, Va.: Council for Exceptional Children, 1973).

[45]Hugh McKenzie et al., "Training Consulting Teachers to Assist Elementary Teachers in the Management and Education of Handicapped Children," *Exceptional Children*, 37 (1970), pp. 37–43.

[46]Matthew Trippe, *The Stigma of Being Special* (A paper presented to the Florida Federation for Exceptional Children, 1965).

[47]R. Rosenthal and L. Jacobson, *Pygmalion in the Classroom* (New York: Holt, Rinehart, and Winston, 1968).

[48]Reginald Jones, "Labels and Stigma in Special Education," *Exceptional Children*, 38 (1972), pp. 553–64.

[49]Reginald Jones, "Student Views of Special Placement and Their Own Special Classes: A Clarification," *Exceptional Children*, 41 (1974), pp. 22–30.

ventional wisdom that classification and stereotyping must lead to negative attitudinal conditions for those who carry the label.

A sufficient number of vocal professional educators have joined in decrying the pernicious potential of labels, regardless of their dependence on logic and values rather than on empirical evidence, so as to constitute a significant force for change in the norms of public school special education programming. Administrators have found themselves in the position of needing to avoid the labeling of pupils, while at the same time acknowledging their dependence on the practice as a prerequisite to securing needed finances for services. Poster art and advertising buttons carrying the admonishment to "label jars, not people" were very popular at the mid-1970s professional conventions of special educators.

Advocacy. The concept of advocacy, as a vital element in securing optimal service and improving the status of populations with special needs, has been promoted from both external and internal sources. According to one point of view, that represented by Wolfensberger,[50] advocacy depends on the actions of persons who are outside the system and not encumbered by job security concerns and organizational loyalties. In discussing the many aspects of advocacy, Biklen[51] elaborates on the necessity of separating the monitor from the monitored, maintaining that it is impossible for an employee of an organization to truly advocate for individuals who are part of the organization's client system. However, he points out that others claim that the head of an organization is the ultimate advocate for the clients. In discussing the role of the state education agency in serving handicapped pupils, New York State[52] placed the responsibility on the Commissioner of Education to be the advocate and guarantor of service for all children of the state.

Regardless of the issue of "being on the payroll," it is clear that a significant body of special education personnel have joined the legal professionals and the lay persons in the thrust for assisting clients in securing their rights. The special educators associated with many of the advocacy projects funded by various branches of the Department of Health, Education and Welfare since 1970 have made an impact on the field of service delivery as well as on their academically based colleagues. The Center on Human Policy at Syracuse University is an example of such a group that has, since 1972, operated as an organization

> . . . interested in studying and promoting services and life patterns which are as normal and non-stigmatizing as possible for all people, but especially for those who have special needs. Among its activities, the Center includes the following: demonstration programs such as group homes for people who have been in-

[50]Wolf Wolfensberger, *Citizen Advocacy* (Toronto: National Institute of Mental Retardation, 1972).

[51]Douglas Biklen, "Advocacy Comes of Age," *Exceptional Children*, 42 (1976), pp. 308–314.

[52]*New York State Board of Regents, Position Paper #20* (Albany: New York State Education Department, 1973).

stitutionalized; advocacy and information for parents of children who have special needs and for all people who have been institutionalized; and training in the social implications of disabilities such as mental retardation for teachers, interested community citizens, physicians, institutional staff, social workers and staff of a variety of programs for both the "typical" and the "special" child.

The purpose of the Center's demonstration programs, advocacy, and training activities is to create an increased awareness of the potential for dehumanization in closed, isolated, segregated environments, and to promote alternatives to segregation. These alternatives take the form of community residential living for those who have been institutionalized, educational opportunities for children with special needs in regular schools rather than in segregated facilities, and free entry for persons with special needs into the variety of community services and life patterns that "typical" people enjoy.[53]

Biklen has outlined a curriculum for training in advocacy activities by listing a number of methods for carrying out the process. The list includes demonstrations, demands, letter writing, fact-finding forums, communications, symbolic acts, negotiations, education, boycotts, lobbying, model programs, legal actions, and demystifying. In compiling such a list he has drawn upon a variety of organizing manuals, that is, actual "how to do it" guides to activism in the securing of rights.

With professional special educators taking an active role in such advocacy activities, the pressure for change that has focused on school and other public agency administrators has become inconvenient and often painful. Particularly significant in this area is the role of the professional in demystifying the pseudoscientific language and procedures which are often used "to intimidate and control consumers rather than to assist communication and development."[54] Thus, the facts show that the advocacy concept must always generate and be driven by forces external to professional education; yet when persons internal to the system become participants, the impact on traditional leadership is significantly increased.

Zero Reject.   The press for progressive inclusion of more severely handicapped children in less restrictive environments has also been initiated largely by forces outside the system. The number of public school systems that have entered into significant programming efforts for profoundly handicapped by the mid-seventies has been very small. However, active interest in the development and refinement of programming approaches for this population, new to the public schools, has been shown by special educators. While the earliest developments most often took place in projects involving an affiliation between university and public school systems, a gradual movement into general school system responsibility for programming has occurred. Most prominent have been the exemplary program developments at Madison, Wisconsin, under the leadership of Lou

[53]Center on Human Policy, *Notes from the Center, #3* (Syracuse: The Center, 1974).

[54]Douglas Biklen, "Advocacy Comes of Age," p. 312.

Brown; at Miami, Florida, under William and Diane Bricker; and at Seattle under Norris Haring and Alice Hayden. These, and other developing programs for severely and profoundly handicapped, have focused on both research and personnel training while providing direct service for children through the vehicle of the University Affiliated Facility model. These university/public school cooperative training models have served to demonstrate how the public school can be more inclusive of severely handicapped children who until this decade would have automatically been considered outside the domain of public education.

The objective complexity of programming for the severely handicapped, as well as the attitudinal obstacles involved, confronts the public school administration as a potent challenge. Questions of funds, facilities, curriculum, instructional methods, medical support services, and personnel competencies all take on new dimensions with the consideration of the severely handicapped. Administrators are faced with a press for program development that has strength from both external and internal sources; this cannot be ignored. The adequate leadership posture can only be one of rising to this aspect of change.

SUMMARY

The driving forces for change, which establish the environment and tasks of the current day leader in the field of special education, consist of such externally based sources as the general social climate, actions of the courts, and legislation at both the state and federal levels. In addition, forces internal to the education establishment, generating from professional doubts, questions, and innovative ideas, suggest new policies, new models, and new approaches to serving new populations. In Chapter 9 the authors present an integrated set of programs and services based upon the concepts and model components identified here. The pervasiveness and postency of these forces seem to leave little chance for anything but accelerating change. The opposing forces that operate to restrain such rapid change and stabilize the environment of the special education leader are discussed in the following chapter.

4

Restraining Forces
to Change

The potency of the forces described in the last chapter as driving the field of special education toward change, and consequently impinging upon leadership personnel as they attempt to execute their role, would seem to be so imposing as to allow nothing short of dramatic change in the traditional operation of the system. However, the restraining forces are also very strong. While these forces might all be characterized under the general category of "status quo maintenance," it may be useful to attempt to separate and analyze each component of these forces. It is probable that certain elements are more strongly ideologically based, while others may be identified as simple resistance to change of any sort. The factors that have a restraining influence on change may be classified into three general types, with overlapping, but sufficiently discrete, characteristics that can be useful for purposes of discussion. For our purposes we will classify these as ideological, bureaucratic, and pragmatic. The order chosen for discussion of these factors may be considered an indication of our personal bias regarding the order of importance of each type of factor as an influencer of what ultimately occurs in the field.

IDEOLOGICAL FACTORS

Ideological factors, those based primarily on human values, can best be discussed from the perspective of the consumer of special education services. Whether it is the handicapped child himself, his parent, or the professional person who is dealing with the issue of services and possible changes therein, the benefits to the client can be viewed as an exclusively ideological issue. The welfare of the professional or the organization in which he works, while related to service delivery capability and quality, is probably not classifiable as an ideological issue.

Of prime importance among ideological factors is the general dilemma of the mixed benefits and costs of specialization. Specialization in any field is developed and increased on the assumption that service quality can be improved through the narrowing and sharpening of the approaches, materials, and behaviors of persons engaged in the delivery of that service. Service programs have flourished as a direct result of universally evident needs for highly specialized techniques for serving the educational needs of many types of handicapped persons. The obvious specialization required to provide instruction for persons who are blind or deaf has been generalized to include the less obvious but demonstrable instructional needs of the physically, mentally, and emotionally disabled.

Educational programs, won by parents of such children, have been successfully established in direct relation to demonstration of unusual instructional needs and the feasibility of developing highly specialized services to meet those needs. The fact that such services tend to lead to separate special facilities, special personnel (with technical skills acquired through training and experience different from teachers of normal children), special materials, and special supporting services not typically found in other educational programs, has been seen as consistant with the child's special status. The disadvantages that the specialized, often stigmatizing, service status brings have been perceived as a reasonable trade-off for the major benefits of the "custom tailored" service. Specialization in educational service delivery has been accepted as a necessary and desirable fact just as in other professional services such as medicine and law. As the study and understanding of special client needs becomes more highly developed, the techniques of instructional intervention and personnel using them become more specialized.

The process of development and maturation of a professional human service system, the establishment of a field of expertise, its institutionalization, and eventually a dependent reliance on it by the client system, follows a natural routine. From the perspective of the client, the maintenance of a system—that is, one that has successfully (or even minimally) ameliorated an acutely felt need—becomes a major consideration. The forces of change in the past decade that have pressed for increased normalization of service systems for handicapped persons constitute a threat to at least some element of the client system. The loss of a valued protection for children in need of highly specialized services has been viewed with alarm by some parents confronted by an ambiguous proposal of some type of "mainstreaming." Suggesting that a less restrictive alternative, such as a resource or consultative service, might be preferrable to a self-contained class for children with specific learning disabilities, proposals have been met with protests by parents. They maintain that their children need as concentrated a service system as possible, and that they will fight to retain the special status that their children's "labels" provide.

The position of private schools, which have grown both quantitatively and qualitatively in a climate of segregation of deviance, is an important element to be considered when changes toward greater inclusion in the mainstream are suggested. Organizations representing the interests of private schools for the handicapped, such as the National Association of Private Residential Facilities for the Mentally Retarded, have come out strongly in opposition to the more vigorous proposals for deinstitutionalization. Citing the particular needs of severely handicapped, and the history of private schools responding to those needs when public services failed to do so, Zneimer[1] has argued that private residential institutions provide an important alternative. This position could easily be construed as primarily concerned with preserving vested interest. In reporting on a study of the use of private sector placements as a means of serving the handicapped in New York, Sage and Guarino[2] pointed to evidence of use of such placements in instances where a presumably less restrictive alternative (such as a class in a public school) would seem to have been possible. However, note that private sector placements constitute a significant resource for many cases, highly preferred by both consumers and professionals on ideological grounds. Interest in maintaining such resources as a link in the total service chain may not be merely a self-serving expression of a special interest group.

An equally strong reaction against deinstitutionalization has been set forth by the Civil Service Employees Association in New York state. They protest that the state policy makers were "dumping" handicapped persons into the community where services were inadequate to meet their needs. The CSEA's newspaper and television advertisements have been charged by their opposition as merely a defense against the threat of job loss.

Whether the benefits of the technically specialized service outweigh those of stigma reduction (that are presumed to be gained through use of the least restrictive alternative model for service) depends largely on the particular case. But it still resolves to a question of values or ideology: where should the line be drawn with a child of given characteristics? The issue is complicated by the fact that handicaps tend to have both an objective and subjective component. A disability may be entirely objective, with indisputable facts as to the manner and degree to which its presence imposes a constraint on the individual's functioning. Beyond this, subjective factors, such as the perceptions of the individual held by his parents, teachers, and others, may constitute the major part of the total handicap. In the case of programming for trainable mentally retarded, children having the same objective characteristics will, in some communities, be accommodated

---

[1]Leonard Zneimer, "Is There a Future for the Residential School in Special Education?" *Phi Delta Kappan*, 55 (1974), pp. 550–52.

[2]Daniel D. Sage and Robert Guarino, "Unintended Consequences: A Law Which Purports to Aid Handicapped Children" *Phi Delta Kappan*, 55 (1974), pp. 533–35.

entirely within regular school facilities. In other communities parents and professionals will firmly believe that such children cannot possibly benefit or cope in a program that does not provide maximum protection from the hazards of the regular school's social and physical environment. The failure to differentiate between objective and subjective components of the handicap tends to support the maintenance of the status quo that keeps the client in a relatively more restrictive situation. Preference for the familiar programmatic response to special educational needs (however limited), especially when supported by the client system, constitutes a major ideological restraint on change in the delivery of service.

BUREAUCRATIC FACTORS

The objective fact of client need, expanded significantly by the influence of subjective perceptions of others, has led to a normative expectation that some form of special service system will exist at each educational level. Even in the least client-centered organizations, where the mission may traditionally be to relieve the general school system of its troublesome pupils, a management structure has become a standard part of the school system. From the perspective of both the specialist and the generalist educator, there are bureaucratic, or organizational maintenance factors which strongly restrain the forces of change.

For the special educator, "empires" have been built on the foundation of an interest in and willingness to serve those who manifest exceptional characteristics. This has occurred with the enthusiastic support of the remainder of the educators, who have been only too happy to be relieved of the problem. Too frequently, especially in the early history of service development, this mere willingness to assume difficult tasks has been the more prominent factor, rather than real expertise in the special education technical matters. As the field of expertise has matured, legitimation of a territorial jurisdiction has become even more firmly established. The professionalization of special education, complete with technical jargon, certification, standards of practice, codes of ethics, and organizational affiliations, though ostensibly directed toward improved service for the client, has also tended to enhance the image of the field and persons within it. The utilization of medically related terms, such as "minimal brain dysfunction" and "dyslexia" and the development of quasimedical techniques of intervention, such as psychomotor training or patterning, have also clearly served to promote the "white coat" image of the special education practitioner. This mystique, or belief that a specialist is required to accomplish a difficult task such as teaching a retarded child, whether justified or not, has contributed to the status of those identified with the profession. Furthermore, it has permitted the establishment of certain tangible benefits such as salary increments, advancement opportunities, and status gains made possible only by the existence of a separate structure, parallel to the regular system of education. This factor is manifested in all levels of local, state, and federal education agencies, as well as in related institutions concerned with personnel preparation and research.

Therefore, a restraint on forces of change can be seen in the attitudes of professionals confronted with the possibility that any particular change might encroach upon the privileges that professional identity provides. Persons whose status depends on a highly specialized domain may be threatened by the changes that a normalization movement might entail. A shift of emphasis from a familiar to an innovative service delivery model imposes a job threat, as does a shift in the characteristics of the client population. For the special education teacher familiar with self-contained classroom instruction for the educable mentally retarded, vigorous program development for the profoundly handicapped and increased emphasis on resources consultant service models may trigger an upsetting uncertainty regarding continued professional status. For the administrator in a program consisting of a heavy deployment of personnel serving mildly handicapped, the decentralization of such personnel to the school building level for administrative purposes may constitute a similar threat on the basis of jurisdiction.

In the same settings where well-developed special education programs provide status for specialists, they provide welcome relief for regular educators from the burden that the handicapped impose on the system. Guarantees of such relief through union negotiations of teacher employment contracts becomes a factor in some communities; it constitutes a major restraining force for systems attempting to develop innovations in service delivery. Union interest in maintaining familiar patterns of service delivery receives support from both regular and special education teachers. Regular classroom teachers have little difficulty arguing that, given the unusual needs of handicapped children, the system has the responsibility of providing for them elsewhere and that the regular classroom should not have to cope with the disruption which their presence creates. Special teachers, whether fearing that administration-proposed innovations only disguise a plan to reduce jobs and save money, or fearing that difficult retraining will be required, argue that the changes will impose a threat to client service. Against such apparent altruism on the part of teachers, other arguments for innovation fade rapidly and the status quo is maintained.

PRAGMATIC FACTORS

The final determination of the course of action in the field, whether characterized by dramatic change, incremental shifts, or rigid maintenance of past practice, will be a mixture of ideological and bureaucratic factors, based on the pragmatism of maximum gain for all concerned. Practices that have produced valued results, or have appeared to have done so, will be continued.

There is little question that power and influence have accrued through the establishment of identity. Nowhere has this been better demonstrated than at the federal level in the Office of Education, where the political effects of identity have caused the administrative offices concerned with handicapped students to be elevated to Bureau status and the subsequent increase of Congressional authorizations, appropriations, and mandates for services. Martin[3] has pointed out the significance of this effect in relation to the passage of Public Law 89-750 in late 1966, mandating the establishment of the Bureau of Education for the Handicapped. Later, Public Law 93-380 included provisions setting the rank of the head of the Bureau at the Deputy Commissioner level and at a particular pay grade (G.S. 18), which has had the effect of guaranteeing policy input within the federal offices at a hierarchical stratum which could not have been otherwise assured.

Concurrently, authorization for funding of programs of personnel development, research, and direct services from the federal level, included in the legislation, has been clearly dependent on the maintenance of a program identity to which ear-marked appropriations could be connected. Congressional appropriations have depended upon the political action of groups having comparatively narrow special interests in handicapped individuals, an interest that could easily be weakened if the handicapped label is diminished. Crudely stated, the "poster child" is good for dollars. The image has been exploited. Philosophically based forces for change must reckon with the fact that anything which might upset the established identity value could jeopardize the favorable support status that has been enjoyed.

Evidence demonstrates that minority needs tend to be overlooked in the competition for scarce resources unless the special characteristics of the group are highlighted and exploited. This is seen particularly in the case of racial and ethnic minorities, but the minority status of the handicapped can be viewed in much the same manner.

At the state government level, where the major support for special education finance is found, the channeling of support has consistently depended on the earmarking of funds, with maximum attention paid to the special, separate status of the children and programs designed to serve them. Funding formulas that call for categorical identification of expenditures, (a practice necessitated by the need to document the "excess costs" of serving handicapped students) have provided a certain amount of assurance that needed services will be forthcoming. The requirement of a financial audit trail lessens the likelihood that funds intended for a particular purpose might be displaced into a general fund. In states that have used the excess cost method of financing services, such as California, the ability to tie program dollars directly to visible children has been essential to the continued maintenance of service. In other states, where the major financial support to education has been through state authorization and financing of teacher units, categorical identification of special education units has again provided the chief assurance that minority needs will not be overlooked.

Almost all of the states have used a method of financing which requires

[3]Edwin W. Martin, Jr., "Breakthrough for the Handicapped: Legislative History," *Exceptional Children*, 34 (1968), pp. 493–503.

some kind of earmarking of either the recipients of the service (for example, average daily attendance of certified handicapped children) or the providers of the service (specially certified teachers or other personnel) as a means of tracking funds. By so doing, it is generally felt that conditions of service have been improved, and to some extent have been successfully monitored.

One contrary example has been observed in New York State, where in 1962 a total educational finance package was adopted which assured a general increase in overall state funding. It was to relieve heavy local costs, but it abolished categorical funding, leaving the local districts to distribute the total state support among the various authorized programs. Observers of the status of special education in New York in the following decade generally concurred that the lack of categorical funds inhibited special education service development. The absence of a financial incentive for service provision made it easier to postpone services, and the absence of a requirement for accounting for categorical funds also minimized the need for state monitoring. Therefore, an accurate census or other statistical accounting for service delivery was hindered. During that period, the major developments in New York occurred in the regional organization (the Boards of Cooperative Educational Services), the only mechanism under which a type of categorical state funding was possible.

Under conditions where surveillance has been lacking, it is assumed that minority interests have been overlooked. When New York's provisions for special education finance were overhauled in 1974, it was with the generally accepted belief that more specific identification of pupils, services, and funding was needed to guarantee an adequate level of programs.

IMPLICATIONS

The foregoing discussion has dealt primarily with forces that maintain a categorical approach to dealing with human variance. This approach necessitates the identification, labeling, and often the segregation of persons into groups as a prerequisite to the delivery of service. Obviously, these factors do not, in themselves, constitute resistance to change. However, a well-established normative attitude and response to human variance has existed for some time, and the educational institutions' means of implementing programs reflects this attitude. Therefore, normative special education has always been categorical special education. Any other approach constitutes a change from the normative and requires a force to bring it about. The opposing forces—those that are associated with maintenance of status quo—are also associated with the maintenance of categorical identity in special education. Interest in promoting change, as well as interest in maintaining status quo, can be found among each of the involved role groups. Clients, professional specialists, and professional generalists can all find rational basis for standing on either side of the change issue.

The opposing forces are manifested not only in the practice of service delivery at federal, state, and local levels, but also in personnel training and research endeavors. In the university setting, territorial jurisdiction between special and general teacher training departments has become an issue. With the benefit of large infusions of outside funds, mostly from the federal level, special education training programs have flourished in the past decade. Questions of curricular inclusions, whether certain general teacher training courses and practices are applicable for special education trainees (and vice versa), have been noted. Differences in certification requirements, and the question of overlap—whether a special education curriculum is sufficient for both special and general certification, or if two separate, parallel courses of study are necessary—also reflect the specialist-generalist issue. Differences in job markets in recent years and the continued financial advantage enjoyed by federally supported special education departments further complicate the issue.

Given these factors, special educators in universities have guarded their special status existence while at the same time proclaiming a mission of involvement with general teacher training in order to bring the benefits of their special "enlightenment" to the mainstream field. Such a mission has not always been welcomed by generalists who view their own existing and developing practices as adequate; and who also resent the wave of privileged support which special educators have been riding. The charge has been made that the specialists are meddling in the general field after being unsuccessful on their own, and that mainstreaming is an effort to hand back to generalists the pupils that the specialists could not handle.

The concepts of special education infusion into general teacher training programs, as represented by the "Dean's Proposals" initiated by the Bureau of Education for the Handicapped (BEH) in 1974–75, and the Exceptional Child Component in the Teacher Corps in the same years, were received with mixed feelings. The money incentive was attractive to general academic departments, but the reminder that special education had the funds to "buy" cooperation with a curriculum change plan, in many cases only reinforced resistance. A significant advance in reconciling this problem is the establishment of a project by the Teacher Education Division of the Council for Exceptional Children, in 1977, with a new journal devoted to bridging the communication gap between Teacher Education and Special Education.

The interplay of forces has also been evident in the educational administration training programs, where specialist training has developed with the support of categorical federal funds. This has occurred at a time when the philosophic thrust in educational administration generally has been toward increasingly generic training. The push for "administration as administration," with a disregard for adjectival distinctions between "elementary school administration," "secondary school administration," and the like, has been faced with a disconcerting value question since special education administration programs with attractive financial supports began to develop curriculum, certification standards, and a programmatic identity. The overlap question, with attention to optimal mix of specialist-generalist content in special education administration training, has been a important issue. However, of even greater controversy has been the question of special education inclusions in all general administration training. The interaction has been most evident in a General-Special Education Administration Consortium (GSEAC) project conducted by the University Council for Educational Administration (UCEA) from 1971 to 1974 under federal support from BEH. This project, which professed a mission "to develop innovations in preparatory programs in the direction of integrating the complementary fields of General-Special Education Administration,"[4] clearly illustrates the balance of forces between specialist and generalist interests that have influenced change.

Specific objectives of the project were:

1. To improve communication and cooperation both within and among institutions involved in the preparation of special education administrators, involved in the preparation of general education administrators, and those involved in other special education preparatory programs.
2. To improve communication and cooperation, both regionally and nationally, among the faculty and student personnel in the preparation of special education and general education administrators.
3. To improve the continuing education of professors of special and general education administration.
4. To evaluate on a continuous and systematic basis the degree to which the prototype model is meeting its objectives.

The particular observations and conclusions generating from the GSEAC project will be discussed in a later chapter.

As implied earlier, pragmatic factors will usually determine whether or not change occurs. The special education leader, in our judgment, should increase the probability that these pragmatically influenced choices will be based on better, more complete data, with ideological issues being consciously considered. He/she can best bring the needed perspective regarding desirable change to the decision process.

SUMMARY

In the preceding two chapters we have attempted to illuminate the major forces that facilitate and restrain change and movement in the special education role within the total school system. Perhaps the most potent of these forces may prove to be the resistance or reaction generated by the fervent, zealous behavior of the special educators who have been agitating for recognition of the rights of handicapped children.

---

[4]UCEA, *General-Special Education Administration Consortium Project*, A proposal submitted to the Bureau of Education for the Handicapped, University Council for Educational Administration, Columbus, Ohio (1971).

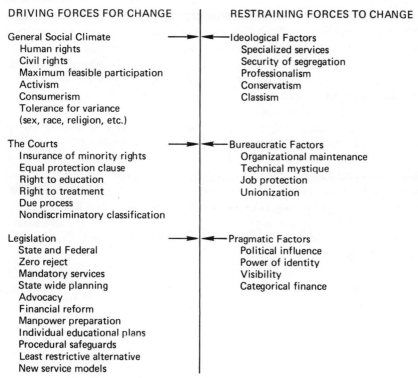

DRIVING FORCES FOR CHANGE	RESTRAINING FORCES TO CHANGE

General Social Climate ——→ ←—Ideological Factors

General Social Climate
   Human rights
   Civil rights
   Maximum feasible participation
   Activism
   Consumerism
   Tolerance for variance
   (sex, race, religion, etc.)

Ideological Factors
   Specialized services
   Security of segregation
   Professionalism
   Conservatism
   Classism

The Courts
   Insurance of minority rights
   Equal protection clause
   Right to education
   Right to treatment
   Due process
   Nondiscriminatory classification

Bureaucratic Factors
   Organizational maintenance
   Technical mystique
   Job protection
   Unionization

Legislation
   State and Federal
   Zero reject
   Mandatory services
   State wide planning
   Advocacy
   Financial reform
   Manpower preparation
   Individual educational plans
   Procedural safeguards
   Least restrictive alternative
   New service models

Pragmatic Factors
   Political influence
   Power of identity
   Visibility
   Categorical finance

Figure 4-1. Forces Influencing the Realization of Free, Appropriate, Public Education for the Handicapped.

The specialization and technical expertise developed by special educators can easily lead to a self proclaimed commitment that "we are the only ones who care for the handicapped." The emotional involvement generated by such a perception, in turn, has quite naturally led to a desire to maintain control over the programs to which that zeal has given life.

The passage of P.L. 94-142 probably marks the completion of the "first revolution." The rights of children and the mandated provision for service have been established; this hard fought battle, making use of crude instruments and power plays, has been won. We must now put aside the approaches that served well in the first revolution, because the second revolution will require something more subtle and sophisticated. To continue to aggress in the manner that permitted initial gains will force a coalition of educational management, teachers unions and other members of the general education community against the special education community. The previous distrust and resentment of the special educator's self-annointed professional role as "guardian of the oppressed" will remain reinforced.

Instead, special educators must execute the second revolution by reflection, consolidation of gains, and the commitment to excel. This can only come through a longitudinal validation process of what does and doesn't work. Until that is carried out, the special educator will be caught in a number of dilemmas. The apparent conflict between the doctrine of least restrictive alternative and the delivery of specialized technical services will require a high level of interpretation and negotiation based on evidence, not on rhetoric.

To summarize the present state of affairs impacting upon the role of special education in the schools, and the place of each factor within the field of driving forces toward change or restraint, we will attempt to graphically portray the major forces. Figure 4-1 lists most of the forces discussed in the previous three chapters. It is not possible to precisely align each driving force against a matching restraining force, as there is much overlap and a lack of clearly distinguishable relationships. The magnitude of each force is also very uncertain and can be expected to vary from one situation to another. However, we believe that the general status of the field, as it relates to the probability of change, is represented faithfully by the forces charted.

5

Developing Alternative Organizational Models for Special Education

INTRODUCTION

In Chapters 3 and 4, internal and external forces have been identified that provide impetus for the reexamination of the special education organizational structure. In this chapter, a process to facilitate special education structural changes is developed. A problem-solving strategy will be utilized within a planned change framework to illustrate the steps in designing new structures for special education. Similarities and differences in the nature of the responsibilities of local, intermediate, and state department mandates will be emphasized, with reference to their impact on developing or changing each level of the special education organizational structure in a state educational management system.

THE PROBLEM-SOLVING MODEL

Havelock[1] has described the most frequently used models of research related to change. They are: (1) the social-interaction model (S-I), (2) the research development and diffusion model (R, D&D), (3) the problem-solving model (P-S), and (4) the linkage model (L), a fourth model that he believes emerges from the previous three models.

---

[1]Ronald G. Havelock, *The Change Agent's Guide to Innovation in Education* (Englewood Cliffs, N.J.: Educational Technology Publications, 1973), pp. 149–77.

The problem-solving model begins with the assumption that basic research principles are valid and the search for solutions must necessarily consider specification of the problem(s). The generation of potential problem definitions is a powerful device in securing initial support for solution-seeking behavior from the significant participants in the problem-solving process. Especially with reorganization efforts, the problem definition is crucial. "All too often, reorganization becomes a political tool to cope with problems that should be faced directly by management."[2] It thus becomes an escape valve for those who fail to acknowledge a problem exists or for those who seek to avoid direct confrontation. The immense frustration and waste of human energy of those affected by the reorganization certainly should be considered before reorganization is undertaken. Therefore, a study of causes, benefits, and costs of reorganization will be required before determining the definitions of the problems that a reorganization may attempt to resolve.

Once the problems have been determined and the support has been secured for resolving them, establishing potential goals and priorities for change follows. Inherent in these goal statements are the success criteria that decision-makers believe are important. Rather than leave these statements of success or value implicit or forgotten until after the solution is implemented a year to two later, they should be culled out and made explicit in order to evaluate subsequent alternative solutions before choosing the final one for implementation.

Given a series of potential alternative solutions, the next step in the problem-solving process is to select and/or implement the best alternative. Each organizational alternative should contain a statement of expected outcomes, impact targets, resources, implementors, enabling activities or vehicles to be used for implementing the action plan, a monitoring sequence, and, ultimately, an evaluation design.

The same goals or values that prompted the need for changing the organizational structure can be used to discriminate between alternative proposals. Feasibility, or likelihood of acceptance, and, finally, costs should also be considered before selection. After choosing the best alternative reorganization plan, a decision to implement (or pilot test) the plan, monitor it, and collect evaluation data ensues. Within the predetermined time frame for implementation, the evaluation is conducted and information is analyzed for feedback to decision-makers to continue, modify, or terminate the selected reorganization plan.

If the decision to continue with the reorganization plan is made, a set of strategies making innovation a permanent part of the total unit of school operation is instituted. If the decision is to modify the reorganization plan, a period of revision and study is necessary before a set of potential adoption tactics are established to facilitate reorganization. Finally, if the decision is to terminate the reor-

[2]Patrick Williams, ed., *New Organizational Structures* (San Jose, California: Lansford Publishing Co., 1973), pp. 1–22.

ganization, another planning cycle must be duplicated and the problem-solving process begins again.

CONSIDERATIONS IN REORGANIZATION

Dale[3] has suggested a number of factors to consider in planning and developing the corporate structures of industrial or commercial enterprises. Those considerations include the following questions: Whose needs will be met? What will be solved? Who will be involved? How will those affected be consulted? What can we learn? How is the future anticipated? What alternatives exist currently or can be developed? What will the reorganization ultimately cost?

Dale has also considered the management style of the leadership persons involved; what the community of constituents will support, the uniqueness of the delivery of programs and services, and the acknowledgement of what the present natural structure of the organization contains.

In light of these considerations, the organization or reorganization of special education at any level in a state service delivery system demands a systematic approach in order to determine the key tasks that are derived from the mission and policy statements of the education agency; this occurs regardless of its place in the service delivery system. Drucker believes that management specialists have learned from twenty years of study and practice that "designing an organization structure is not the first step, but the last. The first step is to identify and organize the building blocks of organization, that is, the key tasks that have to be encompassed in the final structure and that, in turn, carry the structural load of the final edifice."[4]

The remainder of this chapter will be presented and organized with headings corresponding to each of Havelock's[5] six stages of planned change.

Establishing the Need for Special Education Reorganization

In order to answer what needs will be met, an analysis of state, intermediate, and local educational agency key tasks must take place, derived from a review of the particular agency's responsibilities. Until recently, responsibilities at each level involved the key management of planning, organizing, coordinating, and stimulating program development. With the advent of federal and state mandates, monitoring, enforcing, and program evaluation are no longer negoti-

[3]Ernest Dale in *New Organizational Structures,* Patrick Williams, ed. (San Jose, California: Lansford Publishing Co., 1973), p. 21.

[4]Peter Drucker, "New Templates for Today's Organizations," *Harvard Business Review* (January-February 1974), p. 52.

[5]Ronald G. Havelock, *Guide to Innovation,* pp. 21–36.

Table 5-1. Required Responsibilities for Administrators at Each Level of the Service System.

Local Educational Agency (LEA)	Intermediate Educational Agency (IEA)	State Educational Agency (SEA)
Individual educational planning.	Same, for children served by this unit, IEA annual program and service plan based upon LEA needs and requests.	Same as IEA, Annual State Plan, based upon State needs, ensures eligibility for State for 94-142 funds, identifies State's role in program implementation.
Delivery and evaluation of free and appropriate education to all handicapped children.	Same, or only delivery of services to severely handicapped children or lowest incidence types of handicapped children.	Same as IEA.
Assurance that all handicapped children are provided with equal and appropriate educational opportunity.	Same for individual children, IEA provides services for all children not served by LEA, or may with SEA directly monitor LEA programs in accordance with Annual Plan.	Same as IEA's; for all children served directly by State; enforce compliance Federal and State law and administrative regulations through program audit or review.
Personnel development and evaluation.	Appeal agency for parent or LEA.	Same, for parent, LEA, or IEA.
	Same.	Same.
Fiscal planning and control.	Fiscal planning and control. Fiscal audit of LEA. Meet unmet needs at LEA levels.	Fiscal distribution and control of State and Federal funds. Fiscal audit of LEA or IEA.

able management responsibilities. They are, however, differentiated at each level of a state's management system. They are presented below in Table 5–1.

The essential contents of special educational management involve

1. developing and evaluating educational programs and services for individuals and groups of children identified and determined eligible;
2. establishing and maintaining facilities and fiscal resources for housing and finance programs for handicapped children;
3. developing and supporting professional and nonprofessional staff in the delivery of quality educational programs and services;
4. maintaining community involvement and participation in the educational process related to individual educational planning, and maintaining LEA, IEA, or SEA annual planning of programs and services to all handicapped children and youth;
5. developing and negotiating comprehensive programs with other human service delivery agencies of government.

Essentially, the organizational mission at each level in a state's service delivery system is to maximize, fully and appropriately, educational programs and services for all handicapped children.

What will the reorganizing of special education at any one of the three potential levels of a state's service delivery system solve? In Chapter 3, the forces influencing organizational change were presented in some detail. Here, a summary of those external and internal forces which have structural implications for each level in the state service delivery system is presented in Table 5-2.

A review of the forces for change suggests that each level of a state's service delivery system is affected by the changes in the organizational climate that pervades. The LEA's are most directly affected in almost every instance, with IEA's and SEA's being successively less affected.

Establishing the need for different special education organization, for the resolution of the impetus provided by the forces for change, is clear; it has begun. The models described in Chapter 6 serve as testimony to fundamental reorganization of special education in Houston and Boston and as testimony to less drastic changes in Minneapolis and Madison, Wisconsin. In considering reorganization, the questions posed by Dale must be answered in light of the driving forces. The natural structure and the management style needed to accommodate this factor must also be carefully considered since neither the structure nor the leadership in schools have been more fundamentally challenged. The leadership challenges include planning in a cooperative fashion not only within each level but between each level and sharing control of special education, joint evaluation, appeal procedures, and monitoring by others.

Table 5-2.   Driving Forces for Organizational Change in Special Education Having Structural Implications for Various System Levels.

External	LEA	IEA	SEA
Mandates full and appropriate services for all handicapped (3-21).	X	X	X
Mandates consumer participation in individual educational planning and placement.	X	X	*
Mandates consumer participation in annual program planning.	X	X	X
Child or parent advocacy availability for participation in IEP.	X	X	
Organizational advocacy for legislation, litigation, or for securing financial resources.	X	X	X
Managing diversity in and between programs and services.	X	X	*
Mandates State to ensure compliance and enforce legal provisions.			X
Limited fiscal resources.	X	X	X
Internal			
Determining the parameters of special education to other state agencies that have responsibilities for handicapped persons.	X	X	X
Sharing control of programming for handicapped with general vocational education.	X	*	
Reduced categorical emphasis.	X		X
Emphasis on normalization, deinstitutionalization and mainstreaming handicapped.	X	X	X
Integrated administration of special education rather than a separate self-contained organizational structure.	X	*	
Technological issues in evaluating an appropriate education for all handicapped.	X	*	
Less independent specialists or disciplinary control and authority in determining programming and placement.	X		
More emphasis on team functioning.	X	X	

*State Department and LEA's affected if they directly operate program.

Determining and Developing Support for Organizational Change.

The first step in the problem-solving cycle involves the clear specification of those problems or issues that reorganizing education must consider. The discrepancy between what decision-makers want the community to say about the effectiveness and efficiency of special education programs and services, and what currently exists, will further help define the problems. It will also assist in establishing change goals and objectives for reorganization. The "noise-makers" in the system often may not be clearly visible and organized. Therefore, the internal change agents or developers of new or alternative organizational structures must first substantiate who shares the need for change, from all relevant constituencies. Similarities, as well as the differences in their perception of the problems must be debated. Ascertaining their willingness to participate in drafting the action plan and determining what success criteria and expectations must be met for any reorganization effort to succeed should also be agreed upon by the parties involved.

Depending upon the extent of the organization change envisioned, significant others need to be considered. A short checklist is suggested and should include the following categories of significant parties:

1. persons who have perceived and/or demonstrated influence with a constituent group that may serve to gain or lose control over their immediate work scope;
2. persons who have been designated by an election or appointment process to represent a constituency who may be affected by the change;
3. persons from within the system level with demonstrated competence to assist in each phase of the problem-solving process;
4. persons from the system itself in special education who best represent their colleagues and have demonstrated competence in the larger social system of the schools;
5. persons within the system level with the designated responsibility to decide what will be implemented;
6. persons external to the system undergoing structural change from either of the two other levels in the state's service delivery system who are at least indirectly affected by actions taken at either of the two levels;
7. persons external to the system in other human service agencies.
8. persons with expertise in organizational development and/or management external to the system level.

How significant participants become involved demands an analysis of their knowledge, skills, and responsibilities as well as an analysis of the specific tasks and the potential impact of the change on their role. At each step in the problem-solving sequence, therefore, different parties need to be consulted either for input or for reaction and endorsement before moving forward to complete resolution. The intent of developing and obtaining support from significant others is to increase the probability of acceptance and commitment of the individuals involved. They will assist in the adoption of the organizational change by others in the system.

A reorganization task force team, composed of the classes of individuals suggested earlier, would be given certain responsibilities for developing and periodically seeking input and feedback on particular elements during the planning process. Figure 5-1 depicts the planning process and roles of a management task force team working in conjunction with significant others in a state's social system.

Determining and Selecting Change Goals and Objectives

Having established the need for changes in and the identification of the significant participants' role in the problem-solving process, the next step involves the generation and prioritization of change goals so that action planning can occur. A suggested process of goal setting, developed by Lippitt, Fox, and Schindler-Rainman,[6] called *Images of Potentiality*, gets the participants to share

Figure 5-1. Participants' Role in Planning Reorganization of SEA, IEA, LEA Structures.

PLANNING STAGES FOR REORGANIZATION		SEA/IEA/LEA/Bds. of Education	SEA/IEA/LEA Management	SEA/IEA/LEA Professional Staff	Professional Associations	Parent Advisory Committees SEA/IEA/LEA's	Parent Associations and Individual Clients	State/Regional/Local Interagency Management
	1. Established parameters, laws, rules fiscal policy	✓	✓					
	2. Review past practice	✓	✓	✓	✓	✓	✓	✓
	3. Assess needs in anticipation of alternative futures	✓	✓	✓	✓	✓	✓	✓
	4. Set priorities, establish goals	✓	✓	✓	✓	✓	✓	✓
	5. Activities: authority (role responsibilities and decision-making)	✓	✓					
	6. Resources needed: fiscal/human	✓	✓					
	7. Evaluation methods/criteria	✓	✓					
	8. Proposed re-organization plan and accountability	✓	✓	✓	✓	✓	✓	✓
	9. Negotiated re-organization plan and accountability	✓	✓					

(Column header group: Participants Representing)

[6]Robert S. Fox, Ronald Lippitt, and Eva Schindler-Rainman, *Towards a Humane Society: Images of Potentiality* (Fairfax, Va.: N.T.L.—Learning Resources Corporation, 1973).

their perceptions of the future. This tactic provides both a framework and review of essential questions that any organization structure planning needs to consider. What is our mission? What might it be? What should it be? Or, as Dale suggests, how will the future be anticipated? From a state's perspective, Gilliam and Burrello[7] and Burrello, Kaye and Peele[8] describe a special education futures planning process that involves key leadership from federal, state, intermediate, and local levels. Legislators, board members, superintendents, special education administrators, and university trainers were invited to share their projections of the future of education in the year 2000 and the more immediate next five to ten years. These selected policy-makers and educational leaders generated twenty-two alternative futures to guide state agency planning for 1980. The twenty-two goal statements were subjected to further analysis and sent out for additional reaction as reported by Burrello and Siantz.[9] Using a Focus Delphi procedure, eight goal statements reached an 80 percent support level by the special education professional community in Michigan. Five of the top eight statements were also deemed probable by 1980.

Once images of the future of special education have been generated, clarified, and elaborated, and estimates of probability of occurrence and likelihood of support by significant others have been determined, a decision-making process to determine which change goals are most desirable should be initiated.

Vernon and Nutter[10] have developed a rank and weighting process to assist in goal selection. This process accounts for subjective values of key decision-makers as well as for their perception of the probability of occurrence or acceptance of the innovation, goal, or program in the future.

These group planning activities should produce the foundation for the organizational structure. It should result in a statement of the structure's purpose that can then be used in the generation of alternative organizational designs.

Selecting an Alternative Organizational Structure

The first step in organizational designing or redesigning involves the determination of the mission and the key tasks that flow from that mandate. In the previous chapters, increasing responsibilities that educators have been asked to

[7]James Gilliam and Leonard C. Burrello, eds., *Long Range Planning for Special Education, Part I: A Statewide Planning Process,* U.S. Department of Health Education and Welfare, Office of Education, Bureau of Education for Handicapped Grant #OEG-G00-75-00361, (December 1975).

[8]Leonard C. Burrello, Nancy Kaye and Evan Peele, eds., *S.T.A.N.S.E. Initial Report,* State of Michigan, Department of Education Grant #0655-37 and U.S. Department of Health Education and Welfare, Office of Education, Bureau of Education for Handicapped Grant #OEG-007-507294, (August 1976).

[9]Leonard C. Burrello and James Siantz, *Long-Range Planning for Special Education, Part II: A Technical Critique of One Strategy,* (U.S. Department of Health, Education and Welfare, Office of Education, Bureau of Education for Handicapped Grant #EG-G00-75-00361).

[10]David Vernon and Ronald Nutter in *S.T.A.N.S.E. Initial Report,* Leonard Burrello, Nancy Kaye, and Evan Peele, eds., pp. 32–39.

assume for all handicapped children have been presented. Reynolds[11] and Deno[12] have also stressed the service continuum of programs and services needed to serve all handicapped children in the *Least Restrictive Environment* (LRE). The concept of the LRE requires that representatives from the general education social system and the special education subsystem examine how the integration of handicapped children is facilitated.

Placing handicapped children within the Reynolds and Deno service continuum concept has organizational design implications. From an organizational designer's perspective, the problem is one of task and organization differentiation and integration.[13] The extent that programming for either severely or mildly handicapped children is variable from the general educational structure of schools may require different organizational structures. The other factor is the integration of the subtasks of a special education service delivery system: case finding, assessment, certifying, educational planning, placement, programming, and continuous evaluation of individual children (required under tasks' mandatory laws and regulations). Integration of these subtasks varies with respect to the degree of differentiation desired within and between special and regular education.

Increasing demands and variability of approaches to serve all handicapped children will also effect the rate of task integration required to implement successful programs. Different organizational designs for special education may vary within the individual school building, local district, and intermediate units. These factors impede the integration of special education into the regular education service delivery system.

Galbraith conceives of organizations as information processing networks. This theory of organizational design hypothesizes that the "observed variations in organizational forms are actually variations in the strategies of organizations to (1) increase their ability to preplan; (2) increase their flexibility to adapt to their inability to preplan; or (3) to decrease the level of performance required for continued viability."[14] Strategy selection depends upon the relative amount of uncertainty and the costs incurred by each strategy.

The two basic concepts that demand clarification in Galbraith's framework are uncertainty and information. Uncertainty is the relative discrepancy between what information is known to the organization and what information is required to successfully perform organizational tasks. The information needed to make decisions is affected by outputs, or by the number and type of clients to be served

[11]Maynard Reynolds, "A Framework for Considering Some Issues in Special Education," *Exceptional Children*, 38 (1962), pp. 367–70.

[12]Evelyn Deno, "Special Education as Developmental Capital," *Exceptional Children*, 37 (1970), pp. 299–340.

[13]Paul Lawrence and Jay Lorsch, *Developing Organizations: Diagnosis and Action* (Reading, Mass.: Addison-Wesley Publishing Company Inc., 1969).

[14]Jay Galbraith, *Designing Complex Organizations* (Reading, Mass.: Addison-Wesley Publishing Company, 1973) p. 4.

in educational settings: 1) educational, social, and medical assessments required by administrative regulations of different specialists for providing information to determine the eligibility for special education services; or 2) the variability of clients deemed eligible for special education services themselves.

Most organizations—bureaucracy in particular—use prescribed rules and regulations, hierarchical referral, and goal-setting procedures to coordinate the work of their organizational membership. Galbraith suggests that when the organization's key task becomes less certain, the number of exceptions that the hierarchy must deal with increases. When the hierarchy or top management within the organization or unit is overloaded, alternative organizational designs are considered.

There are four organizational designs identified by Galbraith which either reduce the amount of information the organization has to process in order to function, or increase the capacity to handle more information. The goal of the four strategies is essentially the same: to reduce the need for exceptions to the rules, regulations, programs, and services to be channeled upward in the hierarchy. The two organizational design strategies which reduce the amount of information the organization must process are

1. *creating slack resources*, which refers to the "organization increasing the resources available, rather than by utilizing existing resources more efficiently."[15] An example in special education would be special education administrators contracting with part-time school psychologists to administer tests to children when there is a backlog of routine psychological assessments. This does not necessarily occur because of poor management. The problem is related to the lack of information available to coordinate the interdependent aspects of the psychologist's other job responsibilities with this intermittent task of routine reexamination of individual children.

2. *creating self-contained tasks*, which refers to the organization of resources on the basis of client groups, regions, or on project models where all the specialized resource personnel are provided. Rather than have a pool of psychologists who service the entire special education program, a psychologist is assigned to a particular client group or a region within a school district. These changes reduce the scheduling conflicts and the time it takes to determine service priorities between client groups or regions. While specialization is increased, there are fewer scheduling problems in obtaining technical expertise since most resources are assigned to a specific program and location, as in a special facility for severely handicapped children.

There are two design strategies that increase the capacity of the organization to process more information rather than reduce the amount of information or performance required. The two strategies are:

1. *investing in vertical information systems*: this refers to increasing the processing capacity of the organization through combinations of people and machines. This

[15]Galbraith, *Designing Complex Organizations*, p. 24.

strategy is designed to gather information at the point of origin and direct it as swiftly as possible to the appropriate decision-maker in the organizational hierarchy. Computer matching of educational objectives to educational programs and materials should increase the probability and frequency of educational planning and replanning as the objectives are met by children. Teacher time, for developing objectives and searching for and acquisitioning appropriate educational programs and materials for the children's needs, is reduced.

2. *creating lateral relations*: this refers to lowering the decision-making point to the level where the information originates rather than to channeling the information upward for a decision. In special education, lowering many decisions on individual educational planning and placement to the building level rather than maintaining it at the district level, without creating self-contained groups of resources, would be an example of creating lateral relations. The complexity and cost of creating lateral relations escalates with the organization's task information needs. The seven lateral relation mechanisms described by Galbraith are:

   a. Utilize *direct contact* between managers who share a common problem;
   b. Establish *liaison roles* to link two departments which have substantial contact;
   c. Create *temporary task forces* to solve problems affecting several departments or levels of managers at a local, regional, or state organization;
   d. Employ groups or *teams on a permanent basis* for constantly recurring interdepartmental or level problems;
   e. Create a new role, *an integrating role* when leadership between two departments, programs, or levels is problematic.
   f. Shift from an integrating role, to a *linking managerial role* when substantial differential between departments, programs, or level occurs.
   g. Establish *dual authority relations* at critical points *to create a matrix organizational design.*[16]

The organizational structure is dependent on the mission and goals of the organization, structure, information and decision-making processes, reward systems, and the people involved. Achieving the organizational mission is largely dependent on the degree of differentiation and integration of required tasks. The organizational forms therefore vary in relation to predictability of tasks, of technology, and of the social system's support of the mission.

Galbraith[17] in a most recent work has noted again that task variability and diversity are systematically related to structure, leadership style, personality, and decision processes. The conceptual framework for tying these variables into an integrated whole is presented in Figure 5-2.

The choice of an organizational design strategy automatically occurs when the information needed to perform essential tasks and the processes utilized to handle the tasks are matched. Consciously or unconsciously a design strategy is selected. Often the creation of slack resources or the deliberate increase of personnel in periods of abundant resources is evident. The latter two strategies are

[16]Galbraith, *Designing Complex Organizations,* p. 48.

[17]Jay Galbraith, *Organization Design* (Reading, Mass: Addison-Wesley Publishing Company, 1977), p. 31.

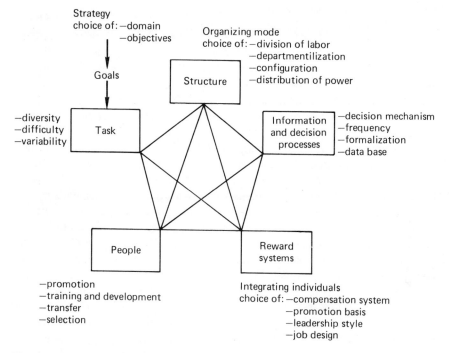

Figure 5-2. Concept of Organization Design. *Reprinted with permission from Jay Galbraith's* Organizational Design *(Reading, Mass.: Addison-Wesley, 1977), p. 3.*

less frequently observed in educational settings. Combinations of functional and self-contained organizational strategies are most often employed in educational settings. The strategy most often selected is one that is the least expensive and least demanding of changes in the management style of the organization leadership.

Implementing and Gaining Acceptance for the Organizational Design

The development of a new organization structure should be viewed as an innovation from its inception. During the problem-solving process, attention to those who will be affected, those whose needs are being met, and the inevitable solutions should be discussed. These questions highlight the basis for gaining acceptance of the new organizational design. Getting the system, its membership, and its constituency ready to accept the innovation begins with the first stage of planned change in the problem-solving cycle. The winning of acceptance is fundamental through each of the subsequent stages of the change process as well. Research on change and innovation suggests that the more the potential recipients of the innovation are involved at each stage of the planning and development process, the more likely they are to be committed supporters of the innovation.

Galbraith has identified seven lateral relation design alternatives to consider when increasing the capacity of the organization for processing information. One alternative, the temporary task force, has already been described. This same organization intervention can be utilized for the development and implementation of a new organization structure. Burrello, Siantz, and Cunningham[18] have described the application of Luke's[19] temporary task force model in work with six intermediate units and a state department in an eight month period. This model of group problem-solving was selected because it allowed each group to select and focus on a problem of importance to them, one which had support from the superordinate(s) in each social system. This support had to be operationally translated into (1) legitimizing the time away from the home district for the planning and development of the innovation; (2) allowing time for periodic reporting and feedback from significant audiences back home; (3) reinforcing its value, by the superordinate; (4) considering the activity as an integral part of the special education administrator's role rather than as another "add on" to an already burdensome workload; (5) using a group of people who had relevant knowledge and skills to contribute for the planning and implementation of the innovation. Therefore, competency, not power status, was the chief criterion for selection of the task force. Line administrators as well as staff supervisors and consultants were involved in the intermediate and local school districts directly; this was where the problem focus might have potentially affected the local district's management of programs, services, or personnel. An analysis of the six intermediate units' and state department task forces' progress and effectiveness can be directly traced to the perceived rewards and support for their task force's efforts and the selection criteria for membership on the task force. Within the seven groups, only three had clear support from the top. All but two had, as part of their membership, either those with the appropriate knowledge and information, or they interfaced their work with significant others back home who did.

Clear definition of the problem, change goals, and appropriate membership are not the only dimensions that ensure success in this particular training and consultation effort with the seven task forces. As both Luke and Galbraith point out, the task force must also develop certain group behavior norms such as active listening, giving and receiving of feedback, shared leadership, consensus decision-making, dealing with conflict, and other planning skills which are more interpersonal or group related than task related. A second analysis of the seven temporary task forces across these dimensions indicates that only three task forces invested time and energy in group development and functioning.

[18]Leonard C. Burrello, James Siantz, and Linda Cunningham, *Final Report: Special Education Simulation and Consultation Project*, Leonard C. Burrello, ed., Special Training Project OEG-072-4309, U.S. Department of Health, Education and Welfare, Office of Education, 1975, pp. 67–83.

[19]R. A. Luke, "Temporary Task Forces: A Humanistic Problem Solving Structure," *Contemporary Organization Development: Conceptual Orientations and Intervention*, W. Warner Burke, ed. (Washington, D.C.: N.T.L. Institute for Applied Behavioral Science, 1972), pp. 149–50.

With both sets of criteria in mind, only one task force's work has been implemented successfully, with minimal resistance, after two years of practice. Much of the success and failure of each task force's effort can be attributed to the components restated by Luke below:

1. competence as the criteria for member selection;
2. a commitment to long-range planning;
3. interpersonal openness;
4. a support-giving executive;
5. task relevant interfacing;
6. open confrontation with resistance to change.[20]

If a temporary task model is selected as the vehicle for the development and /or implementation of a new organizational structure for special education in a school district, much of this discussion will also apply. The problem focus is not restricted by the vehicle. What demands emphasis is the process of participatory problem-solving in redesigning the organization. Both the "legitimizers" and those persons most affected by the new structure, either the "implementors" or "recipients," must be involved if acceptance and commitment are to follow. Involving recipients and middle management personnel in the process is often discussed, but it is also often overlooked.

The temporary task force cannot work in isolation of the organizational environment. The task force must attend to assessing and adapting to changes in the internal and external environment of the organization, such as new board members, or adopting a millage campaign. It must consider group to group interaction within the organization, such as building administrators and resource program personnel. It must consider the individual within the organization with respect to new role expectation, potential rewards, and the necessary support for assisting others to adopt to the new structure. It must also consider the person to person relationships in the key match-ups that are projected between individuals in the new structure. These four basic interfaces between the task force and the existing system and structure are further developed by Lawrence and Lorsch.[21] They are emphasized here to indicate that any new structure will also demand a clear plan of implementation.

Components of the social interaction strategy described by Havelock[22] that emphasize the diffusion aspect of communications between a temporary task force reorganization and significant groups and individuals within the organization also provide ways to involve others in the problem-solving process.

Burrello, Kaye, and Peele[23] have described how both the strategies of

---

[20]Luke, pp. 149–50.

[21]Paul Lawrence and Jay Lorsch, *Developing Organizations: Diagnosis and Action* (Reading, Mass. Addison-Wesley Publishing Company, 1969).

[22]Havelock, *Guide to Innovation*, pp. 149–77.

[23]Leonard C. Burrello, Nancy Kaye, and Evan Peele, eds., *S.T.A.N.S.E. Initial Report*, p. 5.

problem-solving and social interaction or influence were used to assist a state department reorganization. The frequency and type of communication was also carefully designed and transmitted, most often by selected representatives of an entire state management network. Kaye[24] has described the communication process in detail.

The implication of this research to the reorganization of any level of special education is that the change agents must acknowledge and demonstrably involve those affected. Surveys of opinion leaders on key concepts and outcomes, face to face communication by peers and other identified "key communicators," and carefully designed messages should be part of any diffusion strategy on reorganization.

Evaluating the Reorganization Plan

Any reorganization effort will be evaluated either formally or informally by the internal membership and external constituency. While it has been frequently stressed that no one organizational design is ideal, ultimately the design or combination of designs must necessarily, as Drucker[25] posits, structure and integrate three different kinds of work: (1) the operating task, which is concerned with producing results of today's business or this year's annual plan; (2) the innovation task, which projects tomorrow's future objectives or those for the next one to five years; and (3) the top management task, which involves overseeing the implementation of the present, leading in the establishment of the future vision, and setting the course for both the work of today and tomorrow.

The organizational structure and other elements that form the basis for evaluation have been drawn from Dale, Drucker, Galbraith, Lawrence, and from Lippitt.[26] Once an organizational design or combination of designs have been developed and readied for installation, an initial set of standards can then be applied against the structure to determine its potential. A second evaluation should be implemented after a specified period of time. For the earliest period, a set of questions is listed below.

1. Are the positions of role incumbent clear with regard to specific responsibilities, functions, and decision-making authority?
2. Do individuals understand their individual, section, or division roles, as well as the organization as a whole?

[24]Nancy L. Kaye, *Assessing Communication Patterns and Attitudes of Special Education Management Personnel in a Technical Assistance Network* (Doctoral Dissertation, University of Michigan, 1976).

[25]Drucker, "New Templates," p. 50.

[26]Gordon Lippitt, *Visualize Change for Model Building and the Change Process* (Fairfax, Va.: National Training Laboratories—Learning Resources Corporation).

3. Does decision-making authority focus on the key issues, and is action oriented and designed to be carried out at the lowest possible level of management?
4. Are accountability, control, and anticipation of conflict and ways to minimize it provided for?
5. Does the operating task derived from the organization mission reflect a process-focus, as well as product?
6. Is adaptability or flexibility to environmental forces evident to maintain daily harmony and ways to learn?
7. Are ways to increase the individual's growth and contribution an integral part of the structure?

Top central office management, building level administrators, and instructional and supportive staff should be polled and asked to provide feedback stating how well the structure is designed to meet the sample standards listed above.

The community and larger constituency of board members, parents, and organizations should also be polled, particularly with reference to Dale's earlier question: Whose needs will be met and what will it solve? The board must necessarily also be sensitive to the three different kinds of work that structures must provide. Other managers at state, intermediate/county, or local levels should also be invited to test the viability of the structure and its impact in reciprocal relationships that the particular service unit will have in each of the other units.

The second evaluation is primarily a replication of the first, that is, reapplying the standards a second time. The major difference, however, is that criteria statements should be included in the standards set during the initial evaluation. A separate analysis of perceived effectiveness by each significant group—legitimizers, implementors, and recipients of programs and services—should be completed according to the predetermined criteria.

Once the data are collected, the planning and development task force should be reconvened to analyze the information and make recommendations for change. Essentially these recommendations will fall into three categories: (1) continue as is; (2) modify structure or processes; and (3) terminate and begin planning cycle again. If this final step is taken, it will serve as a major indication of the organization's commitment to continue to gain new perspectives and knowledge. This process, if conducted annually, can provide the continuous impetus to be open and responsive to the constituency, and the organization's members can then continue to meet its current and future agendas.

SUMMARY

The planning process described in this chapter and illustrated in Figure 5-1 should be viewed as basic and adaptable to other planning tasks. Later, in Chapter 10, we will illustrate its use in SEA, IEA, or LEA planning efforts.

In this chapter, a process for planning a reorganization of special education has been described, using a problem-solving strategy within Havelock's stages of planned change. This process identifies significant participants and their roles in the planning effort. It also identifies four organizational design strategies related to the amount of differentiation within and between units on organization needs and the integration of tasks within the organizational unit itself. A temporary task force concept was suggested to guide management to the planning of a reorganization effort.

In Chapter 8, the authors will describe an organizational model for special education based upon new models and the planned change and organizational design concepts presented in this chapter.

6

Special Education
Organizational Models:
A Review

This chapter identifies examples of organizational models that have been implemented over the past nine years. These models include structural changes based upon emerging norms and values presented in Chapters 3 and 4. Each model will be discussed in terms of the social system perspective presented in Chapter 1, and in terms of specific organizational components.

Few special education organizational models have been described and disseminated. Still fewer have identified the key environmental forces, and specific norms or values that provided the basic rationale for building the organizational model. None of the models have been subject to objective evaluation or scrutiny.

The models selected for presentation in this chapter include four local educational agencies: (1) the Madison City Schools, Madison, Wisconsin; (2) the Minneapolis City Schools, Minneapolis, Minnesota; (3) the Boston Public Schools, Boston, Massachusetts; and (4) the Houston Independent School District, Houston, Texas. An intermediate educational agency model (the Board of Cooperative Educational Services #2 Southern Westchester County, New York) and a state educational agency model (the Michigan Special Education Services Area) are also presented as examples.

These six models have been selected for presentation for four reasons. First, descriptions of three of the six models have been described in literature elsewhere but the remaining three have not been disseminated widely. The BOCES #2 Model is one with which both authors had extensive familiarity.

Second, descriptions of specific environmental forces, institutional norms, and values, upon which the models were based, were available for analysis. These descriptions facilitate their adaptability to other districts that were searching for an alternative special education organizational structure. Third, the four local district models were clear attempts by outstanding special educators to bring the structure of special education services into harmony with the driving forces for change toward a more open society. As illustrated in Figure 4-1, forces in the general social climate, such as the expanding civil rights movement (including the handicapped), and a tolerance for variance characterized these models. Finally, all six models appeared to include common strategies designed to facilitate the education of handicapped children in the least restrictive environment.

A discussion of assumptions that have guided the development and organization of special education in state departments to local school districts must be speculative. Few descriptions of administrative organization and structure are explicit with regard to values, goals, or norms that can be identified as the basis of the special education organization. For this reason, a discussion of assumptions has been extracted from analysis of special education organizational charts and descriptions that the authors have observed, evaluated, researched, or designed themselves in consultation with others.

LOCAL EDUCATIONAL AGENCY ORGANIZATIONAL MODELS

The Madison Model

Systemic Values in the Madison Model   The first of the local educational agency models, the Madison School System, is the smallest of the four systems described; the system has an average daily attendance of thirty thousand. The basic assumption that provided the impetus for reorganization of the district's administrative structure was that the schools should be responsive to community interest and quickly dispatch resources to deal with individual consumer concerns. The changing values within special education were: (1) reducing the segregated class program profile to a continuum of services such as Reynolds[1] and Deno[2] have described; and (2) moving from a medical categorization or specific defect approach to service delivery to an ecological- or systems-based approach. The organizational assumptions were that: (1) the organizational structure should be able to anticipate and plan for the future utilizing new forms of management; and (2) the previous administrative structure did not facilitate the

---

[1]Maynard Reynolds, "A Framework for Considering Some Issues in Special Education," *Exceptional Children*, 38 (1962), pp. 367–70.

[2]Evelyn N. Deno, "Special Education as Developmental Capital," *Exceptional Children*, 37 (1970), pp. 229–40.

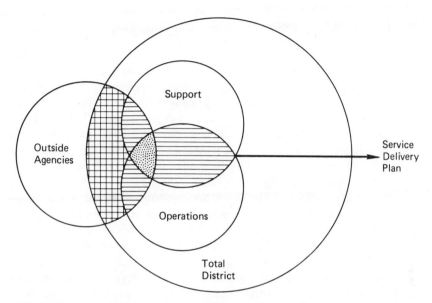

Figure 6-1. Visual Portrayal of Interrelationship Between Operations and Support Divisions. *Reprinted from Tilley, B.K., "The Madison Plan for Organizing and Delivering Specialized Educational Services" in* Special Education in Court, *Volume 2, eds., Johnson, R. A., Gross, J. C., and Weatherman, R. F., p. 284, with permission.*

special education delivery within the regular school building program in a cooperative fashion.

Structure of the Madison Model.   The school district was reorganized from a district-wide attendance area into four regional attendance areas, each headed by a generalist administrator in charge of operations. Besides the operations unit, three other organizational units were described by Tilley:[3] (1) total district offices and functions; (2) supportive divisions, such as curriculum, personnel, special education, federal programs, and the like; and (3) outside agencies, such as state educational agency, community agencies, and so forth. The Department of Special Services was similarly reorganized with a special education coordinator in each of the four regional units. The function of special education within these regions was to provide direct services to mildly handicapped children and to support the general school program for all children. A visual illustration of the interrelationships between the operation unit and the supportive unit (special education) is presented in Figure 6-1. A fifth unit was also estab-

---

[3]Bill K. Tilley, *The Madison Plan for Organizing and Delivery of Specialized Educational Services*, Vol. 2 in Leadership Series in Special Education, eds. R.A. Johnson, J.C. Gross, and R.F. Weatherman (Minneapolis, Minn.: University of Minnesota, 1973), pp. 275–88.

lished providing for comprehensive programs for severely handicapped children. A fifth special education coordinator was appointed to head this unit.

The nature of responsibilities and decision-making authority in the planning, allocation, implementation, and evaluation of a regional service delivery plan was negotiated between the heads of the area operations divisions and the head of each supportive division. While each division's responsibilities and decision-making were not spelled out, Tilley did emphasize that special education services retained personnel allocations and budget control district-wide. This authority was given to the Director of Special Services by the superintendent of the district. Other assurances were also given stating that all supportive divisions could seriously negotiate with operations personnel.

The Madison Special Education Services organizational model moved from a district-wide disability program model to a combination of functional organizational structures and a self-contained structure within and between regional areas and district-wide areas. In the regional service areas (where self-contained units could complete all tasks through the resources organized within the region) special services were organized providing for a variety of specialized inputs (functionally organized and distributed across buildings within the region) for the general programs in the region. The regions could also obtain and provide, on a functional basis, specialized resources to each other from other supportive divisions district-wide.

The fifth unit of the special service division was also designed to be a self-contained unit where most, if not all, of the resources were housed in one administrative area. This served the severely handicapped district-wide. A most significant development has recently occurred since the initial inception of this model in 1972. In the fall of 1977, the fifth unit in this structure was disbanded due to the system's success in integrating all severely handicapped children into the regular school-based programs of the four regions.

The author of this Madison model also includes significant management initiatives designed for facilitating cooperative planning that deals with changing circumstances and problems as they arise. As discussed in Chapter 5, Galbraith[4] has identified these initiatives as lateral relationships (or organizational design procedures) that increase the capacity of the school system to process information and make decisions. These procedures prevent the overloading of the hierarchy with multiple policy exceptions or other internally or externally established administrative rules and regulations. Examples of these design procedures are (1) creating a direct negotiation process between operations and supportive division heads for the pre-planning of services; and (2) creating temporary task forces of relevant personnel for the attack of a specific problem between, or external to, levels in the organization.

[4]Jay Galbraith, *Designing Complex Organizations*, (Reading, Mass.: Addison–Wesley, 1973).

The Minneapolis Model

Systemic Values in the Minneapolis Model. At approximately the time the Madison Public Schools were reorganizing generically, the special education leadership services in Minneapolis were preparing their own major reorganization. Minneapolis represents a somewhat larger district in this review of local educational agency organizational models; it has an average daily attendance of approximately sixty-five thousand students.

The impetus for the Minneapolis plan of reorganization has been clarified by Johnson and Gross[5] in their specific criteria summarized below. Johnson and Gross sought to design a model of administrative structure that was (1) organizationally, philosophically, and conceptually sound; (2) responsive to the program operations level evidenced by a decentralization of decision-making (which facilitates the use of special education services for regular education); and (3) demonstrable of the reduced reliance on the categorical labeling process. The goals included maximizing strengths and interests of administrative and program personnel, reducing the competition for unrelated outcomes at the expense of child-centered outcomes, accounting for the fiscal resources behind each activity, and the performance of administrative and supervisory staff.

These administrators engaged in an analysis of management and program instructional support activities. A total of sixteen activities were identified as important management or program activities. These activities are better understood in categories of educational administrative behavior established by Hemphill, Griffiths, and Fredericksen.[6] Four concepts were derived from the functional analysis of hundreds of tasks collected from work samples that elementary principals reported. The four task groups were

1. developing educational programs and services;
2. maintaining facilities and fiscal resources;
3. developing and supporting personnel; and
4. maintaining community relationships.

In Figure 6-2, the four task domains from Hemphill, Griffiths, and Fredericksen, and the two classes of leadership functions set by Johnson and Gross provide the matrix for analyzing management and program activities. Ten of the sixteen activities are primarily program specialist functions. Five items are shared with the other functional leadership role that is identified as generalist or management related. Six are specific to the management role and are not shared

[5]Richard A. Johnson and Jerry C. Gross, *Restructuring Special Education Leadership Resources: The Minneapolis Model*, Vol. 2 in Leadership Series in Special Education, eds. R.A. Johnson, J.C. Gross, and R.F. Weatherman (Minneapolis, Minn.: University of Minnesota, 1973).

[6]John D. Hemphill, Daniel Griffiths and Norman Fredericksen, *Administrative Performance and Personality* (New York: Bureau of Publications, Teachers College, Columbia University, 1962).

PROGRAM SPECIALIST	GENERALIST
1. Developing Educational Programs and Services.	
Case Management	Program Advocate
Student Placement	Expeditor and Facilitator
Curriculum Development	
Materials Evaluation	
Program Planning*	
Program Evaluation*	
2. Maintaining Facilities and Fiscal Resources.	
	Budget Development and
	Monitoring State
	Reporting Systems
3. Developing and Supporting Personnel.	
Personnel Development and	Personnel Recruitment
Supervision*	
Personnel Evaluation*	
4. Maintaining Community Relationships.	
Parent Education and	Public Relations
Consumer Planning	Information Clearinghouse
Agency Liaison	

*Shared tasks between generalist and program specialists.

Figure 6-2. Matrix of Task Domains and Leadership Functions.

with the program specialist. The scope of responsibilities differentiates the generalist's role from that of the program specialist.

Structure of the Minneapolis Model. The entire school district was regionally organized with a generalist-manager in charge of each of the three areas. He reported to a deputy superintendent who also had responsibility for all program planning, and responsibility for supportive and instructional services such as special, vocational, and compensatory education. The remaining central office personnel included associate superintendents for personnel, business associates, and other specialized supportive and district technical assistants. The generalist-manager and the program specialist-supervisor differentiation was translated into a two-tier structure. The two levels that evolved acknowledged the need for generalist and program specialist personnel in both regular school-based programs and in programs for the low-incidence or severely handicapped child. The authors of the Minneapolis model have illustrated its structure in Figure 6-3.

It is important to note that before this reorganization, the Minneapolis special education department had recently incorporated school psychological and

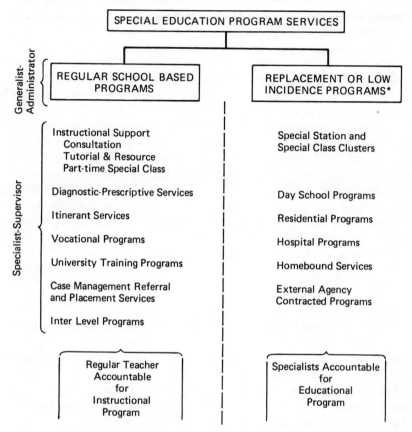

SPECIAL EDUCATION PROGRAM SERVICES

Generalist-Administrator

| REGULAR SCHOOL BASED PROGRAMS | REPLACEMENT OR LOW INCIDENCE PROGRAMS* |

Specialist-Supervisor

Instructional Support
   Consultation
   Tutorial & Resource
   Part-time Special Class

Diagnostic-Prescriptive Services

Itinerant Services

Vocational Programs

University Training Programs

Case Management Referral
and Placement Services

Inter Level Programs

Special Station and
Special Class Clusters

Day School Programs

Residential Programs

Hospital Programs

Homebound Services

External Agency
Contracted Programs

Regular Teacher
Accountable
for
Instructional
Program

Specialists Accountable
for
Educational
Program

*Includes programs and services of severely handicapped students in all categories.

Figure 6-3. Working Model—Leadership Structure. *Reprinted from Johnson, R. A., and Gross, J. C., "Restructuring Special Education Leadership Resources: The Minneapolis Model," in* Special *Education in Court,* Volume 2, eds. Johnson, *R. A., Gross, J. C. and Weatherman, R. F., p. 269, with permission.*

social work services as well as related health services under the umbrella of a special service program. Within the reorganization, these integrated specialists enhanced scheduling, team planning, implementation, and accountability in program areas.

The Minneapolis model, like the Madison plan for the delivery of specialized programs and services, has combined organizational design strategies. The regular school-based programs depicted in Figure 6-3 contain elements of a functional and self-contained design. The low-incidence (or replacement) programs and services constitute a self-contained organizational design where all tasks and resources are organized into one unit.

The key organizational issues in the self-contained design are the allocation of resources for the maintenance of the desired support levels and the integration of all staff into the total program. When combining self-contained and functional-organizational design models, the key management problem is how to allocate resources and resolve authority relationships. In functional designs alone, authority over staff is always in question: Should the operating head of a unit that requests services from a specialized group of system-wide resources be under the authority of a centralized administrator?

Since the implementation of both the Minneapolis model and the Madison model, the top management in the school districts have moved on to other positions. Of the two districts, the Minneapolis model has undergone the most significant changes. These changes involve the loss of the related specialists in psychological, social work, and other health services. These personnel have been removed from special education and given separate status under the associate superintendent to whom the current special education director reports. Other personnel shifts include the elimination of a former deputy superintendent position as well as other central office reporting differences.

The Boston Model

Systemic Values of the Boston Model. The administrative reorganization of the Special Services Department in the Boston School System represents one of the most recent evolving examples of structural change. Additional time will have to pass before the effects of the reorganization can be properly evaluated, but the forces leading to the reorganization and the calculated steps taken in response to those forces are worthy of discussion. They provide an example of rather major organizational change.

Prior to the adoption of a basic reorganization plan in 1974, the Boston public schools (with approximately 78,000 students) had known a typical structure for special education leadership. Categorical departments based primarily on classifications of disability were led by specialists associated with such handicaps. Impetus for change of that traditional structure generated from studies by both internal and external evaluators of the administrative process. The focus of such studies on the special education service delivery system was accentuated by the passage of legislation (Massachusetts Chapter 766) which was well ahead of most states in its emphasis on moving away from categorical classifications of children and programs. While the implementation of the reorganization plan did not begin immediately (it took place incrementally through 1977) some assumptions were identified that guided the process of change toward certain objectives:

1. Decentralization of the Department of Special Services will lead to more effective and efficient service delivery as well as greater accountability.
2. Central office must be capable of providing the necessary technical and expert support to the districts so as to maximize program implementation.
3. Central office must be capable of monitoring the implementation of policies and

procedures regarding special services and make appropriate modifications when necessary.[7]

An additional assumption in the Boston situation was that the central administrative unit overseeing special education services would also encompass those related functions, that is, health, attendance, psychological assessment, counseling, that in many systems were not organized integrally with the major instructional aspects of special education. The conceptualization of a total range of services that cut across the entire student population but had proportionately greater concern with those with special needs was made more concrete by the regulations implementing Chapter 766; this prescribed broad multidisciplinary input to the evaluation and placement decision process.

In Boston, more than in other systems in the Commonwealth, additional pressures for organizational change generated from court actions charging the system with failure to provide mandated services for the handicapped. Proposed remedies in response to the court orders depended mostly on the nature of leadership roles and functions in the system and, therefore, further influenced the structural changes that evolved.

Structure of the Boston Model.   To accomplish the decentralization objective, each of the nine community districts of the system was assigned a District 766 Coordinator, who would be responsible to the Community District Superintendent. The major role of this position was to coordinate and monitor the process of pupil evaluation, educational planning, and placement on a district-wide basis, in accordance with central office procedures, and to state Core Evaluation Team regulations. Further execution of the decentralization process was accomplished by the appointment of Core Evaluation Team Chairperson Designees, each functioning under a building administrator. These persons accept and process referrals for core evaluations, coordinate the writing of educational plans with state regulations and system procedures, and facilitate all other aspects of evaluation, placement, and service delivery within the assigned individual school building(s).

As described in an announcement of promotional ratings for administrative positions, the Department of Special Services had renewed its structure, departing from instructional programs organized and administered by categories of handicap, and shifting to administration according to level of service offered. Three major areas were created, each constituted by two or more units responsible for function:

1. Student Support Services (Educational Investigation and Measurement, Pupil Adjustment Counseling, Guidance, Core Evaluation Teams, Health Services, and Attendance).

[7]Boston Public Schools, *Administrative Reorganization of the Department of Special Services*, 1976.

    2. Special Schools and Programs (Boston Special Schools and Programs, Contracted Educational Services).

    3. Mainstream Programs (Resource, Interlevel, and Itinerant Programs).[8]

Figure 6-4 illustrates the manner in which the areas constitute a set of vertical teams. Each area is administered by a director, who reports to the Associate Superintendent for Special Services. Under the three directors are associate directors who administer the various units comprising each area, for example, Core Evaluation teams, Contracted Educational Services, Resource Programs. Horizontal teams, made up of all positions at each level, constitute another set of management relationships. Within the department, these three levels of leadership personnel perform primarily management and administrative functions. Figure 6-5 depicts the estimated percentage of emphasis on such functions for each management level.

At the lower levels of the management teams, supervisors and coordinators are seen as having less than 50 percent management functions, since their role is primarily to provide supervision and technical assistance. At a fifth level, lead personnel are even less concerned with management function as their technical role takes precedence.

In addition to the management and administrative functions, each level is assumed to exercise coordinative functions. As Figure 6-5 suggests, levels A, B, and C would be concerned with all types of horizontal and vertical coordination within and among the departments in the areas and the units represented. By contrast, personnel at levels D and E would be primarily concerned with indirect horizontal coordination and horizontal coordination within program coordination.

The ultimate effects of the new structure's leadership behavior on administration-teacher-pupil interactions are currently being identified and examined.

The Boston model is primarily organized around a functional design strategy. The management personnel within levels B and C are responsible for planning, supervising, and evaluating programs across the nine community districts. Management personnel within levels D and E, however, are primarily organized with a matrix design strategy. Level D and E personnel are responsible for reporting purposes to both the community district superintendent and to centralized special education managers at management level C.

The net effect of having both functional and matrix designs utilized in the same system is two-fold:

    1. With a functional design, conflicts may arise between the community superintendent and management personnel at levels A and B over the distribution and direction given to centralized personnel working in the nine community district

---

[8]Boston Public Schools, *Superintendent's Circular*, no. 154 (April 27, 1977).

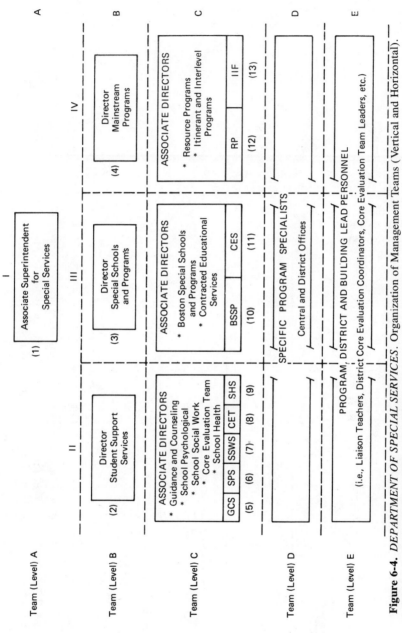

Figure 6-4. *DEPARTMENT OF SPECIAL SERVICES.* Organization of Management Teams (Vertical and Horizontal). *Adapted from* Master Plan, Component B, *The Boston Project, 1977.*

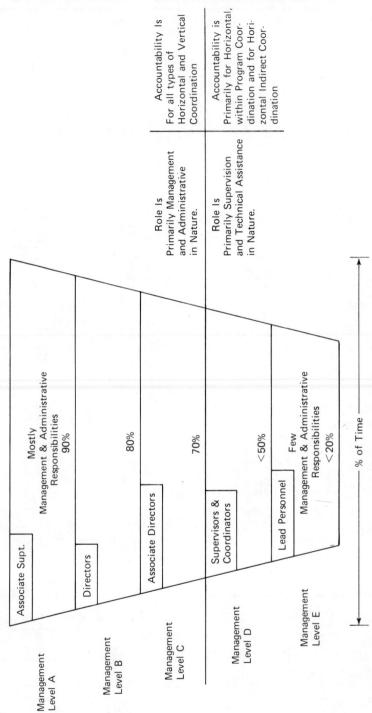

Figure 6-5. *DEPARTMENT OF SPECIAL SERVICES,* Scope of Responsibility for Management/Administrative Functions and for Vertical Horizontal Coordination. *Adapted from* Master Plan, Component B, *The Boston Project, 1977.*

units. This is because the community district superintendent has little authority over personnel distributed and directed out of the central office.

2. With a matrix design, personnel at management levels D and E must deal with conflicting priorities in their daily activities, created by the dual authority structure over them, that is, the district superintendent and the centralized special education management personnel at levels B and C.

Definitions of the types of coordination responsibilities that are assumed to be operating are:

Vertical Coordination: coordination of personnel and other resources within one operational area or organizational component, where a superordinate-subordinate leadership chain exists.

Direct Horizontal Coordination: coordination of personnel and other resources across two or more operational areas or organizational components whose leadership personnel are administrative peers, and where one person has the responsbility for coordination.

Indirect Horizontal Coordination: coordination of personnel and resources across operational areas of organizational components whose leadership personnel are administrative peers and where all such peers are equally responsible for coordination.

Horizontal within Program Coordination: coordination of personnel and resources within one operational area or organizational component, where one person is responsible for coordination.

The major question of the Boston reorganization lies in its implications for facilitating the overall leadership process in the absence of categorical classifications based on specific handicaps. It places an emphasis on the types of service and leadership functions involved. The transition from one type of organization to another can be difficult in any event. An adequate evaluation of its results must await full implementation of the proposed structure.

The Houston Model

Systemic Values of the Houston Model.   The Houston Independent School District is the largest of the four organizational models presented here. The Houston schools serve more than 215,000 children daily, and that number is increasing since Houston is one of the country's fastest growing cities.

The Houston plan is not a complete description of a special education school district organizational structure. The reason for its inclusion here is that the Houston schools, like all Texas school districts, had been faced with a legislative mandate to program for all children within the least restrictive environment by 1976. Beginning in the 1972 school year, Houston began to develop an adaptive system that would serve not only identified handicapped children, but would provide alternative instructional programs for all children.

The Department of Special Education became the Center for Human Resource Development and Educational Renewal (CHRD). Its new functions were intended to retrain classroom teachers into professionals who could, with minimal assistance, maintain previously referred children. They also designed multidisciplinary teams to assist in supporting teachers and children in need. Finally, they developed a proactive unit to plan and develop still other alternatives.

This model of organization also called for a break from the categorical model of program organization. It suggested that a functional organization model be developed to support both teachers and children. It required the development of lateral relationships rather than a further delineation of hierarchical relationships between teachers, supportive personnel, and building administrators. Task force teams of supportive personnel initiated a series of retraining sessions for teachers and subsequently replicated the training classroom in the teachers' home schools. These task force teams also provided direct technical assistance in the teachers' classrooms after they trained the teachers to transfer their training to the work situation.

The basic assumptions inherent in the Houston plan show that the organization mission for special education from 1972 to 1974 was not to maintain separate programs of services. In this model, the focus of the intervention was placed equally upon the trainer and on the trainee. The intent was preventive, not ameliorative. The process was retraining regular classroom teachers by applying basic learning principles to adult and child alike. The organizational design, therefore, was developed to facilitate those objectives.

Structure of the Houston Model. In 1972, the Houston schools were organized into six regions, each containing some thirty-five thousand to forty thousand children. Each region was headed up by an area superintendent. Within each region, an area special education administrator was identified. Seven classes of personnel were assigned to each area director: education diagnosticians and resource program personnel, psychologists, social workers, associate psychologists, special education counselors, and program supervisors. The area director was primarily a generalist manager like those identified in the Minneapolis model. The central office organization of special education reflected the three divisions or components in the areas described by Meisgeier.[9] The three divisions in each area were (1) program planning, (2) training, and (3) administration. The counterparts at the area level were (1) program planning and implementation through the Precision Learning Centers; (2) special and regular classroom educational renewal and training through Teacher Development Centers; and (3) integration and coordination of specialized diagnostic and program personnel (through administration liaison between area superintendents and the area special education director) with the program supervisors. These six area di-

[9]Charles Meisgeier, "The Houston Plan: A Proactive Integrated Systems Plan for Education," *Instructional Alternatives for Exceptional Children*, ed. E. Deno (Arlington, Va.: Council for Exceptional Children, 1974).

rectors reported to the assistant director in charge of program planning in the central director offices. Two other assistant directors for training and administration reported to the central director, who in turn had great access to the general superintendent of the Houston schools.

After top management in both the general superintendent's office and the central director's office of special education in the CHRD were changed, a new structure emerged. The net effect of the change was the lowering of the place of special education in the administrative hierarchy. Another major outcome was that the area directors of special services now reported to the area superintendent rather than to the centrally-based special education administrator. The current assistant superintendent for special education maintains three divisions: program planning, community services, and administration and articulation with the area directors for special services.

The Houston model has also been a combination of functional and self-contained organizational designs. The area directors have been responsible for all programs and services within their region. The central office administrators have been primarily concerned with overall regional program planning, linkage with the external agencies and associations, and supportive administration and coordination. These responsibilities have been functionally distributed across the district.

The Houston plan was not designed to focus on the most severely handicapped low-incidence children. It was, however, the most ambitious long-term systematic attempt to fundamentally redefine special education as a direct provider of services to *all* children and as a supportive, consultative, and training agency for *all* teachers. The major continuing impact of the Houston model is the widespread use of resource programs and its precision learning center concept. Dollar and Klinger[10] have reported that special education services increased from 10,500 to 21,000 children between 1972–76 using the same staffing pattern that was initially organized under the Houston plan. An average of two resource teachers and an aide were provided for in each building. The major stumbling block in the total implementation of the Houston plan was that the innovation was so fundamental, so rapid, and so complete. Given the large number of persons involved, a sustained effort of this magnitude could have as many adversaries as it does advocates. The extent of its success may never be fully recorded since the district did not continue to support the intervention at its projected level after the top management in general and special education left their positions. Without the continuing support of top management and the Board of Education, less than complete adoption of the Houston plan was to be expected. Still, the commitment to continue many positive aspects of the plan by many building ad-

[10]Barry Dollar and Ronald Klinger, "A Systems Approach to Improving Teacher Effectiveness: A Triadic Model of Consultation and Change," in *Psychological Consultation: Helping Teachers Meet Special Needs*, ed. Clyde A. Parker, (Reston, Va.: Council for Exceptional Children, 1974).

ministrators and their staffs shows the initial impact of the intervention in the education of children in Houston.[11]

The Houston plan represents the most distinctive and dramatic example of a special education mission significantly different from others prevalent in practice. This model is the most functionally organized example found in recent administrative practice. Many components of the Houston plan are adaptable to other districts. The focal point in the Houston plan is the place of the trainer in the arrangement of conditions which either facilitate or hinder the growth of children.

AN INTERMEDIATE EDUCATIONAL AGENCY MODEL

The Board of Cooperative Educational Services (BOCES) Model

Systemic Values of the Board of Cooperative Educational Services (BOCES) Model. The BOCES concept is a model of intermediate unit services operating in a number of states and designed to assist local school districts in the delivery of services to children. The BOCES had to develop programs that local districts could not provide individually for themselves. Special education in BOCES grew rapidly in the mid-sixties as direct service providers. The primary growth occurred through the rapid development of programs for the learning disabled and the emotionally disturbed. In New York, building programs also facilitated program development for the severely retarded after 1967 when enabling legislation provided the impetus for BOCES building programs. In the early 1970s, with the mainstreaming emphasis, consumer pressure for the return of children to their home districts and pressure for new funding formulas provided an incentive for local districts to keep children in their home districts. Therefore, the program disability model of the BOCES as the exclusive organizational design for special education services is becoming less appropriate.

The BOCES #2 intermediate unit in southern Westchester County, New York, served between 759 and 800 students from twenty-six constituent school districts in the early 1970s. In 1968–69, the BOCES special education program was distressed over the lack of appropriate educational facilities, the fragmentation and discontinuity of the curriculum from initial placement to present placement, and the lack of accountability in the constituent school districts.

In 1969, 50 percent of all children being served by the intermediate unit were housed in churches and segregated old school buildings. No child was ever assured of continued placement from the primary program to the intermediate or secondary one. Educational programming suffered from lack of coordination, quality control, and sequencing. If the child was in an intermediate unit secon-

---

[11]Charles Kelso, Personal Interview, April 1976.

dary program, parents were concerned about the program's relationship to their district's secondary program. Also, parents desired a regular school placement within their home district, especially for young children. They wanted equal resources and facilities provided by their local district or by a neighboring district school.

Given these parent values, the Board of Education directed the special education leadership to formulate a one- and five-year program projection, complete with facility needs for all handicapped children from both the intermediate and constituent school districts.

Structure of the BOCES Model.   Prior to reorganization, the special education organizational structure was primarily based upon disability categories and the age of the student. The director, two assistant directors, and six instructional coordinators were a combined management and program supervisory team responsible for six intermediate centralized programs, two- and three-unit primary and secondary center locations, and twelve to fifteen district classroom units ranging from one to two classes per constituent district.

With the advent of the regional facility plan, the other parental concerns increased. The need to adopt an organizational structure providing for program continuity within the intermediate unit, and the need to integrate with the constituent school districts became key factors in the reorganization effort.

The model proposed in 1970, which has since undergone slight modification, was based on an analysis of the projected program goals, the previous administrative and supervisor practices, and the regional facility plans.

In order to ensure program continuity and individualized education programming, leadership and administrative or management tasks were divided into three categories:

1. Management (M), setting policy and procedures, directing personnel, supervising budgeting, establishing facilities, supervising purchasing, accounting, and evaluating staff performance;
2. Pupil Personnel Services (PPS), processing referrals, identifying and differentiating handicapped conditions, setting up mental health consultation, developing and evaluating pupil personnel staff, providing a liaison with local schools, developing individual educational plans, and reporting systems; and
3. Supervision and Curriculum (SC), planning the program within primary, intermediate, and secondary levels, and between BOCES operations and constituent school districts, developing professional staff and in-service training, researching, and evaluating the program.

After this analysis was completed, major tasks, responsibilities, and decision-making authority were identified. Figure 6-6 illustrates the organizational structure as it was designed. The director's chief management task was to coordinate the management team (consisting of four assistant directors) and to maintain liaison with the central intermediate unit administration and constituent district superintendents. The two assistant directors for programs (secondary and

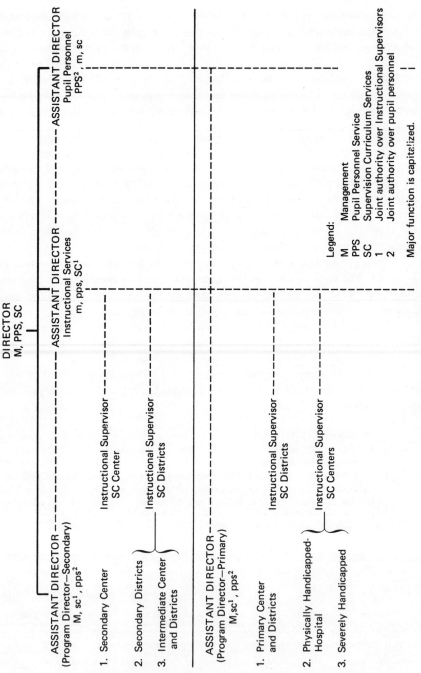

Figure 6-6. BOCES Organization.

primary) were management focused and primarily concerned with program organization and coordination of instruction and supportive personnel for the development of comprehensive individual educational plans and a total program. The assistant director for instructional services was primarily concerned with program continuity within primary and secondary programs. These were directly operated by the intermediate unit. The development of program alternatives within constituent school districts, allowing children to move from the intermediate unit's programs back to the home district or region, was the second major responsibility of this office. Instructional supervisors worked in conjunction with both assistant program directors and instructional services. The assistant director for pupil personnel initially was to maintain all of the office's previous pupil personnel functions.

Personnel changes, a reduced pupil population, and the increasing responsibility of the pupil personnel staff in constituent school districts created two changes in the original structure within one year.The pupil personnel staff was assigned to the program administrators; this increased their availability, scheduling options, and visibility as team members in either the primary or secondary program. The remaining key functions assigned to the assistant director for pupil personnel were reassigned to the assistant director for instructional supervision. Once the constituent districts geared up their individual educational planning and placement, the development of alternative educational arrangements in constituent school districts was again stressed as a high priority. Curriculum development and measurement of student progress within predetermined instructional objective domains were also emphasized.

The significance of the BOCES model is twofold. First, the organizational demands on the intermediate unit have required internal coordination and integration as well as cooperative leadership in program development and accountability for the districts' handicapped children. Second, the model reflects an alternative organizational design. It combines self-contained administrative units in the primary and secondary programs with a new set of lateral relationships in a matrix organizational design. The matrix design is evident in this model—since dual authority relationships were established for instructional supervisory and pupil services personnel—with program administrators and each of the other two assistant directors in charge of instruction and pupil personnel respectively. Even with subsequent modification in the number and type of management personnel, dual authority relationships continued for instructional personnel.

The key organizational problem in the matrix design is one of conflicting priorities between managers who retain authority over shared personnel. In the functional organization design, authority relationships are always in question when the operating head of a unit requests services from a specialized group of system-wide resources under the authority of a centralized administrator. Persons under a dual authority structure in the matrix may experience frustration due to conflicting priorities of their respective management heads. In the functional design, personnel establish an allegiance to one chief although they may work in other settings where the operating administrator has no authority over their work.

A STATE EDUCATIONAL AGENCY MODEL

Prior to the advent of state mandatory laws and federal law (especially Public Law 94-142), state departments of education had organized their special education divisions much like intermediate local education agencies. The program disability categories served as the basis of the state's structure. The state department staff also approved requests for state reimbursement from the local education agency on the basis of children served or teacher classroom unit. This was done according to the type of handicapped or the type of disability certification that the classroom teacher held.

Besides program approval, the state department's divisions of special education have traditionally collected data for state and federal legislature reporting. State staff have also been instrumental in program development for and consultation with intermediate and local general and special education management, and with instructional personnel. They continue to play an important technical assistant role in program development through this direct consultation and in-service training capacity in sparsely populated and rural areas of the states. They collect and disseminate information concerning services rendered and model programs to both professional colleagues and parents. They continue to work in conjunction with parent and voluntary organizations concerned with the handicapped.

The most significant problem facing state organizational structure developers is the organization of two seemingly incompatible functions: planning and technical assistance versus program monitoring and compliance with state and federal mandates. Arizona, Florida, and Indiana are examples of states that do not differentiate the functions. These states have active state-initiated program review procedures. Other states, such as New York, Wisconsin, and Illinois, apparently have separated these functions into two divisions of the SEA organizational structure. The Michigan organizational model was selected to illustrate how one state had attempted to resolve this dilemma by separation of responsibilities into functional units.

The Michigan Special Education Services Area Model

Systemic Values of the Michigan Special Education Services Area Model. In the future, perhaps even more significant than the state department's compliance approval function will be the responsibility to produce a state plan and to evaluate services. Both functions will be further strengthened by P.L. 94-142. The state plan now reinforces SEA's projecting and reporting functions. State and federal law makers and executives want an annual report indicating a state's progress toward full and appropriate education for *all* handicapped children, regardless of where a child resides.

Since the advent of the state mandatory law and P.L. 94-142, the Michigan Special Education Services Area, like its counterparts in many other states, has undergone fundamental changes in the nature of the state agency's relationship to intermediate and local educational agencies. In the past the state department staff could cut off support to the local level for blatant violations of the state education law and code of regulations; now the mandatory law provides the authority to ensure compliance. The law's demands for minimum standards require more than a cursory review of a school district's program before state approval can be met.

In Michigan, mandatory law, developed through an initiative petition of over two hundred thousand persons, is one of the most extensive state laws. It requires educational services for all handicapped children from birth through age twenty-five. The law, except for minor provisions, goes beyond the requirement of the federal mandates in P.L. 94-142. The public development and regulations show a highly visible participation of professional and lay persons. Each of the characters in the planning, implementation, and evaluation of services for the handicapped (state, intermediate, and local lay and professional persons) is being held accountable to ensure its success.

The continued increase in funding, especially from the federal level beginning with the Elementary and Secondary Education Act of 1965, its subsequent amendments under Title VI for the handicapped, and P.L. 94-142, has had its impact on the state education agency. In Michigan, state and regional programs for low-incidence populations of deaf-blind children have required adjustments in the state special education organization.

In the late sixties the state was organized into two divisions: state-assisted programs and federal-assisted programs. The state assistance branch, based upon staff funding and state support of local and intermediate programs, was responsible for data collecting, planning, developing and enforcing rules and regulations, approving programs, consulting, in-service training, and programming public information. This branch was functionally organized statewide, staffed on the basis of program disability areas, and included in the 1970s' school psychology and social work programs. With the two latter additions, certification of professional staff also became a function of the state staff.

The federal assistance branch, unlike the state assistance branch, was not organized functionally within program disability areas. It was organized on the basis of project titles corresponding with their respective funding source under federal law. Therefore, staff for Titles I, III, and VI were identified and developed. Each project was organized to perform specific functions related to project development, grant announcements, receipt, approval, disbursement, monitoring, evaluation, and reporting.

In 1975, the state director of special education began to consider reorganization of the Special Education Services Area. The assumptions on which the reorganization effort was based were: (1) the changing emphasis in functions under current state and coming federal mandates required different staff attitudes, knowledges, and skills; (2) the working relationship within state staff and between state staff and intermediate and local agency professional and lay personnel had changed; (3) the state department was a partner in the state service delivery system with other professionals and parents; (4) the state's responsibilities under the state and federal law would be the basis of a functional organizational structure rather than the source of support for programs, services, or staff; (5) the information processing demands from internal and external agents required a different reporting relationship between the director and his staff.

Structure of the Michigan Special Education Service Area Model.   The state director initiated the reorganization process with an analysis of the state department's responsibilities toward the state superintendent and his staff. He included other participants from the state's management network of administrators and supervisors at the intermediate and local levels. The Statewide Technical Assistance Project in Special Education (STANSE) was utilized to obtain feedback and make subsequent revisions in the model. For a more complete discussion of this statewide planning process, see Burrello, Kaye, and Peele.[12] This model was to become operational in 1978. Appendix A contains a description of Michigan's organizational structure, including responsibilities and decision-making authority for the director and each of the three section heads.

In Figure 6-7, three sections have been proposed. First, the Program Analysis, Planning, and Consultation section has been developed. The chief functions of that unit, in order of priority are (1) assessing statewide needs; (2) planning state and intermediate school districts; (3) programming staff to the second and third sections of services areas; and (4) providing technical assistance and consultation to intermediate, local personnel, and other interested parties such as parent and professional associations.

In section two, the Program Approval and Compliance section approves intermediate school district planning, planning of local agency programs and professional certification programs, monitoring compliance to the intermediate plan or local program statements, granting deviations, conducting investigations and hearings on noncompliance allegations, updating rules and regulations, and providing public information. The Program Development and Training section works with the other two sections in the development, administration, and evaluation of model programs and services. Once programs are deemed worthwhile and once they match other state needs, this staff is responsible for facilitating dissemination through public forums and in-service training. They are also responsible for assessing training needs, initiating cooperative planning with uni-

[12]Leonard C. Burrello, Nancy L. Kaye, and Evan Peelle, *S.T.A.N.S.E. Statewide Technical Assistance Network in Special Education: Initial Report 1975–76*, Grant No. 065537 State of Michigan and Grant No. OEG007507294, U.S. Office of Education (Ann Arbor, Mich.: The University of Michigan, 1976).

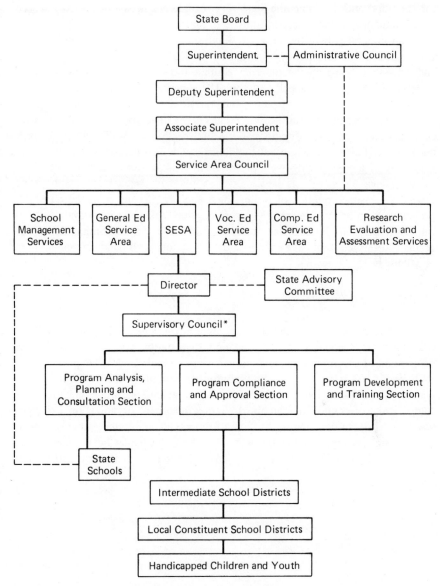

*Supervisory Council consists of the Director and the three Section Supervisors.

Figure 6-7. Michigan Special Education Services Area (SESA) Organization.

versities, and professionally developing the state staff. Regional projects, including the Michigan component, are also coordinated by this unit.

Besides the reorganization into three sections, two other major modifications have been made in this new model. In order to integrate two state schools for the blind and deaf into the state service delivery network, the two school superintendents no longer report directly to the state director. They, instead, become an integral part of the Program Analysis Planning and Consultation unit. The objective is to increase the dialogue between all state management personnel and the state schools management to facilitate the state's planning a continuum of services for all handicapped children. The superintendents report to the director's office only on matters of policy and communications.

The second major modification relates to the development of a supervisory council, composed of the director and his three section heads. Together they represent the management team that facilitates statewide operations internally and externally with other management personnel in the state service delivery system.

An evaluation of this new model should have been undertaken during 1978–79. A subcommittee of professional and lay persons from the STANSE project were to have measured the extent to which this reorganization effort has improved the state-intermediate-local planning and the communications programs and services that have enhanced the education of all handicapped children in Michigan.[13]

SUMMARY

In this chapter, four local educational agencies, one intermediate unit, and one state department model of special education organization were described. A short description of conditions, values, and structure of each model was provided. In each case, movement from a traditional program disability model of organization was identified as the basis of administrative organization. Movement from the categorical self-contained structure to more functional organizational designs was noted in each description. In three of the models presented, other organizational design strategies and tactics were identified. In Chapter Seven, a complete discussion of special organization problems affecting reorganization will be presented.

---

[13]Annual Report of STANSE: Ronald Nutter, Principal Investigator, State of Michigan and University of Michigan (1977).

APPENDIX A

Description of Michigan Organizational Structure[1]

STATEMENT OF DIRECTOR OF SPECIAL EDUCATION SERVICE
AREA (SESA)

RESPONSIBILITIES AND DECISION-MAKING AUTHORITY

1.0 DEVELOPING AND INTERPRETING POLICY

1.1 The Director is responsible for the preparation of policy statements on all matters in the SESA for the State Board of Education. Policy statements are developed by the Director in consultation with Associate Superintendent and Superintendent. This responsibility, while traditionally a responsibility of each Director in a Service Area, will soon be organized into a new administrative manual for the SESA.

1.2 The Director is the primary liaison with the two State professional associations of administrators, MAASE and the MAISEA, in order to maintain a formal vehicle of communication between field management and the Chief State Special Education Office. This authority is person-

[1]Taken from L. C. Burrello, N. L. Kaye, and E. Peelle. The Initial Report: Statewide Technical Assistance Network in Special Education, submitted to Michigan State Department of Education and Office of Education, Bureau for the Education of the Handicapped, 1976.

111

ally assumed by the Director. The Director assumes individual decision-making responsibility with each of these groups on policy and management of SESA.

    1.2.1 Program staff will serve as technical resources to these two associations. Their decision-making authority will be consultative to their individual supervisor in SESA.

  1.3 The Director is responsible to serve as the chief executive officer of the Special Education Advisory Committee to assist the SESA in the development of policy statements for State Board action. The Director has the individual delegated authority given to him by State Board policy.

2.0 REPRESENTING SESA IN SED AND OTHER STATE AGENCIES.

  2.1 The Director is required to participate in the Superintendent's Administrative Council of the SED 13 Service Areas. The Council is a forum to provide SED administrators with an opportunity to share perspectives and issues.

  2.2 The Director is required to participate in Associate Superintendent's Management Group consisting of Special and General Ed, Voc. Ed, and Compensatory Education and Departmental Services. This group, established by Administrative Memo from the Associate Superintendent, is designed to establish common management procedures between and within these five service areas.

  2.3 The Director is responsible for representing SESA on various State Interagency Committees and Task Forces to coordinate State Services to common populations of children and common populations of children and adults. This is a traditional responsibility of the Director of SESA (Governor's, Board Office).

  2.4 The Director is responsible to brief, consult, and prepare correspondence and reports for the State Board and Superintendent offices within the State Department of Education as well as for the Executive and Legislative branches of the State Government on technical matters regarding the interpretation of law, rules, regulations, and Board policy statements. These responsibilities are traditionally delegated to the Director.

3.0 MANAGING AND DEVELOPING THE SESA

  3.1 The Director is responsible for the establishment of the structure and organization of procedures for the implementation of the policy and procedures of the State Board of Education. The Director has individual delegated authority over the administrative implementation in the SESA. This authority is established in the Director position description.

  3.2 The Director is responsible to inform and consult with the Superintendent and Associate Superintendent on *exceptions* to established procedures.

  3.3 The Director is responsible for the supervision and evaluation of the five

Supervisory personnel employed by SED and assigned to SESA. The Director has individual delegated authority which he will retain in the overall planning and coordination of the four SESA sections.

3.3.1 The Director is responsible for convening the Supervisory Council on a regularly scheduled basis. He will be responsible for setting the agenda on matters related to

a. overall policy development
b. planning
c. selection and assignment of personnel
d. final budget preparation
e. SESA communications to Board, Superintendent, Executive Office, Legislature, and all field personnel and advocate groups;

and criteria for decision-making will collectively be discussed with the Supervisory Council. He will ultimately make the necessary final decisions which affect all sections of the SESA.

3.3.2 The Director is responsible for convening the Supervisory Council for emergency problem-solving sessions or when he determines significant issues or exceptions to establish SESA policies and procedures when warranted.

3.3.3 The Director is responsible for scheduling individual monthly sessions with each of his five supervisory personnel for individual supervisory review and professional development.

3.3.4 The Director is responsible to identify staff facility needs and submit requests to the Deputy Superintendent for authorization of the necessary space from Departmental Services.

4.0 DEVELOPING AND MAINTAINING COMMUNITY RELATIONSHIPS

4.1 The Director is responsible for major policy development and communication with major parent and advocate groups. These are traditional responsibilities assumed by the Director.

4.2 The Directors, with the Supervisory Council, will appoint primary liaison to each of the major disciplinary or disability professional and parent groups from the program staff.

4.3 The Director is responsible for the preparation of public information statement on issues affecting SESA with the Associate Superintendent for Public Affairs. The Director will involve the Associate Superintendent for Instruction and Superintendent when appropriate.

5.0 GENERAL SUPERVISORY RESPONSIBILITIES

5.1 The Director delegates to each Supervisory Head and to the Superintendent of the State Schools for the Blind and Deaf the following responsibilities and decision-making authority:

5.1.1 Each Supervisor is responsible for establishing a structure and organizing procedures for the implementation of State Board policies and procedures within their respective areas of responsibility (See Draft of Organizational Chart).

5.1.2 Each Supervisor is responsible to inform and consult with the Director on *exceptions* to established procedures.

5.1.3 Each Supervisor is responsible for developing role responsibilities and decision-making authority over specific activities with individual staff members assigned to their sections.

5.1.4 Each Supervisor is responsible for the periodic and annual evaluations of individual staff performance.

5.1.5 Each Supervisor is responsible for maintaining necessary records and completed forms, applications, and Board agenda items as per Department requirements.

PROGRAM ANALYSIS, PLANNING AND CONSULTATION SECTION (P.A.P.C.)

1.0 PROGRAM ANALYSIS

1.1 Develop and maintain a statewide special education needs assessment program.

1.1.1 Coordination of statewide data collection

1.1.2 Analysis of program outputs

1.1.3 Delivery system analysis

1.1.4 Identification of resources needed to maintain the delivery system
   a. Fiscal needs
   b. Personnel
   c. Other resource needs

2.0 PROGRAM PLANNING

2.1 Intermediate district planning

2.1.1 Consult with intermediate district planners regarding intermediate district-wide planning of special education programs/services

2.1.2 Develop ISD planning format in cooperation with other units to assure data is in appropriate form for other units

2.1.3 Review preliminary and final drafts of ISD plans to resolve technical problems and provide suggestions to strengthen the plan

2.1.4 Conduct Public Act 18 visitations in all intermediate school districts with emphasis on:
   a. ISD planning
   b. Program operation

2.1.5 Summarize data in ISD plans which will be needed to develop state plan

2.2 Statewide planning

2.2.1 Conduct statewide hearings/conferences to assess program priorities as identified by consumers and educators

2.2.2 Develop and update the state plan
    a. Develop a yearly draft
    b. Public review of State Plan draft
    c. Revise and prepare final draft for State Board approval

2.2.3 Identify special education budget needs in conjunction with Management Services
    a. Projections for succeeding year for Bureau of the Budget by October 1 each year
    b. Continual update of financial projections
    c. Reporting of financial status current and past year

3.0 PROGRAM ANALYSIS AND PLANNING FOR MAINTENANCE AND OPERATION OF SPECIAL EDUCATION SERVICE AREA

3.1 Coordinate needs assessment planning and consultation activities with Michigan School for Blind and Michigan School for Deaf

3.2. Provide technical assistance to other units for Annual Program Plans, Budgets, and other internal management activities

4.0 CONSULTATION

4.1 Provide leadership in program development for consumers and educators such as insuring the quality of programs statewide

4.2 Serve as liaison and provide leadership to consumers and educators needed to improve special education programs and services in various disability and program areas

4.3 Provide technical assistance to Program Compliance and Approval Section in order to:
    4.3.1 Participate in approval of ISD plans upon request
    4.3.2 Participate in investigations and hearings upon request
    4.3.3 Assist in development of forms, legislation and publications, rules and regulations upon request

4.4 Provide technical assistance to Program Development Section and help to:
    4.4.1 Assist needs assessment for federal reports
    4.4.2 Participate in developing and reviewing of university training programs
    4.4.3 Identify Part D Institute needs
    4.4.4 Serve on interagency and inter-service area projects and committees
    4.4.5 Assist in the development of forms, publications, etc.

4.5 Provide technical assistance to other service areas and departments regarding educational needs of handicapped children

4.6 Provide public information in disability areas and program development in cooperation with Legislation and Public Affairs Units

4.6.1 Update guidelines

4.6.2 Develop public information documents, films, etc.

5.0 RESPONSIBILITIES AND DECISION-MAKING AUTHORITY OF THE SUPERVISOR OF PROGRAM ANALYSIS, PLANNING AND CONSULTATION SECTION

5.1 Management of the Section

	RESPONSIBILITY	DECISION-MAKING AUTHORITY
5.1.1	To assign and to assure that all work is completed on time and according to specification; and to do periodic and annual review of the staff.	Individual, delegated by the Director.
5.1.2	To select and assign staff, and to approve all itineraries, leave, forms, etc.	Individual, delegated by the Director.
5.1.3	To develop and implement procedures for evaluation of the activities of the Program Planning and Consultation Analysis Section.	Advise Director.
5.1.4	To inform the Director on the status of progress of major activities.	Advise Director.
5.1.5	To consult with the Director on exceptions to established procedures or major problems.	Advise Director.
5.1.6	To prepare Section budget for incorporation into the SESA budget.	Jointly with the Supervisory Council and the Director.
5.1.7	To provide, inform, or advise the Director on policy documents, publication, prior to submission to Superintendent's office, State Board, managers in State Educational system and public information to all other significant groups.	Advise the Director and inform.
5.1.8	To conduct process and product evaluations of Section's activities and share with the Supervisory Council and the Director.	Advise Director.
5.1.9	To coordinate technical assistance to local and intermediate school districts.	Jointly with Section staff, individually and collectively.
5.1.10	To coordinate technical assistance to colleges and universities.	Jointly with Section Chief of P.D.T.
5.1.11	To coordinate technical assistance to citizen groups.	Jointly with the Supervisory Council.

5.1.12 To coordinate technical assistance to parents of the handicapped for programs in all disability areas. — Jointly with the Supervisory Council.

5.1.13 To coordinate State School programs and services in planning, technical assistance and evaluations, statewide. — Jointly with school superintendents.

5.2. State Plan and Intermediate School District Planning

RESPONSIBILITY	*DECISION-MAKING AUTHORITY*
5.2.1 Official interpretations of the State Plan.	Advisory to Director, State Superintendent.
5.2.2 Coordinate, implement, and evaluate the State Plan.	Individual, delegated by the Director.
5.2.3 Final draft of the State Plan.	Jointly with the Supervisory Council.
5.2.4 Develop, coordinate and evaluate ISD planning activities.	Individual, delegated by the Director.
5.2.5 Coordinate all data collection activities and approve all data collection forms going to school districts.	Advisory to the Supervisory Council and the Director.

5.3 Data Management System

RESPONSIBILITY	*DECISION-MAKING AUTHORITY*
5.3.1 Develop and maintain data collection and analysis system in order to plan State Delivery System; respond to inquiries, Federal Compliance, etc.	Individual, delegated by the Director.

5.4 General SESA Management

5.4.1 Coordinate final SESA internal budget for Supervisory Council review and recommendation to Director.

PROGRAM COMPLIANCE AND APPROVAL SECTION (P.C.A.)

1.0 PROGRAM APPROVAL: ISD PLANS OR LEA PROGRAMS

1.1 Review and recommend the appropriate State Board action regarding approval of ISD plans by 10/1 each year.

1.2 Identify specific deviation from the General School Laws (1973) and transmit to ISD or LEA.

1:3 Review revisions from ISD to insure compliance.

1.3.1 Consult with technicians concerning changes.

1.4 Review objections to ISD, attempt to mediate an agreement and recommend actions to the state director—the actions to be taken by the board.

1.5 Design and update the approval criteria to be used to evaluate ISD plans.

2.0 PROGRAM COMPLIANCE

2.1 Program Monitoring

2.1.1 Review program application(s) to determine compliance with General School Laws (1973) as amended.

2.1.2 Review program application(s) to determine compliance with staffing patterns identified in ISD Plan.

2.2 Non-compliance

2.2.1 Process, investigate, and make recommendations on all requests for non-compliance to General School Laws (1973) section 340.252b.

2.3 Deviation

2.3.1 Process, investigate, and make recommendations on all requests for deviations from the Special Education Code.

2.4 Due process hearings

2.4.1 Process, review, and conduct due process hearings in accordance with Rules 24 and 25.

2.5 Process, investigate, and make recommendations on all complaints in accordance with State Board Policy.

3.0 LEGISLATION, RULES, AND REGULATIONS

3.1 Recommend modifications in rules and submit recommendations to Program Analysis, Planning and Consultation Section.

3.2 Develop a standard statement of interpretation or rules.

3.3 Develop vehicles for the dissemination of rules and regulations.

3.4 Development of legislative proposals in conjunction with Legislation and Public Affairs.

4.0 INFORMATION ASSISTANCE

4.1 Provide assistance to parents and advocates of handicapped persons in understanding enforcement procedures of the General School Laws (1973).

5.0 INVESTIGATION ASSISTANCE

5.1 Assist ISD in developing and implementing investigation procedures.

5.2 Provide inservice training to perform investigations.

6.0 SPECIAL EDUCATION PERSONNEL APPROVAL

6.1 Process temporary approvals for teachers and teacher consultants with recommendation of technical assistance staff.

6.2 Process temporary and full approvals for school social workers and school psychologists with recommendation of technical assistance staff.

6.3 Process temporary approval and full approvals for supervisors and directors.

7.0 MAINTAIN LIAISON WITH TEACHER CERTIFICATION SERVICES

7.1 Review and approve new special education personnel training program at colleges and universities for compliance to rules.

8.0 MANAGEMENT OF THE SECTION

RESPONSIBILITY	DECISION-MAKING AUTHORITY
8.1 To assign and to assure that all work is completed on time and according to specification; and to do periodic and annual review of staff.	Individual, delegated by the Director.
8.2 To select and assign staff, and to approve all itineraries, leave forms, etc.	Individual, delegated by the Director.
8.3 To develop and implement procedures for evaluation of the activities of the Program Planning and Evaluation Section.	Advise Director.
8.4 To inform the Director on the status of progress of major activities.	Advise Director.
8.5 To consult with the Director on exceptions to established procedures or major problems.	Advise Director.
8.6 To prepare Section budget for incorporation into SESA budget.	Jointly with Supervisory Council and Director.
8.7 To provide, inform, or advise the Director on policy documents, publication, prior to submission to Superintendent's office, State Board, managers in State Educational system and public information to all other significant groups.	Advise Director.
8.8 To conduct process and product evaluations of Section's activities and share with Supervisory Council and Director.	Advise Director.

9.0 COMPLIANCE TO THE GENERAL SCHOOL LAWS

RESPONSIBILITY	DECISION-MAKING AUTHORITY
9.1 To coordinate complaints, investigations, deviations, hearings, and objections to ISD plans.	Individually delegated.
9.2 To make recommendations regarding complaints, investigations, deviations, hearings, and objections to ISD plans.	Advise Director.
9.3 To assign staff to review intermediate school district plans to assure adherence to the General School Laws.	Individually delegated.

9.4 To develop and disseminate standard statements of law and rules and regulations.	Jointly with the Supervisory Council to Director.
9.5 To assure all special projects are included in the ISD plans at the original submission or through the process of modifications to the ISD plan.	Jointly with Section Chief of P.A.P.C.
9.6 To coordinate activity of the section with other state department sections and service areas and with the U. S. Office of Education rules and policies.	Individually delegated.

10.0 GENERAL SESA MANAGEMENT

10.1 Develop and coordinate legislation and rule modification for Supervisory Council review and recommendation to Director.

PROGRAM DEVELOPMENT AND TRAINING SECTION (P.D.T.)

1.0 PROGRAM DEVELOPMENT

1.1 According to the compliance requirements of USOE/BEH, provide information for the State Plan under Title VI-B (EHA) in collaboration with the planning and evaluation section.

1.2 Participate in needs assessments of State and Field personnel to determine program annual priorities. Utilization of the regional needs assessment conducted by USOE/BEH should be considered.

1.3 Develop and assist State and Field personnel in the acquisition of State and Federal resources to aid in the implementation of needed programs.

    1.3.1 Design and disseminate procedures to assist in the application to secure State and Federal resources.

1.4 Develop and assist State and Field personnel in the acquisition of State and Federal resources designed to facilitate the support for experimental and innovative projects and programs.

2.0 ADMINISTRATION OF SPECIAL PROJECTS

2.1 Regional Deaf/Blind

    2.1.1 Application, review, administration and evaluation of Regional Programs for Deaf/Blind

2.2 GLALRC

    2.2.1 Application, review, administration and evaluation of Great Lakes Regional ALRC Program

2.3 Title I, P.L. 89–313

    2.3.1 Application, review, administration, allocation of resources, monitoring and evaluation of P.L. 89–313 programs.

2.4 Title VI–B, P.L. 93–380

    2.4.1 Application, review, administration, allocation of resources, monitoring and evaluation of Title VI Programs.

        a. B Programs—State priorities and Statewide projects

           1. Program initiation, expansion and improvement

           2. Technical Assistance

        b. C Programs—Michigan RRC

           1. Staff inservice

           2. Technical Assistance

        c. C Programs—Michigan D/B

           1. Technical Assistance

           2. Staff inservice

        d. F Programs—Michigan ALRC

           1. Technical Assistance

           2. Staff inservice

2.5 Title VI–D, P.L. 93–380

    2.5.1 Application, review, administration and evaluation of Part D Training Grants.

2.6 Cooperative Program Development with Vocational Rehabilitation and Vocational Education.

2.7 Statewide Training Programs

    2.7.1 Develop and contract for the inservice training needs of professional personnel in ISD and local school districts.

    2.7.2 Develop and contract for the inservice training needs of SESA staff.

    2.7.3 Develop procedures to assist in the application to secure State and Federal resources to meet inservice training needs.

    2.7.4 Develop a Cooperative Planning process with Michigan institutions of higher education to insure communication between field and university personnel in meeting both the pre-service staffing needs of ISD and local school district programs as well as the continuing education of personnel in service.

    2.7.5 Identify and coordinate the liaison personnel with universities in the State.

3.0 MANAGEMENT OF THE SECTION

RESPONSIBILITY	*DECISION-MAKING AUTHORITY*
3.1 To assign and to assure that all work is completed on time and according to specification; and to do periodic and annual review of staff.	Individual, delegated by Director.

3.2 To select and assign staff, and to approve all itineraries, leave forms, etc.	Individual, delegated by Director.
3.3 To develop and implement procedures for evaluation of the activities of the Program Planning and Evaluation Section.	Advise Director.
3.4 To inform the Director on the status of progress of major activities.	Advise Director.
3.5 To consult with the Director on exceptions to established procedures or major problems.	Advise Director.
3.6 To prepare Section budget for incorporation into SESA budget.	Jointly, with the Supervisory Council and Director.
3.7 To provide, inform, or advise Director on policy documents, publication, prior to submission to Superintendent's office, State Board, managers in State Educational system and public information to all other significant groups.	Advise Director.
3.8 To conduct process and product evaluations of Section's activities and share with Supervisory Council and Director.	Advise Director.

4.0 ADMINISTRATION OF SPECIAL PROJECTS

RESPONSIBILITY	*DECISION-MAKING AUTHORITY*
4.1 Responsible for the overall administration of all statewide projects.	Individual, delegated.
4.2 To incorporate annual priority and other significant data into individual Federal projects for State and local educational agency usage.	Individual, delegated.
4.3 To participate in our delegating a liaison from the staff to participate in various inter and intra state committee meetings, conferences and task forces germain to federal/state special education program planning and implementation.	Individual, delegated.

4.4 To coordinate activity of the section with other state department sections and service areas and with the U.S. Office of Education.

Individual, delegated.

4.5 To complete all State documents regarding federal program implementation to the State Board of Education.

Individual, delegated.

4.6 To complete all federal documents regarding federal program implementation to the U.S. Office of Education, Bureau of Education for the Handicapped.

Individual, delegated.

5.0 *GENERAL SESA MANAGEMENT*

To be assigned as needed.

7

Special Organizational Problems

Special educators can properly credit themselves with prominently aiding in the developments that eventually become standard good practice throughout education as a whole. The concepts of individualized instruction, certain technologies for delivering instruction in a maximally individualized manner, and the whole philosophy of students' rights, which affect the entire educational establishment, have largely been the product of the advocacy thrust of the professionals and clients concerned with handicapped students.

By contrast, in meeting the challenge of development of organizational structures for administering programs, special educators have *not* been particularly creative. Considering the demand for innovative structures that the wide variety of service needs impose, the administrative organization within various systems (aside from those discussed in Chapter 6) remains surprisingly routine. Conspicuously absent (except for the Houston example) has been any contribution to organization theory or practice for *very* large systems. More attention has been given to the particular problems of rural, sparsely populated regions, where the issue has been the aggregation of sufficient population base for the provision of client services. The special problems of administering cooperatively organized systems, such as joint agreement arrangements, cooperatives, and intermediate education units, have been given some attention, but still warrant study and attempts at innovative solutions.

Different kinds of organizational problems, each calling for different approaches for solution, are worthy of discussion.

THE LARGE URBAN SYSTEM: THE DECENTRALIZATION DILEMMA

A major issue of the past decade has been the search for optimal administrative units to achieve responsiveness to clients, effective service delivery, and efficient management. In large systems this has been translated as "how to decentralize." Increasing awareness by the general public regarding the almost automatic failings of large bureaucracies, the rise of consumerism, and the drive for "maximum feasible participation" by clients in decisions affecting their welfare, has led administrators and policy makers in very large school systems to the conclusion that some form of decentralization is an absolute necessity. Since decentralization must be accomplished, only the questions of what form and precisely how it should be carried out are left

The specific factors that constitute the core of the decentralization issue have been discussed in detail by Cronin[1], Nystrand and Cunningham[2], and by Gittell.[3] In these and other works the distinction has been drawn between political decentralization, which involves true community control with grass roots participation in major policy matters, and the less dramatic process of administrative decentralization, in which major policy matters are retained by a central board and only administrative details are delegated to local school executives. While only a couple of examples of true political decentralization are usually cited (New York City and Detroit), it is generally acknowledged that the pressures that brought about these experiments, with their highly equivocal results, have caused a great number of other systems to take positive steps toward administrative decentralization. Perhaps such steps were taken as a hedge against more revolutionary attacks on establishment control, as a window dressing token. The positive examples of such administrative decentralization can be interpreted as honest attempts to achieve more effective service delivery by careful and conservative adjustments to the executive processes.

While major urban school systems have been conscientiously wrestling with these organizational issues, special educators have not been prominent in the debate. This is understandable due to the special educators' usual concern with securing an adequate population base for the establishment of a service for a low-incidence need. Special educators have helped to establish organizational

[1]Joseph M. Cronin, *The Control of Urban Schools* (New York: Free Press, 1973).

[2]R.O. Nystrand, and L.L. Cunningham, "Federated Urban School Systems: Compromising the Centralization-Decentralization Issue," in *Toward Improved Urban Education*, ed. F.W. Lutz (Worthington, Ohio: Charles A. Jones, 1970)

[3]M. Gittell, *Participants and Participation* (New York: Center for Urban Education, 1967).

structures that centralize by consolidation or by the formation of intermediate units, cooperatives, joint agreements, and the like. Concern has tended to focus on how to get a sufficiently large organization for feasible service delivery purposes. In terms of gross numbers, systems already having sufficient size to deliver services effectively and efficiently were few, and therefore relatively ignored by those special educators interested in organizational matters.

As the trend toward decentralization of large systems accelerated during the late 1960s, the question of how to treat special education services under the new organizational structures became very pertinent. Little in the way of empirical data or well-founded theory was available as a guide. A study conducted by the Los Angeles City system[4] had partially dealt with the question, and had gathered opinions of persons regarded as expert judges of special education in large systems. However, conclusions drawn from information generated by that study were extremely tentative, due to the wide variety of opinions expressed and practices described.

When the most dramatic attempt at full-scale political decentralization, with community control, was launched in New York City in 1967 and finally institutionalized by legislation in 1969, special education and a number of other central system components were specifically excluded from the plan. Among the conditions cited as demonstrating the failure of the New York City reorganization to really involve community control, and to merely constitute a form of administrative decentralization, is the exclusion of high schools, special education, vocational education, and such from the reorganization package. The fact that certain aspects of the total school program required centralized control and administration, was used by critics as evidence that the professional establishment, the central board, the central administrators, as well as the teachers' union, were unwilling to change for fear of secure power loss. Another argument maintains that certain portions of the total public school program and/or certain functions of administration cannot be expected to adequately occur in other than the largest possible organizational units. Whatever the interpretation, in the nation's largest decentralization effort, special education retained its centralized base of operations.

The first notable national study on this issue was initiated under joint sponsorship of the Leadership Training Institute/Special Education at University of Minnesota and the Council of Great City Schools, who convened a conference on Special Education in School System Decentralization in Boston in December 1973. Funds from the Exceptional Children's Programs, Bureau of Adult and Occupational Education, U.S.O.E., supported the activity that brought together special education administrators from many of the nation's largest school systems.

---

[4]Frank M. Hodgson, "Special Education—Facts and Attitudes," *Exceptional Children*, 30 (1964), pp. 196–201.

The report of that conference[5] included results of a survey conducted in 1973[6] which contained returns from twenty large school system directors of special education, twelve of which described their general school system organization as decentralized. While summarization of the survey data was difficult due to the open-ended nature of the survey, some interesting general observations were set forth.

In the process of planning for general decentralization, special educators were significantly involved in a minority of the systems. Often, they were included only by courtesy, if at all, since special education was not going to be decentralized with the rest of the system. While the style of each city's decentralization was unique, in most cases the special education organization was altered very little. In five cities no change occurred at all. In others, there were administrative shifts into the area structures, with planning and coordination functions still centralized. A breakdown of fourteen functions indicated that total decentralization of most functions occurred in only one or two systems. Many systems retained functions at a centralized level, but, in even more systems, the pattern for assignment of administrative functions was described as shared between central and area offices.

The survey also noted that increased emphasis on mainstreaming practices, with inherently increased interaction between special and general administrators, required role clarification between central and area personnel, to deal with unavoidable role ambiguities. It appeared that the degree of function decentralization varied between high- and low-incidence programs, as might be expected. Any programmatic innovation that might be anticipated as a result of the flexibility in relatively localized authority did not occur. A rational explanation for this would be that the newness and incompleteness of the decentralization for special educators had them focusing primarily on coping with role, communication, and visibility problems rather than on programmatic innovation. Territorial maintenance was suggested as a major concern for special education administrators in newly decentralized systems, regardless of whether the special education department was included as a part of the reorganization package.

The information gleaned from the forementioned survey, as well as the concepts advanced by presenters and reactors at the Boston conference, seems to suggest that decentralization (to whatever extent it includes special education) and program innovation (to whatever extent an institutional response is made to the forces that demand it) create a need for an organizational design, applicable to large systems, that can accommodate for the division between centralized and decentralized administration.

[5]Maynard Reynolds, *Special Education in School System Decentralization* (Minneapolis, Minn.: Leadership Training Institute, 1975).

[6]Nicholas Nash, "Decentralization and Special Education in the Great City Schools: A Summary of Survey Results," in *Special Education in School System Decentralization*, ed. M. Reynolds (Minneapolis, Minn.: Leadership Training Institute, 1975).

Such a design could be based on a number of different organizational principles, which might be classified generally into two types: One type of organizational principle emphasizes form, that is, the type of child served or the type of service delivered. The other type of principle emphasizes the functions of leadership involved.

If we limit our discussion to large school systems, for example, those over seventy-five thousand enrollment, we will be speaking to an existing concern for a good number of administrators, a concern representing a major portion of the nation's programmatic efforts in special education. We may assume some form of two-layered organization, with overlapping central and regional jurisdictions, each with administrative personnel, with a governing board at the central level, and possibly (though probably not) an additional board at the regional (decentralized) level. Each decentralized region should have a total pupil base of 20,000 to 40,000. Units smaller or greater than this probably distort most of the rationale upon which large system decentralization is based.

In most systems, the relationship between the central and regional offices of special education and the school building administration is more staff than line. The operational accountability of the building principal for all programs, including special education, is maintained with a direct line to regional and/or central general administrators, but not to the special education administrators.

Given this basic total system organization, how can we best organize special education? What should be assigned centrally, and what should be handled regionally?

Organization Based on Form

If we choose an organizational principle based on form, rather than function, there are at least three rational means by which we could handle the administrative process. Each of these approaches is based on some form of client or service classification, delineated either on statistical incidence, clinical disability, or type of service indicated.

A differentiation on the basis of *statistical incidence* can be made with simplicity and logic. Conditions of pupils occurring in low incidence, for example, much less than one percent of the general school population, could be assigned for all administrative purposes to the broadest based, centralized management unit. Such assignment would be based on the assumption that a client population requiring similar type of service should consist of at least 100 pupils (ages three to twenty-one) in order to constitute a viable planning and service unit. For example, severely hearing impaired children, whose incidence in the population might approximate .1 percent, would not be likely to total more than 30 in a decentralized region of 30,000 and should therefore be assigned for service programs to the larger central system. On the other hand, children whose common educationally related needs occur in one percent or more of the general population would constitute a group of at least 200, ages three to twenty-one. They would, therefore, become an entirely viable service unit within the decentralized area, and should have their needs adequately met without resorting to the larger organization.

Applying this incidence criteria would probably result in centralized administration for programs for orthopedically handicapped, trainable and profoundly retarded, autistic, multiple handicapped, home and hospital bound, visually impaired, and severely hearing impaired. Service by decentralized region would probably be viable for educable retarded, emotionally disturbed, specific learning disabilities, speech handicapped, socially maladjusted, and gifted. It is immediately evident that a classification problem may occur as we attempt to differentiate between speech and hearing problems, where mild hearing conditions, supplemental to speech impairments, would fall into the high-incidence side, while only slightly more severe hearing conditions would belong to the centralized, low-incidence population. A similar difficulty may occur as we attempt to distinguish between levels of emotional disturbance, mental retardation, and physical handicap; for most purposes the method would probably work, given the unfortunate way we are habituated to classifying children.

A slightly different approach would be to ignore incidence and classify strictly on the basis of *clinical types of disability*. Such a plan would permit the deployment of instructional and supervisory expertise to the level at which the population was assigned. It could result in much the same assignment between levels as that found in the statistical approach, since the rationale for assignment would have to take incidence into consideration. It could also warrant some differences on the basis of presumed common need of a disability group, regardless of degree of severity. Using such logic, all services for the mentally retarded might be assigned to decentralized regions, since together such pupils would constitute a large population; perhaps the same could be justified for all levels of social-emotional maladjustment and functional speech handicaps. This might leave physical and sensory impairments to the larger centralized level, where, it could be argued, they would permit a focus on methodological and prosthetic intervention in the instructional program rather than curricular modification. However, logical breakdowns occur in that model also. The severely autistic and profoundly retarded child would not receive optimal service from the resources available in an organizational unit of only 30,000 pupils.

A third approach based primarily on form, though related to instructional functions, would be to classify the *type of instructional service*, ignoring both incidence and clinical category of disability. Such an approach has viability only where the total system is able to adopt a full continuum of services, including consultative resource, itinerant and resource instruction, as well as self-contained, full-time classes and school centers. Under this approach all services that are delivered in an essentially self-contained mode, isolated from the mainstream and providing for children who have minimal contact with regular classes, would be operated by the central administration. Services that are most articulated with the mainstream, such as resource teachers, itinerant teachers and consultants, would be administered by the decentralized unit, where proximity to regular teachers and administrators could be optimized.

Within the decentralized regions, there is again a choice of design strategies for the decision makers. If the objective is to maximize the integration of the services, then the matrix design presented in Chapter 5 is most appropriate. Here the building administrator would have all specialized resources assigned to the building, but he/she would be under a dual authority structure reporting to both the central office and the regional office. A second design strategy is the functional distribution of all specialized service personnel from the regional office of the special education leadership to the individual building level. The third strategy is the self-contained unit where integration of services is not desired, and where a self-sufficient program of services for any or all of the handicapped students is organized within individual buildings or in separate facilities in each region.

The assumption is made that persons responsible for special education will be employed at both the central and regional administrative offices, that some division of labor is needed, and that the assignment of responsibility can be attached to programs of services and/or classifications of children.

Organization Based on Function

A different approach to division of labor between central and regional offices is the viewing of the total task in terms of the leadership functions to be fulfilled, without regard to the instructional organization or clientele being served. A simple classification using this dimension would be the identification of the separate processes that constitute the total leadership role, and then the determination of whether the nature of the tasks permits a reasonable differentiation between a central versus regional locus of execution.

The most frequent division of leadership functions has been between the administrative versus the supervisory processes. The earliest studies and attempts at a taxonomy of special education leadership skills and functions—by Mackie and Engel,[7] Graham,[8] and Mackie and Snyder[9]—have drawn this distinction at both the local school system and at the state agency levels. Wherever these two

---

[7]Romaine P. Mackie and Anna M. Engel, "Directors and Supervisors of Special Education in Local School Systems," *U.S. Office of Education Bulletin, 1955*, no. 13 (Washington, D.C.: USGPO, 1956).

[8]Ray Graham, "Functions of the Director of Special Education," *A Guide–Directing the Education for Exceptional Children in a Local School District* (State of Illinois: Superintendent of Public Instruction, 1956).

[9]Romaine P. Mackie and Walter E. Snyder, "Special Education Personnel in State Departments of Education," *U.S. Office of Education Bulletin, 1956*, no. 6, (Washington, D.C.: USGPO, 1957).

roles have been described there has also been an inherent hierarchical relationship, with the administrative functions seen as superordinate to the supervisory ones. This has held, in spite of the obviously trivial nature of certain administrative tasks and the relatively crucial impact of technical supervisory processes on the quality of service delivered.

While the administration-supervision dichotomy may provide a useful way of classifying and concentrating on leadership activity in a single strata organization, or within one strata of a multi-strata organization, it does not provide a rationale for differentiating what can best be classified as centralized versus decentralized in systems using a two-layered model.

A significant break with traditional organization has been described in the Minneapolis system by Johnson and Gross,[10] where the new model has been employed as a means of minimizing disability categories and relating maximally to the various levels of the service delivery system. The model divides the total service system into two major dimensions: (1) those which are based in regular schools and are in support of the regular class teacher and principal (mainstream programs), and (2) those for which a specialist is accountable, due to the low incidence, special physical setting, and largely categorical nature of the clientele. Within each of these two major program dimensions a generalist-administrator, having management functions, and a specialist-supervisor, having technical functions, are described.

The Minneapolis model has among its objectives the decentralization of the decision-making process and the development of resource allocation systems that are designed to focus financial resources at the point of program operation. However, the model does not speak to the problem of the two-layered system since its intermediate total size (about sixty thousand enrollment) has not warranted the same decentralization of the entire special education organization as that in the nation's larger systems. While the mainstream programs in the Minneapolis system are considered decentralized, responsibility is delegated to the school building level rather than to a regional office constituting an "in-between" layer. However, the breakdown of functions into clusters (associated with the generalist versus the specialist) in the Minneapolis model may offer a type of framework for the larger, two-layered systems.

The Dade County (Miami), Florida system constitutes a good example of a two-layered system in operation. As one of the six largest school systems in the nation, with a total student enrollment of about two hundred and fifty thousand in 1976, it contained six decentralized area offices, each with a superintendent and staff, which execute the policies developed by a central, county wide board of education and executive officers. The Department of Exceptional Child Educa-

[10]Richard A. Johnson and Jerry C. Gross, *Restructuring Special Education Leadership Resources: The Minneapolis Model*, Vol. 2 in the Leadership Series in Special Education, eds. R.A. Johnson, J.C. Gross, and R.F. Weatherman (Minneapolis, Minn.: University of Minnesota: 1973).

tion was made up of a centralized office with a director and staff of ten to twelve coordinators, each assigned responsibilities largely on the basis of disability category. Since these personnel function across all six geographic areas of the system, and were concerned with a staff of teaching and other direct service personnel totaling approximately twelve hundred, their mode of operation was largely limited to policy development, program planning, monitoring and evaluating. The feasibility of involvement with direct supervision and consultation with any kind of thorough coverage was doubtful. The role of the director in such a large system actually resembles that of a state agency director. Indeed, the population of this district is greater than that of at least a dozen states and the geographic area covered by the district exceeds that of Rhode Island and Delaware.

The analogy to the state agency role is extended by the existence of the second level: Area Offices for Exceptional Child Education. On the staff of each of the six area superintendents was an Area Director of Exceptional Child Education and a small cadre (three to five) of teachers on special assignment (TSA's); their function was to provide technical support, and supervision/consultation to the direct service personnel in that area. A large part of the job task for these leadership persons, especially with the requirements of P.L. 94–142, was focused on case conference, placement decisions, and individualized program planning. With this task, there is less specific association of a staff member with a categorical disability at this level. The TSAs and area level directors functioned as generalists across a variety of handicaps, particularly with the programs for the more numerous, mildly handicapped. Since each area included a total student enrollment of approximately forty thousand with about two hundred special education teachers, the organization at that level could well be as extensive as that for the entire system in larger school districts. With a student base of this magnitude it might be argued that almost all services for the handicapped could be organized and supplied without dependence upon the more broadly based central office.

With personnel operating on these dual levels, plus an active state agency playing its role in relation to the district on much the same basis as in the other much smaller districts of the state, it could be anticipated that delineation of functions, responsibilities and authority between the levels would be an issue requiring negotiation, clarification, and sometimes arbitration. While certain functions (for instance, development of proposals for system wide adoption) would clearly belong to the central office, and certain others (routine pupil placement decisions, for example) would clearly belong to area offices, there remain gray areas of jurisdiction that could legitimately be claimed by either level. An example might be a decision regarding allocation of personnel between two alternative programs where a system-wide thrust might not coincide with expressed preferences of the professional staff within one of the geographic areas.

In the Dade County example an additional factor should be noted. Two or three school campuses in each of the six areas have been developed as "Exceptional Child Centers." There, in addition to the regular elementary or junior high school facilities and programs, a concentration of services exists for the more severely handicapped; for instance, for the deaf, the trainable mentally retarded, and the orthopedically handicapped. The services require facilities that warrant some degree of centralization for effective and efficient service delivery. As these "Centers" have increased in size to ten or fifteen teachers and paraprofessionals, the assignment of an extra assistant principal to this part of the school program has become a standard practice. Persons assigned to these supervisory positions have been selected with due regard to their qualifications as teachers of the handicapped. In this manner, still another "layer of technical expertise" is added to the leadership structure of a significant portion of the system's total program. Theoretically, a teacher of handicapped children in such a center might secure technical leadership support from any of four levels: (1) the assistant principal in the building, (2) the area office of exceptional child education, (3) the system (county) office of exceptional child education, and (4) the state education agency. This is in addition to the *general* system supervision represented by the building principal and general line authorities over that office.

It may be that this amount of leadership support is necessary. The needs for both general management and technical support are great. However, in such a structure there is vulnerability to redundancy, conflicting direction, gaps, and otherwise inefficient operation of the support system. This can be minimized only by careful attention to the problem and clear specification of role and territorial jurisdiction. The management system presents a complex problem. While such relationship issues will require periodic, if not continual, adjustment and renegotiation in a dynamic system, some basic principles determining responsibility may be established as constants.

Looking at the total scope of leadership functions associated with any organization, certain processes fall logically into the domain of the broadest, most centralized organization units; others fit into the directly operational level. Policy development, for example, surely is a function of the centralized office. In contrast, personnel selection usually needs to be carried out by administrators closest to the field of action. As we move from general administrative principles for all organizations to education particulars, including the specific mission of special education, the determination of each level's processes becomes unclear. At the central level, we could place those functions concerned with planning, development, and evaluation, leaving decentralized offices with the functions of management and direct supervision. Such a dichotomy would distinguish policy matters from operational matters, at least in a crude sense.

The distinction of each level's responsibilities is reduced by the broad scope of certain concepts. For example, while planning would normally be concerned with overall long-range programmatic issues, daily operational survival also includes planning. Similarly, the evaluation process is normally concerned with programs calling for a broad-scale central perspective, but specific units to be evaluated (for example, instructional personnel) would best be examined by leadership staff nearest the action.

To elaborate on some of the activity which would be found at the central level, following this model, we would see planning and policy development as it relates to resource allocation, curriculum, and general program evaluation. Budget development and staff allocation would be specifically handled within the context of resource allocation, as would the function of in-service development of existing staff. The functions of program advocacy, public relations and interagency liaison, would also probably be best executed from the broadest central level.

At the decentralized regional level, the operational management functions would include personnel selection and placement, personnel evaluation, case management and pupil placement, instructional supervision, resource management (including such tasks as materials procurement, facility procurement) and consumer (parent) relations. Figure 7-1 illustrates the general result of this functional approach.

If the functions of the two levels of administrators were as separated as the above dichotomization might imply, real problems of articulation would ensue. Operational managers would be faced with carrying out programs in which they had no voice in development. In actual practice, the centralized personnel would involve input from regional managers as they engaged in planning and development activity. Conversely, the regional personnel would seek the counsel of central administrators as they executed certain management tasks such as personnel evaluation. The crucial consideration is that the responsibility be fixed at one level for each function, leaving few, if any, functions in an ambiguous shared domain. Even if both levels might be involved in a particular activity, the division of authority and function should be clear.

The authority relationship between regional and central offices becomes an awkward problem, regardless of the division of functions that is established. If maximum articulation and coordination within special education is the most desired characteristic of a good system, it would be advantageous to have the regional office special education administrators report to the chief administrator of central special education. Such an arrangement would enhance internal communication, ensuring maximum consistency between policy planning and implementation. Since programmatic operations in special education differ from those in the mainstream and warrant separate and special handling, a line relationship between central and regional personnel would be useful. This would encourage a perception of special education as a separate, parallel system, apart from the mainstream.

If the desirable characteristic of a good system is maximum integration of special education, with program ownership by the general administration in whose buildings and geographic regions the special programs are housed, then the regional special education administrators should relate to the general administrators of the same regions. Neither the general superintendent of a region nor the principal of a building can become very deeply invested in a program that merely occupies space in his territory and is essentially governed by a separate outside office.

It is difficult to achieve an acceptable balance of responsibility and authority that ensures sufficient operational involvement of the "locals" for maintaining a sense of ownership, yet ensures sufficient policy planning and evaluation involvement by the "centralists" for the maintenance of equal opportunity for quality services for all pupils.

Figure 7-1. Functional Organization of Management for Special Education in Large Systems.

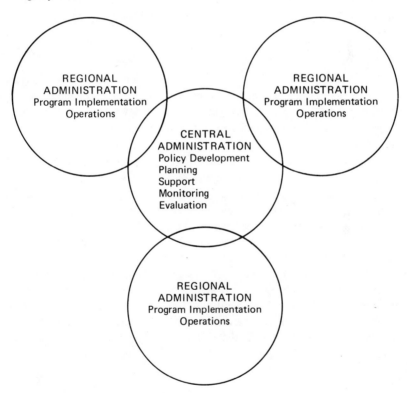

EACH MANAGMENT FUNCTION IS CONCERNED WITH FIVE BASIC ADMINISTRATIVE TASKS:

1. Developing the Educational Program—the Curriculum Task
2. Developing and Maintaining the Fiscal Resources—the Business Task
3. Developing and Maintaining Physical Resources—the Facilities Task
4. Selecting, Assigning, Developing, and Negotiation with Staff—the Personnel Task
5. Developing and Maintaining Community Support—the Community Relations Task

THE INTERMEDIATE EDUCATION UNIT:
THE LIMITED PURPOSE DILEMMA

The Intermediate Education Unit (IEU), one of the possible vehicles for ensuring free appropriate public education for all children, has a number of different forms having certain common characteristics as well as some individual, significant variations for administrative practice. Like the central office of large two-layered systems (such as Dade County, described earlier), the intermediate unit is a link in the chain of organizational structure between the state agency and the local service delivery. However, depending on the legal structure of each state, an intermediate unit may have other advantages and disadvantages of function. In some states it may not exist at all. In Dade County, as in a number of states other than Florida, the county is legally the local education agency, with subdivisions existing only in the largest counties where decentralization is deemed necessary. Montgomery County, Maryland, is another example where, although administrative decentralization has created service unit subdivisions, the county system is legally the LEA and an IEU as well.

The more germaine example of the IEU, for special education concerns, is any of the types in states that have smaller systems as the basic legal structure for LEAs. They have utilized the IEU concept, in whatever form, as the means of aggregating a sufficient population to organize services that would otherwise be economically and programmatically infeasible in a single LEA.

Lord and Isenberg[11] and Gearheart[12] have described the history of cooperative organizations for special education service delivery. The recurring theme in the development of the various models, whether stated openly or not, has been the implicit goal of achieving capacity programming in a manner possible only in large systems while retaining the benefits of the smaller LEA. The preference for local autonomy, which pervades the public attitude toward school systems nationally, has been a major factor in the creation of the IEU. Recognizing that the small size of most of the nation's districts precludes any adequate program development for the handicapped, for vocational education, and for a variety of other support services (such as pupil personnel services, research, data processing, and instructional resources and materials), yet resisting strongly any suggestion of large scale consolidation, the IEU concept appears to provide an acceptable compromise. It is the conflicting nature of the needs and preferences which makes compromise necessary. That creates special problems for leadership, which we shall illuminate.

[11]F.E. Lord and Robert M. Isenberg, *Cooperative Programs in Special Education* (Washington: The Council for Exceptional Children and the Department of Rural Education, National Education Association, 1964).

[12]B.R. Gearheart, *Organization and Administration of Educational Programs for Exceptional Children* (Springfield, Ill.: Charles Thomas, 1974).

Intermediate Units vary among states on a number of dimensions, such as scope of program involvement, governance, fiscal base, and organizational structure. The significance of these variations for special education leadership is our major concern.

Scope of Program

In most instances the IEU development has been in response to an unmet need. These needs have tended to be focused around a particular service, such as special education or vocational education. As a result the IEU has tended to provide for special services only, rather than become an integral part of the entire educational system. Where this has been the case, as in the Board of Cooperative Education Services (BOCES) in New York and Colorado, and the Regional Education Service Agency (RESA) in West Virginia and Iowa, the limited scope places the agency and the leadership personnel in a tangental role, somewhat apart from the other major business of the regular school system. Personnel employed by IEUs are identified only with the special purpose program and often in the same "second class citizenship" status as the students for whom the services are provided. This phenomenon has been observed in the language of both professionals and clients who make references to pupils or programs as being either "BOCES" or "Public School," as if the IEU were not a public school operation.

In other states the scope of the IEU may be broader and more integral to the total education system, constituting an all purpose link between the SEA and LEA. Where this is the case, for instance, in Michigan and in Pennsylvania, the image of the IEU is less constrained, although the major role may still be in special services.

The signficance of the limited purpose image of any IEU for the special education leader lies in the problem of credibility in impacting the mainstream educators when issues arise regarding service delivery in the least restrictive alternative. The special educator in any system must overcome the specialist image. In the IEU, if the entire organization is perceived as "outside" the main system, the problem is compounded.

Governance

The legal structure of IEUs vary greatly among the states. The manner by which governing boards are selected, by appointment or election, whether by component LEAs or at large, and the degree of SEA involvement in the selection of boards and executive officers, all have bearing on the manner in which the special educator can carry out his function in such systems. Where the IEU is an integral part of the state to local chain of command, serving as an extension of the

SEA into the field, rather than merely a cooperative group to which LEAs may choose (or not) to belong, the capability of the IEU administrator to impact the direct service field is enhanced. However, this "official" status also carries the disadvantage of being apart from, and somewhat superordinate to, the mainstream system. Whether the benefits outweigh the constraints in such a situation is hard to assess and will probably depend on other marginal situational circumstances. The governance structure will certainly influence the degree to which regular educators and parents feel that the special education program operated by the IEU is accessible, integral, and relevant from their perspective.

The ultimate in separate governance, and a unique model for dealing with the problems of population base, is the St. Louis County (Missouri) Special District. Established in 1957, and requiring special state legislation, the district has legal, fiscal, and governance structures similar to all other school districts in the state, but it geographically overlays all the regular districts of the area. The district not only operates the special purpose programs (vocational education and education for the handicapped), but has the same tax levying and capital construction bonding capability as regular districts.

The benefits of independence which such a special district enjoys are reflected in the type of special programming that has to be developed. The legal and organizational separation from the mainstream educational programs would constitute a barrier of some magnitude in cases where interaction between the regular and special programs has been desired. The capacity for easy flow along levels of a continuum of special services would seemingly be constrained, with negative influence on the least restrictive alternatives in programming decisions.

The St. Louis County model has been heralded for two decades as a solution to the programming problems of smaller systems. The disadvantages of utilizing a "separate but equal" special purpose system have been outweighed by the technical capabilities achieved. The philosophic thrust associated with P.L. 94–142 can be expected to shift the balance of those relative values, if the least restrictive alternative truly becomes predominant.

Fiscal Status

The IEU structure in some states provides for a tax levy and a participation in the state funding structure on a basis similar to that of other LEA administered service. In other cooperative organizations (such as New York's BOCES) the funding of services is primarily by tuition receipts from the LEAs on the basis of pupil services provisions, and prorated administrative charges, with no separate taxing authority or share of state support. In the latter case the stability of operating income is dependent on the continued participation of LEAs in "buying" the service from the IEU provider. This potential instability is cushioned somewhat by the requirement of shared administrative costs as a prerequisite, nonrevocable condition for original membership, regardless of continued participation in pupil-tuition services.

When deciding to participate in IEU provided services versus LEA initiated services, the fiscal issue often takes on more importance than other program quality factors. Economic concerns (often the *perceived* rather than an *actual* cost-benefit balance) may dictate the program emphasis if not the continued existence of a special education program within an IEU. For instance, the dramatic growth of BOCES programs in New York had occurred at a time when the financial advantage of BOCES participation (intentionally established to encourage program development and overcome local reticence) was clearly greater than participation with the LEA. The incentive worked so well that major BOCES growth occurred in some of the suburban regions where the population base in the LEAs could have supported their own programs. The primary intent of using BOCES in rural regions, where cooperative organization had been the only answer, was somewhat subverted by the vigorous embrace of the model by those systems which needed it less, but recognized the financial advantage. With changes in the total funding structure in 1974, making the financial advantage of local versus BOCES participation more equivocal, a shift of participation was observed. The shift toward local programming could be attributed to an awareness of the least restrictive alternative. However, it is more likely that financial considerations were often the basis for decision rather than program quality or client preferences.

In the final analysis, the fiscal issue will influence whatever role the IEU special educator may play in the total service system.

Organizational Structure

In practice, the effect of a particular model of a state IEU will depend very much on the daily details of operational performance. Possible leadership functions may be greatly influenced by whether physical space for services is owned by the IEU, rented by the IEU from component LEAs, or procurred from third (non-school) parties. These and similar mundane provisions may impact significantly on the relationship surrounding pupils, direct service personnel, and various involved leadership persons. Responsibility for executing routine management functions, when pupils become "assigned" to a separate organization, extend to the staff who may be employed by one organization (the IEU) but are housed in or deployed to another (the LEA). The practical problem of supervision of teachers, including evaluation of provisional employees, is amplified when the legal superordinant (IEU administrator) has less contact with such employees than another administrator (the LEA principal) in whose territory the person is working.

The establishment and continued clarification of policy in these regards is crucial where IEU-LEA interaction is a part of the service package. The complexity of such policy will vary as a function of range of service alternatives. While procedures regarding a single option (such as self-contained special classes) can be established with relative ease, the complete service system may have an array of perhaps seven levels of intensity in service alternatives, each requiring slightly different leadership support provisions. When transfer from one system (the LEA) to another system (the IEU) is a necessary transaction for every case in which a special service of any sort is needed, the assignment of jurisdiction or the assumption of responsibility for first-level intervention (referrral, assessment, and the like), as well as terminal-level actions (that is, reassignment from special to regular programs), becomes an important policy consideration. The bureaucratic preference for maintaining control of gatekeeping functions on one's own side of the interorganizational boundary must be considered in establishing the procedures governing such interactions. This in itself constitutes a special problem in the intermediate unit leadership process.

Within the general laws, regulations, and policies governing IEU operations in each state, there are structures regarding broad decisionmaking. These will usually need to be particularized to cover the kinds of concerns that are relevant and crucial to the special education service system.

The problems of leadership in the IEU or any type of cooperative, interdistrict service unit are inherent in the concept and largely unavoidable, regardless of particular structure, fiscal status, governance, or scope of program. Isenberg described the characteristics generally considered desirable for assuring efficient operation of such organizational frameworks:

1. Broad and comprehensive responsibility for both elementary and secondary education and their specialized aspects.
2. Broad and generally oriented professional administration.
3. An area of operation large enough to permit the efficient development of most services local school systems cannot provide for themselves.
4. Adequate and dependable financial support with some degree of flexibility in its use.
5. The ability to adapt programs and direction as circumstances and needs change.
6. A sufficient stability to assure the continuation of service in spite of changes and realignments among participating local school systems.
7. A responsiveness to the needs and desires of local school systems as seen from the local level.
8. The ability to secure a staff sufficiently competent to have something substantially worthwhile to offer participating districts.[13]

We would submit that although these are valid characteristics, their presence will not resolve the administrative problems of limited special purpose, separate governance and fiscal status, ambiguous structure, and the resulting complexity of interorganizational relationships.

[13]F.E. Lord and Robert M. Isenberg, *Cooperative Programs* p. 21.

THE RURAL SCHOOL SYSTEM: THE SPARSE POPULATION DILEMMA

The establishment of intermediate education units has constituted a direct assault on the problem of getting special education services to those in need where the individual school district population is too small to warrant full services. However, there are many situations where even such a scale of organization cannot adequately deal with the problem. In sparsely populated regions, even after maximum redistricting or cooperative organization has been accomplished, the distribution of pupils needing service is such that the usual means of transporting them daily to any type of specialized group instruction becomes infeasible.

The management of services in such regions therefore resolves to a considerably curtailed range of alternatives, such as residential facility placements, extraordinary transportation or communication mechanisms, or itinerant-consultant procedures for bringing the service, on a periodic basis, to where the child is. The primary variable determining the choice among these alternatives is the severity of need for specialized services or the intensity of service required. The other variables include the comparative benefits that can be anticipated, and the trade-off in costs, both in dollar resources and in psychological, social, and educational concomitants of possible alternatives.

It is probable, for example, that if a blind or deaf child is the only one within a 100-mile radius whose instructional needs appear to require highly technical expertise, a residential placement (public or private) may be the only choice. However, the possibility of daily air transport could in certain circumstances be weighed against the costs and benefits of residential services. Where the intensity of specialized instruction is less clear, the choice may be between the residential or transportation solution versus electing for a much lower intensity of service that might be provided by an itinerant consultant, who could work directly with the child as well as consult with the regular teacher. However, this would be on an infrequent periodic schedule. The cost-benefit considerations in such situations are very complex and involve balancing the possible, the desirable, and the contrast of dollar versus psychological costs. They also involve making judgments on the basis of flimsy and often controversial data.

It would appear that the nature of the problem for very rural school systems is one of

1. Identifying available alternatives for service.
2. Innovating beyond ordinarily existing alternatives.
3. Evaluating trade-offs between equivocal alternatives.
4. Making decisions between alternatives, neither of which can be considered optimal, but hopefully may suffice.

Leadership in rural systems must be provided by persons who either cannot be exclusively concerned with special education issues or must be spread very thinly over broad geographic territory. The nature of the role demands wide knowledge, a high level of innovativeness, and judgment capability based on analysis of complex human variables. These demands for leadership are perhaps more difficult than those for typical special education organizations, yet the realities dictate that such leadership must come from persons minimally prepared to provide for it.

Rural leadership situations place a high value on broad general knowledge of alternatives rather than a higher level of specific technical skill. The analogy of the "general practitioner" in medicine is probably appropriate to this case. However, the question may become one of differentiating between administrative leadership and direct service provision, and determining whether these two functions can best be executed by the same person or by different persons.

As special education has reached beyond the boundaries of major school systems, a common model for some rural areas in this country has been the use of itinerant teacher/consultants; they had served primarily as sensitizers of other educators to the special needs of certain children. By fulfilling a diagnostic and referral function, as well as a general advocacy function, for children regarded as "problems" by their regular teachers, and then providing for consultation and short-term direct instruction, these special education personnel have become the only service for handicapped children in rural regions. The concept has been sophisticated and organized more effectively in recent years in the Vermont Consulting Teacher model.[14] This approach has been particularly suited to the needs of sparse population areas where the clustering of handicapped children into groups for special instruction is difficult. This model is a significant departure from traditional models in that it emphasizes the responsibility of the regular teacher for instruction of a wide range of deviant children. It utilizes the specialist as a consultant to the regular teacher for the assessment of the child's status; it plans and programs the instructional treatment; and it then guides the teacher in executing it. The model's emphasis on staff development and supervision of the regular teacher causes the specialist's function to overlap between a direct service role and a leadership role.

The need for a special education administrator is obvious where the model is implemented. The consulting teacher, as specialist, becomes the major service provider, while the major administrative functions can be executed by the general administrator who oversees all educational services, including those special services provided by the consulting teacher. If the consulting teacher does possess the skills for executing the leadership (consulting) role, and if the organization gives that person the opportunity to fulfill all aspects of the role, the problem of leadership in sparsely populated areas can be greatly diminished. The consulting teacher can easily assume the major responsibility for functions that in other sys-

---

[14]Hugh McKenzie, et al., "Training Consulting Teachers to assist Elementary Teachers in the Management and Education of Handicapped Children," *Exceptional Children*, 37 (1970), pp. 37–43.

tems would be associated with first-level supervision, including the process of deciding programming alternatives. The need for higher-level supervision under such circumstances would not ordinarily go beyond that which a competent generalist could provide.

Models describing a continuum of service delivery alternatives do not deal with the specific problems of rural areas. Little seems to have been published on the problem. Weatherman and Hollingsworth[15] have disseminated proceedings of a conference held at the University of Minnesota in 1975 which addressed critical factors of service delivery where complicated by distance and low population density. A variety of approaches to regional planning and service delivery are described in the report, but a general model guiding such needs is not provided. Erdman, Wyatt and Heller[16] have also discussed some of the issues of program administration in small school systems, but the focus in that publication is limited to one category of the population of handicapped pupils.

We will attempt to provide a comprehensive four-dimensional model for service delivery for handicapped children in rural areas that will consider all the relevant variables. (Figure 7-2) The resulting figure is a diamond, with the first dimension, the number of children to be served, varying as a function of each remaining dimension. As one moves toward the center of the diamond from either tip, the number of cases increases as more children are served in each type of alternative. The upper triangle of the diamond is essentially the classic Reynolds framework.

The second dimension deals with the population density. The more sparsely populated the area, the fewer children need service within each programming alternative, irrespective of severity of handicapping condition, since the issue is the access of children to services at a school-based program.

The third dimension is concerned with the severity of the handicap. Least severely handicapped students would receive services in a school-based program, while the more severely impaired would require service in institutional-based facilities, irrespective of population density.

The fourth dimension involves the location from which the services are provided. Most students will be served from school-based or regional-based programs that encompass a major portion of the model. The more severe the condition or the more sparsely populated the area, the fewer the number to be served by such facilities, and therefore the greater use of home-based or institution-based programs.

Some of the terms used in the model may need to be explained. Telecommunications, which are home-based, can be provided in three ways. One is a

[15]Richard F. Weatherman and Sue Ann Hollingsworth, *Administration of Special Education for Rural and Sparsely Populated Areas* (Minneapolis, Minn.: University of Minnesota, 1975).

[16]Robert L. Erdman, Kenneth E. Wyatt, and Harold W. Heller, *The Administration of Programs for Educable Retarded Children in Small School Systems*, (Arlington, Virginia: The Council for Exceptional Children, 1970).

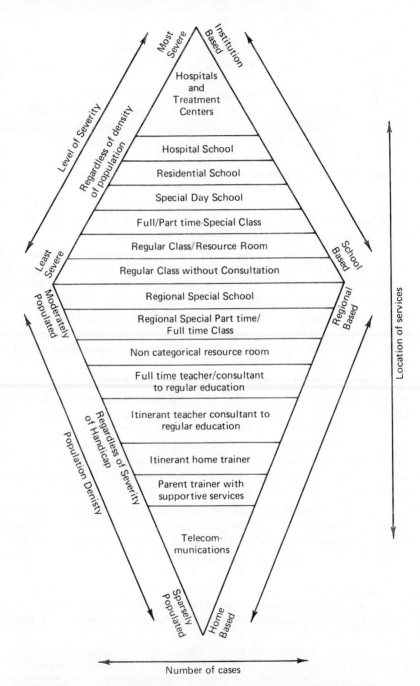

Figure 7-2. Continuum of Services in Rural Areas. *Copyright, Vicky L. Ondell and Leonard C. Burrello, 1978. From C.A.S.E. Information and Dissemination Delivery of Special Education in Rural and Sparsely Populated Areas.*

telephone that is installed in the child's home. Communication can then be carried on between the teacher and student over long distances.

The second method of telecommunication is a television placed in the home. Depending on the sophistication and resources of the geographical area, different approaches can be taken. One approach is to transmit educational programs to the television. The state or local district will be responsible for making the programs and televising them. Wisconsin has programs similar to this that are televised to the schools.

Another approach concerns itself with broadcasting the classroom setting to the home. Again depending on resources, the audio-communication could be one-way from the classroom to the home, or two-way, from the classroom to the home and from the home to the classroom. This would enable the student to ask questions during lessons and receive an immediate response. The severe winter of 1977 resulted in Ohio implementing educational services by way of television. With school closed for an extended period of time, the students were instructed by their teachers by watching T. V. This resulted in the students receiving school instruction despite the weather conditions.

The third method of telecommunications involves administrative services. If an administrator is needed for services in his district, (for instance, a case conference) and is unable to be present for these services, the telecommunications process can be used. The administrator can conduct a case conference forty miles from his office without physically attending the conference.

The parent trainer with supportive services involves the parent as the primary teacher for the student. The supportive services are those provided by the school district in which a teacher visits the home periodically to record student progress and consult with the parent trainer.

The itinerant home trainer can be viewed as a variation of a homebound teacher, where the teacher visits the house on a routine schedule and instructs the student in the home. The homebound teacher model has been used extensively to instruct non-handicapped students who, because of temporary illness or accident, are out school for short periods of time. The home trainer can be used for those handicapped students who have no direct access to education in a school-based or regional-based setting.

The itinerant and full-time teacher consultant can be used in a similar fashion to the Vermont teacher-consultant model, which will be discussed in Chapter 9. The difference between the itinerant and full-time teacher-consultant is primarily a matter of the availability of financial resources of the school district. It should be noted that in providing services to regular education a new concept can be employed—that of having the teacher-consultant train peers to help instruct the handicapped student. Bloomfield Hills, Michigan has developed a program in which student peers are trained by special education personnel at the high school level to become communication facilitators between deaf students and regular classroom teachers. This could be adapted to train peers to help regular classroom teachers deal with handicapping conditions other than the deaf.

The regional special part-time/full-time class can be employed where an area has just enough students to fill a classroom but not enough to fill a single school, and where there is too great a transportation distance between the schools. The result is an alternative living program whereby a handicapped child lives with surrogate parents during the school week and receives the education in that district. The school district reimburses the surrogate parents for expenses for having the handicapped child living with them. On the weekend, the child goes back to his natural parents. This type of service delivery has been implemented in Wassau, Wisconsin and in Delaware. A regional special school may also be an alternative for a multi-county/LEA area.

The appropriate organizational unit for housing and administering services in such sparsely populated areas is not necessarily the local school district. Unless mechanisms for cooperative service delivery to a wide area from the LEA level are arranged, it is likely that a service, such as the Vermont Consulting Teacher model, would best be managed from an intermediate unit or possibly the SEA level.

For certain purposes, the establishment of communication systems via telephone and cable television will be a major consideration. While such procedures have been used routinely for pupils needing home and hospital instruction, the extension of this technology is possible into circumstances where an instructional specialist could guide both the child and a regular teacher or paraprofessional through learning sequences not found in the repertoire of the nonspecialists. The development of such technology is the responsibility of the existing Learning Resources centers of the Bureau of Education for the Handicapped. But the determination of whether a technology reaches the child becomes a matter of knowledgeable local leadership.

SUMMARY

Whether the solution to difficult service needs is to be found in esoteric transportation schemes, unusual communication mechanisms, residential placements, or deployment of personnel into different kinds of roles, the delivery of services in sparsely populated regions will involve decisions based on a different cost-benefit scale than that of ordinary systems. This calls for a high level of awareness for possible innovations, a readiness to experiment, and creative adoption and/or adaptation of innovations. The challenge for leadership under such circumstances, from whatever level of the organizational hierarchy, is in the generation and utilization of ideas rather than the following of convention. This may be the place where the best of special education leadership can be demonstrated.

8

A Projected Model: Organizing Special Education as a Supportive Service for All Children

INTRODUCTION

In this chapter, we will attempt to share a planning perspective leading to an alternative organizational structure for the delivery of equal and appropriate educational opportunities for handicapped children and others with special needs. The set of assumptions that will guide the development of this structure will be drawn from a futures orientation. The implications of the futures perspective in designing the educational organizational structure will then be identified. A set of specific goals for education of all children and a description of programs and services ensuring the identification and placement of handicapped children into the least restrictive environment will follow.

THE FUTURES PERSPECTIVE

A futures perspective is based upon the generation of alternative projections of desirable outcomes that any community of people seek to achieve. Since any decision is a future-oriented act, it is irresponsible not to consider the future in present plans. Adelson believes that the critics of futures thinking come to two wrong conclusions. First, he contends that futures thinking is not "some sort of fantasizing or abstruse kind of activity which some people do on behalf of everybody, and that it may or may not have any real impact on the present."[1] On the contrary, he posits that the real reason for futures thinking is to make decisions in the present.

> Thinking about the future is not irresponsible as a way out of the present. Since all decisions are necessarily future oriented, by not thinking about the future in a systematic and open way, we are being irresponsible; or people who do think that way, rather than the other way around, are irresponsible.

Futures planning must, then, consider the alternative desirable futures first, then consider which futures can be supported and planned.

The futures perspective is a recent topic of discussion in education. Social scientists and behavioral engineers have led the development of futures research and technological development. Research institutes such as Rand and Batelle have pioneered in this research. Major works forming the basis of this discussion is based are Michael[2], Hencley and Yates[3], Hack[4], and others. In special education more recent applications of the futures research include Hobbs[5], Gilliam and Burrello[6], Siantz[7], Morrow and Yates[8], Schipper and Kenowitz[9], and Rhodes[10].

[1]Marvin Adelson, "Perceptions of the Year 2000," in *Long Range Planning for Special Education*, eds. J. Gilliam and L. Burrello, (U.S. Office of Education Grant #OEG-GOO-75-00361, 1975).

[2]Donald Michael, *On Learning to Plan and Planning to Learn* (San Francisco, Calif.: Jossey–Bass Publishers, 1973).

[3]Stephen Hencley and James Yates, *Futurism in Education: Methodologies* (Berkeley, Calif.: McCutchan Publishing Corporation, 1974).

[4]Walter Hack, *Educational Futurism 1985: Challenges for Schools and their Administrators* (Berkeley, Calif.: McCutchan Publishing Corporation, 1971).

[5]Nicholas Hobbs, *The Futures of Children* (San Francisco, Calif.: Jossey–Bass Publishers, 1975), pp. 222–83.

[6]James Gilliam and Leonard Burrello (eds.), *Long Range Planning for Special Education*. Part 1: A Statewide Planning Process, United States Department of Health, Education and Welfare, Office of Education, Bureau for Education of the Handicapped Grant #OEG-GOO-75-00361, December 1975.

[7]James Siantz, *Long Range Planning for Special Education: Technical Critique of One Strategy, Part II* (Doctoral Dissertation, University of Michigan, 1976).

[8]Henry Morrow and James Yates, *Pupil Appraisal 1975 to 1990, A Delphi Study* (Austin, Texas: Regional Resource Center, 1976).

[9]William Schipper and Leonard Kenowitz, *Special Education Futures: A Forecast of Events Affecting the Education of Exceptional Children: 1975–2000* (Washington: National Association of State Directors of Special Education Inc., 1975).

[10]William Rhodes, *The Future of Childcare* (Conceptual Project in Emotional Disturbance at Institute for the Study of Mental Retardation and Related Disabilities, Ann Arbor, Mich.: The University of Michigan, 1975).

Alternative Societal Futures

The specific alternative societal futures listed below provide a perspective on what the authors see as the basis for organizing special education services.

1. Increasing awareness that our world is becoming more and more interdependent, requiring an analysis of long-term effects rather than political or temporary effects of advances and new discoveries.
2. Supporting more public policy that reinforces the individual right to be different, and encourages not mere tolerance, but a positive valuing of difference.
3. Anticipating more change through the application of new planning and communication technologies.
4. Fostering a climate of cooperation and community participation in setting direction and requiring accountability of business and industry, government and public agencies that work in the best interest of the community.
5. Stressing the value of education and the retraining of people as careers change throughout their life.
6. Continuously developing alternative forms of community living.
7. Applying more technological advances to daily life.
8. Increasing sophistication of computer technology for storing, retrieving, and planning for the future.

Future Images for the Education of All Children

Specific implications of projected societal futures for the education of all children call for increasing:

1. cooperation between boards of education, school management and teacher organizations, and the larger community for education policy formulation and designing of alternative forms of education.
2. commitment to individualize education for all children.
3. accountability of public school systems for *all* children.
4. participation of parents in education planning involving their children.
5. utilization of alternative settings for education.
6. support for the individual teacher in planning, organizing and evaluating instructional performance of students.
7. the number of career alternatives for instructional staff from individual classroom teaching, to a variety of alternative roles supporting instruction.
8. commitment to assess the process of instruction through action research, professional development, and evaluation.
9. utilization of information processing systems to manage flow of communication between instructional-supportive management and community.
10. role of the school-community as the central force in interagency cooperation, leading to comprehensive programs for children, youth, and aged.

THE SPECIAL EDUCATION LEADERSHIP ROLE

The special education leadership role facilitating the education of all children must first begin with the underlying value that individualized education should be the goal for all children. Secondly, special education must continue to stress the accountability of the schools to service all children. Many children are in need of alternative education programs and services not found in general education classrooms. Teachers and counselors alike have identified 30 to 40 percent of children in schools today as needing an alternative form of instruction. Rubin and Balow[11] have results that indicate that 41 percent of 967 children in kindergarten through the third grade were identified as having school learning and behavioral problems. Over 24 percent were already referred or placed in some form of specialized service. Burrello and Peelle[12] surveyed a junior high school program when teachers and counselors indicated that a significant proportion of pupils were "only sitters," not participating fully as students. Among 404 students so identified out of 1200 in the seventh through ninth grades, the primary areas of concern were: self-concept, attitude toward school, low achievement, attendance, and discipline.

Much of the needed instructional service can and should be carried on within regular classrooms. Teachers, however, need some assistance in the rapid assimilation and application of information as well as alternative means to managing the multiple and diverse needs of children. Children whose learning needs differ in terms of their acquisition rates, style, retention, comprehension, and application or transfer of training, demand alternative strategies and tactics to maximize their learning.

The complexity of the task is indisputable. The educational system is too fragmented and unorganized to meet the demands of the job. The competition for students failing in the regular education programs has resulted in unnecessary duplication and resource waste between remedial and compensatory education efforts, and between vocational and special education efforts. Regular instructional staff has been alternately threatened and disappointed with the delivery of these alternative programs for children with special needs.

Gallagher has drawn the analogy of the infantry, which in the military has a complex set of support systems working together to maximize its impact on a prescribed target. "It is all too clear that the educational support systems necessary to get complex tasks done are not there . . . just as the infantry can fail because they're not backed up with good support services, so can the classroom

---

[11]Rosalyn Rubin and Bruce Balow, "Learning and Behavior Disorders: A Longitudinal Study," *Exceptional Children* (December 1971), pp. 293–301.

[12]Leonard C. Burrello and Evan Peelle, *Final Report, Special Education Simulation and Consultation Project*, ed. Leonard C. Burrello (Special Training Project OEG-O-72-4309, U.S. Department of Health, Education and Welfare, Office of Education, 1975), p. 50.

teacher fail if he is not backed up with good support services."[13] Gallagher suggests that three major functions must become a part of school operations: planning and evaluation, training, and research and development.

These authors believe that special education can play a significant role in developing and implementing those needed functions. Reynolds believes this change has already begun to occur. The movement to special education as a support system suggests teaming with regular teachers. Four implications of this change have been identified by Reynolds. They are:

1. special education personnel will be less identified with categories of exceptionality.
2. regular teachers will, both through formal training and work experience with special educators, become more knowledgeable and resourceful in dealing with exceptional pupils.
3. special education personnel will be selected and prepared for more indirect influences in the schools, as in consultation and change agent roles.
4. major restructuring will occur in the college training programs for special education personnel, becoming less categorized and more integral with general teacher preparation.[14]

Special education should be reorganized as an integral support system for all children. This must begin with reinforcing the schools' responsibility to serve all children. Initially, the shared or centralized responsibility of special education demands a change in role and function. If the schools are responsible for serving all children in the least restrictive environment, school administrators must assume the required responsibility and authority to organize, operate, and evaluate all programs for all children at the district or building level. Special educators should then plan, organize, and evaluate their contribution as a support system to the regular administrative and instructional staff.

The organization and the accountability for special education should be to:

1. provide support and assistance to regular education personnel to help them teach and organize instructional services for the handicapped students and other students with special needs.
2. establish direct services that allow for the unique learning and behavioral needs of the students in the least restrictive environment.
3. set up a team effort of parents, students and professionals for the planning and placement of the handicapped student.
4. initiate alternative settings and services at the building and district level.
5. provide for evaluation of a student's progress and decision points for the exiting from the settings in various programs and services.

[13]James J. Gallagher, "The Search for the Educational System that Doesn't Exist" in *Imprint*, (CEC Information Center, January 1972), pp. 4–5.

[14]Maynard C. Reynolds, *Trends in Education: Changing Roles of Special Education Personnel* (Columbus, Ohio: The University Council for Education Administration, 1975).

6. enable the professional staff development to increase teacher and administrator competencies.
7. develop a field-based-action research program that tests the application of basic learning principles to instruction, behavior management, and mental health of students, parents, and professionals.
8. negotiate and obtain external participation of other state and community agencies for the support of instructional programs, mental health services for children, and social welfare services for parents and children.
9. provide direct consultative services to parents and students to assist them in becoming better participants in the educational planning process.
10. apply criteria derived from considerations of process and least restrictive environment to all individual educational planning and placement alternatives developed at the individual building or district levels.

SPECIAL EDUCATION ORGANIZATION

The organizational model for special education is drawn from a number of sources. This model is largely based upon the futures perspective and the responsibilities identified earlier. Specific components of the organizational models presented in Chapter 5 have also been incorporated here. Four organizational designing principles were reviewed in Chapter 6, highlighting Galbraith's information processing theory. When considering organizing special education for the future, the organizational design must include a combination of those principles. Whatever the strategies selected, cost will certainly be a factor. Yet regardless of cost, a strategy will be observed in any structure that is designed. In this model, three design strategies have been utilized. They are:

1. the creation of lateral relations in building level supportive programs and services for mildly handicapped children and others with special needs;
2. the development of self-contained tasks in organizing district level programs for low-incidence, severely handicapped populations; and
3. the investment in vertical information systems for the processing of information on factors that influence the individual educational planning at either the building or the district level.

Building Level Supportive Programs and Services

The first strategy, "creation of lateral relations," is selected because the delivery of building level supportive services increases the accountability of educators for all children with special needs. By lowering the level of decision-making down to where the information exists, rather than maintaining it in the central office, resources can be more appropriately integrated into the unique climate the building administrators and staff create. While many forms of lateral

relations will be employed in this model, the primary form will be the establishment of a dual authority relationship. In order for the integration of specialized
resources to take place, the building administrator must become a member of the
instructional team responsible for educational planning and placement in the individual school building. The net effect of this change is to create a power balance between the assistant superintendents for operations and the assistant
superintendent for supportive services, each of whom advocates a different
cause.

Each decision related to program or services may not be predicted in advance; it may demand resolution on its own merits. Rather than refer each cir-
cumstance up the school system's hierarchy, the matrix design institutionalizes
an adversary system.

> The resultant goal conflict implements search behavior to discover current informa-
> tion and to create alternatives to resolve the conflict.
> The joint decisions of the adversaries will reflect global considerations to the
> degree that power is distributed across the roles in proportion to the importance of
> the sub-goals for global goals and to the degree that the role occupant employs be-
> havior which leads to joint problem-solving. The power balance is, in a sense, an
> unachievable razor's edge, but it needs only to be approximated. The power at-
> tributable to each role is determined by the selection of the occupant, the design of
> information systems to support the role, initiation and approval powers in the plan-
> ning and control process, control of money to effect goals, and the establishment of
> formal authority relations.[15]

In the matrix shown in Figure 8–1 the Assistant Superintendent of Elementary and Secondary Curriculum and Assistant Superintendent of Supportive Services participate equally in these specialized processes.

In establishing dual authority relations it is important to identify the critical
points of potential controversy. They are: (1) estimating the need for supportive
and alternative programs and services; (2) allocating resources; (3) evaluating the
building administrator's utilization of those resources efficiently and effectively;
and (4) judging the effectiveness of the supportive programs and services on
teacher or student performance.

Other forms of lateral relations include encouraging direct contact between
building administrators and the director of supportive services, identifying
liaison to link the two departments, and employing permanent teams to work on
individual educational planning and evaluation that affects the interdepartmental
utilization of supportive services.

This third lateral relation strategy, the permanent interdepartmental team,

[15]Jay Galbraith, *Designing Complex Organizations* (Reading, Mass.: Addison–Wesley Publishing Company, 1973), p. 105.

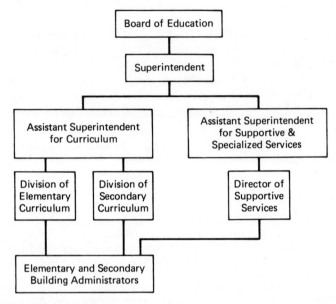

Figure 8-1. Establishing a Dual Authority Structure.

is the fundamental vehicle that Burrello and Gilliam[16] have recommended in their two-part model illustrating an educational planning process. This model and a detailed description of each of its components will be presented later in this chapter.

District Level Program and Supportive Services

The second strategy, "creation of self-contained tasks," is appropriate for organizing district-wide programs and services for the clearly identifiable severely and multihandicapped children. This strategy incorporates programs and services involving a new client group to many school systems. This group of children demands a skilled instructional and technical assistance staff committed to long and frequent criterion trials in order to demonstrate changes in performance. By reducing the variability of professional performance (or a functional distribution of resources), increased time and focus can be spent on a difficult population of children. Burrello, Tracy and Schultz[17] have suggested that this population is truly an empirical test of our professional capacities. For the next ten years both social acceptance and methods of instruction should be continually

---

[16]Leonard Burrello and James Gilliam, "Administering Special Education Programs—An Interrelated Service Model" (Unpublished Paper, 1974).

[17]Leonard Burrello, Michael Tracy and Edward Schultz, "Special Education as Experimental Education: A New Conceptualization," *Exceptional Children*, 40 (1973), pp. 29–34.

developed, validated, and diffused to enhance the movement of these children into more normalized environments. Positions expressed by Sontag, Burke, and York,[18] Meyen and Altman,[19] and Sontag[20] further elaborate the needs, under the federal mandate P.L. 94–142, for equal and appropriate education for all children.

Like building level services, district level services are also designed to keep children moving toward the least restrictive environment. The special education leadership personnel are responsible for planning, organizing, operating, monitoring, and evaluating the educational programs developed for all children in district level programs. A critical task is determining and applying the district's criteria for the movement of children from district level programs into building level programs. This is especially significant for the most severely handicapped children, who in many states have only recently become the responsibility of the public educational system.

Types of Programs and Services

The supportive programs and services function of special education involves *direct services to administrators and teachers* through consultation and technical assistance for the programming of all special need children. This would include the development of alternative individual educational programs in the regular classroom which are designed, pilot tested, and disseminated through joint training by special educators and regular teaching staff. Kuik,[21] Kuik and Burrello,[22] and Nutter[23] have reported on a two-year intervention with regular classroom teacher teams for the development of positive attitudes and increased administrative skills in adapting the school environment to all children with special needs.

The supportive programs would also include *indirect services to teachers* by designing and demonstrating how regular classroom teachers can program for children with unique learning problems, developmental lapses, or who need special learning programs before maximum participation in the regular classroom is

[18]E. Sontag, P.J. Burke and R. York, "Considerations for Serving the Severely Handicapped in the Public Schools," *Education and Training of the Mentally Retarded* (February 1973), pp. 20–26.

[19]E. Meyen and R. Altman, "Research Implications," *Education and Training of the Mentally Retarded*, 11, No. 1 (February 1976).

[20]E. Sontag, "Federal Leadership in Education" in *Hey, Don't Forget About Me: Education Investment in the Severely and Profoundly and Multiply Handicapped*, ed. M.T. Angel (Reston, Va.: Council of Exceptional Children, 1976), pp. 146–61.

[21]Duane Kuik, *The Effects of In-Service Training on the Development of Integrative Plans for Exceptional Children* (Doctoral Dissertation, University of Michigan 1976).

[22]Duane Kuik and Leonard Burrello, *Training General Education Personnel as Mainstreaming Change Agents* (Final Report to Saginaw, Michigan Public Schools, 1976).

[23]Ronald Nutter, "A Bayasian Decision-making Process in the Planning and Placement of Children With Special Needs" (Unpublished Doctoral Dissertation, University of Michigan, 1977).

possible. These programs are primarily demonstration classrooms where children are programmed up to 50 percent of the school day under the aegis of a resource teacher. The resource teacher program is a training program for individual children or groups of children. It can be modeled in the regular classroom or in the alternative program where the child is placed. Consequently, regular teachers will have to observe and eventually demonstrate skills incorporating the design and program of instruction in the regular classroom. If they are unable to implement the instructional program in the regular classroom, recycling consultation services may be recommended by the building based resource team.

Supportive services also include *direct services to children and their parents* through itinerant personnel. Itinerant therapeutic assistance may be provided at the building level. These services, while directly impacting on children, should be measured in terms of student achievement, adjustment, and adaptability in the least restrictive alternative in which the child spends most of the school day.

Training and direct services may also be extended to parents by either school district or external agency personnel. The planning and organization of these services will be the responsibility of the district office, but the actual operation will be coordinated by the building administrators regardless of their internal or external affiliation.

In summary, four components of supportive services are provided to teachers, children and parents at the building level. They are: (1) consultant teacher services, (2) demonstration resource teacher programs, (3) itinerant services, and (4) training. In each case, the ultimate criterion of success is the support of the regular teaching personnel in the design and implementation of these alternative educational programs and strategies.

The special education leadership is responsible for planning with building administrators the type and number of supportive services needed, coordinating the consultation and technical assistance, and training for individual educational planning and implementation.

Direct consultation to the building administrator on matters of eligibility, due process, supervision of staff, demonstration projects, and the like will depend on building administrator and staff requests as well as pressures or complaints from parents and other advocates. The special education administrator will retain authority over monitoring the movement of children in and out of individual buildings to district programs, and will retain annual review of building supportive services in accordance with state and federal law. The special education office will also be the district's internal hearing office for appeals by parents and other child advocates regarding individual plans and placements made at the building level. The special educational office will serve as the district's liaison in any other levels of appeal arising from a disputed plan or placement. Budget planning for supportive resources at both district and building levels will be the district's central office responsibility, but the actual budget operation will be the responsibility of the building administrator.

A summary of the leadership functions of special educators, divided by the type of support to regular educators' operations—directly operated by special educators by level, is presented in Table 8–1. Each function for each setting and each responsible administrator and personnel affected is identified.

Summary of Model Components

The organizational structure is divided into two distinct components, each employing a different design strategy to either increase or decrease the capacity to process decision-making information.

In the division of supportive services, the objective is to reduce the amount of functions that must be performed for different client groups by skilled professionals. With a "full complement of specialties, the schedule conflicts across client groups disappears, and there is no need to process information to determine priorities."[24]

In Figure 8–2, depicting the organizational structure between instructional and supportive services, Galbraith shows a developmental process utilizing lateral relationship leading to the matrix design. A district attempting to use this structure could begin by organizing to

1. Create a temporary force to solve problems affecting several departments. (See Luke[25] for requirements for establishing and operating a temporary force.);
2. Employ a management team on a permanent basis for constantly reoccurring interdepartmental problems;
3. Create a new role, an integrating role, when leadership is needed to implement lateral processes;
4. Shift from an integrating role to a linking managerial role when faced with substantial differentiation among departments, their functions, resources, etc;
5. Establish dual authority relations at critical points to create the matrix design.

Development of Information Processing Capacity

The third design strategy, the development of vertical information systems, is designed to also increase the information processing capacity of the organization and its units. This strategy has four components, according to Galbraith:

1. Decision frequency, or timing of information flowing to and from the decision mechanism.

---

[24]Galbraith, *Designing Complex Organizations,* p. 16.

[25]R.A. Luke, "Temporary Task Forces: A Humanistic Problem Solving Structure," in *Contemporary Organization Development: Conceptual Orientations and Intervention*, ed. W. Warner Burke (Washington, D.C.: National Institute for Applied Behavioral Science, 1972).

Table 8-1. Summary of Special Education Leadership Functions by Type and Level.

	Function	Settings	Administrator Responsible	Specialized Personnel
Supportive Building Level	Consultative or Instructional	Regular Teachers Class Setting	Building Administrator	Consultant Teachers Resource Teachers Itinerant Consultants & Therapeutic
	Consultative or Instructional	Alternative Educational Setting	Building Administrators Program or Project Director	Itinerant Consultants & Therapeutic
Operation District Level	Administrative Program – Supervision Instructional Administrative Coordination	Applied Experimental Settings Itinerant Consultation and Therapeutic Setting	Program Administrator in Special Education Program Administrator in Special Education	Specialized Teachers Itinerant Consultation and Therapeutic Psychologists Social Workers Therapists Teachers Therapeutic Medical Health Welfare
Coordination Building or District Level	Therapeutic Administrative Coordination	External School Treatment Settings	Assistant Superintendent for Supportive Services	
Supportive District Level	Consultative Training and Development	Regular Teachers, Settings, School & District Settings, Off-site, Visitation, Instructional Materials, and Media.	Assistant Superintendent for Supportive Services	Persons from the school district with acknowledged expertise Consultants University Personnel

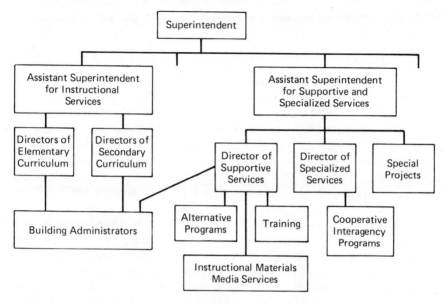

Figure 8-2. Formal Authority Structure of Matrix Organization.

   2. Scope of the data available to the decision mechanism;
   3. Review of formalization of the information flow to and from the decision mechanism;
   4. Capacity of the decision mechanism to process information and select the appropriate alternative.[26]

At the building level, the most significant component in this strategy is the decision-making mechanism. Burrello and Gilliam[27] have described the basic mechanisms as separate, yet interdependent, building and district level educational planning teams. These permanent teams utilize professionals, parents, and students (where appropriate) to plan individual educational programs, to designate the supportive personnel, and to periodically reevaluate the plan's implementation.

Information needs for team decision-making must be identified, and assignments must be made for data collection, storage, and reporting on a continuous basis. Promising computer formats are currently being developed in Maryland[28] and New York.[29] Managing information for individual educational planning is a significant problem for special education administrators.

[26]Galbraith, *Designing Complex Organizations,* p. 31.

[27]Burrello and Gilliam, "Administering Special Education Programs,"

[28]Linda Jacobs, *Management Information System*, Anne Arundel County School District, State of Maryland, Baltimore, Maryland, 1974.

[29]Robert Hanson, "Learning Management System in Southern Westchester," in *BOCES, Port Chester, New York 10573* (Presented paper at Syracuse University, Syracuse, New York, May 20, 1977).

The vehicle that provides the cohesion between roles, services and settings is the Educational Planning Committee (EPC) concept. Each building should develop its own Building Educational Planning Committee (BEPC), and the school district should establish a District Educational Planning Committee (DEPC). These committees should facilitate a student's academic and social development by evaluating the conditions that are interfering with progress, deciding on the services appropriate for the student, and recommending an individual educational plan and placement. Both committees should elucidate the responsibilities for each person involved with the student and should develop procedures to ensure that the student's rights are not violated. It is imperative that the members of the BEPC's and DEPC's function as an interdisciplinary team with the primary objective of planning the most appropriate and effective program for all special-need students.

Membership on the committees should be comprised of representatives of the school system, including a representative of the administration, diagnostic personnel, regular education personnel, special education personnel, the parents and/or their representatives. When appropriate, the student would sit with the committee and be actively involved in the decision-making process concerning his/her educational program. At the building level, the BEPC should be chaired by the building principal. At the district level, a program administrator should chair the DEPC.

The planning process for the handicapped student and others with special needs has serious consequences for the student, parent, and school. The effects of labeling, the right to an equal educational opportunity, and the rights covered under "due-process" considerations must be carefully attended to in the Educational Planning Committee's planning and decision-making. Procedures should be designed to ensure that checkpoints are established for consistent and efficient performance and that participants on the committee have defined responsibilities and role functions. A procedural format is needed to describe the steps to be taken, the required action and persons responsible for that action, and an explanation of the required action. The procedure must describe parent consent for student evaluation, the referral process, the evaluation report, the educational planning and placement conferences, the parent's right to appeal, and the decision to recommend services. Written, individualized performance objectives and provisions for evaluation of a student's progress and placement should also be included. Gilliam[30] has designed a promising evaluation tool to determine the contribution of individual participation in BEPC or DEPC.

The differences between the Building Educational Planning Committee and the District Educational Planning Committee are:

1. Membership on the BEPC is comprised of personnel who function primarily in the building. DEPC participants should include personnel from the experimental

[30]James Gilliam, *Influence and Contributions of Participants in E.P.P.C.*, (Doctoral Dissertation, University of Michigan, 1975).

classrooms, central office administrative staff, instructional specialists, and diagnostic personnel who are involved in each referral from BEPC's and external agencies.

2. Recommendations from the BEPC should focus on services that can be provided or developed within the child's home school with the staff and settings available. The DEPC should consider planning and placement for students whose handicapping conditions precludes them from receiving services in their home school.

3. Recommendations for out-of-district services and placement in external schools (day school in clinics, hospitals or other treatment centers, etc.) would be coordinated through the DEPC. Re-entry of a student from out-of-district settings should also be coordinated by the DEPC.

4. The responsibility for convening and directing the BEPC is with the principal, while DEPC responsibility belongs to the special education administrator and/or a designated program administrator.

5. Movement of children from individual buildings to district programs should involve a joint meeting of BEPC and DEPC's representatives, chaired by the central office administrators responsible for supportive and specialized programs and services on a rotating basis.

SUMMARY

In this chapter, a model was presented for organizing special education with supportive and specialized services and programs for special-need children. A matrix organization design was described because it increases the capacity of the schools at the individual school building level to integrate supportive programs and services into the total building instructional program. A second organizational design strategy, a self-contained task unit, was also shown describing district-wide specialized programs and services for the severely and profoundly handicapped and other experimental projects. They assured a coordinated single focus group of professionals to test and retest potential interventions that can eventually affect all children and personnel. A third design strategy, a vertical information processing system, was described. Such a system increases the school system capacity to process information at two decision-making levels of the system: at the individual building-based and district-based educational planning committee levels. This will involve the continued development of computer technology for the rapid assimilation of data for planning and scheduling of scarce resources.

In the next chapter, a detailed description of the alternative supportive and specialized services are presented, utilizing Building Educational and District Planning Committees.

9

Integrating District-Wide and Building Level Programs and Services

INTRODUCTION

This chapter describes a planning process that links building based needs with district resources and describes those programs and service concepts developed by special educators that provide alternative arrangements for all special-need children. The components of this current statement are drawn from Burrello and Gilliam[1] and from Deno's[2] edited volume on instructional alternatives, particularly those emphasized by Adamson and VanEtten,[3] Meisgeier,[4] Prouty and

---

[1] James Gilliam and Leonard Burrello, eds., *Long Range Planning for Special Education*. Part 1: A Statewide Planning Process, United States Department of Health, Education and Welfare, Office of Education, Bureau of Education for the Handicapped Grant #OEG-GOO-75-00361, December 1975.

[2] E. Deno, ed., *Instructional Alternatives for Exceptional Children* (Minneapolis: Leadership Training Institute, 1973).

[3] G. Adamson and G. VanEtten, "The Fail-Safe Programs: A Special Education Service Continuum," in *Instructional Alternatives for Exceptional Children*, ed. E. Deno (Minneapolis: Leadership Training Institute, 1973).

[4] C. Meisgeier, "The Houston Plan: A Proactive Integrated Systems Plan for Education," in *Instructional Alternatives for Exceptional Children*, ed. E. Deno (Minneapolis: Leadership Training Institute, 1973).

McGarry,[5] McKenzie, Egner, Knight, Perelman, Schneider, and Garvin,[6] and Lilly.[7] For the basic flow and conceptual scheme of the specialized district level service components, we have relied on Hewitt's[8] engineered classroom concept.

Underlying all of our discussion should be a commitment to the *empirical search* and determination of other future structures and processes that increase our knowledge and skill towards easing the learning of others. The latter is best expressed in Burrello, Tracy, and Schultz,[9] *Conceptualization of Special Education as Experimental Education*.

INDIVIDUAL EDUCATIONAL PLANNING PROCESS

In Figure 9-1 the process of individual educational planning is presented. The basic components of the model (besides the decision mechanisms of the BEPC and the DEPC) are represented on the extreme left and right. On the extreme left, the range of the general education programs and the basic process of student enrollments into the regular classroom is made. Next, the regular classroom is depicted. It is assumed that teachers, through both formal and informal means, initiate an individual educational planning process to identify children's learning strengths and weakness. This is done to arrange for alternative approaches to meet the needs the teachers have assessed. On the extreme right, the range of building and district level supportive and/or alternative programs and services are provided. They are introduced only after the BEPC or the DEPC decides to refer the program or service on an individual basis.

The Cooperative Educational Planning and Placement Process is depicted as the integrating process between the general education system on the left and the supportive services sub-system on the right. The integrating process is presented in the center of Figure 9-1. It is initiated after problems develop that demand inputs beyond the teacher's own information capacity. The teacher, principal, parent or child may identify, through observation and feedback, that a problem in achievement or socialization may be evident. The problem-solving

---

[5]R. Prouty and R. McGarry, "The Diagnostic/Prescriptive Teacher," in *Instructional Alternatives for Exceptional Children*, ed. E. Deno (Minneapolis: Leadership Training Institute, 1973).

[6]H. McKenzie, A. Egner, M. Knight, P. Perelman, B. Schneider, and J. Garvin, "Training Consulting Teachers to Assist Elementary Teachers in the Management and Education of Handicapped Children," *Exceptional Children*, 37 (1973), pp. 137–43.

[7]M.S. Lilly, "A Training Based Model for Special Education," *Exceptional Children*, 37 (1971), pp. 745–49.

[8]Frank Hewitt, *The Emotionally Disturbed Child in the Classroom: A Developmental Strategy for Educating Children with Maladaptive Behavior* (Boston: Allyn and Bacon, 1968).

[9]L. Burrello, M. Tracy, and E. Schultz, "Special Education as Experimental Education: A New Conceptualization," *Exceptional Children*, 40 (1973), pp. 29–34.

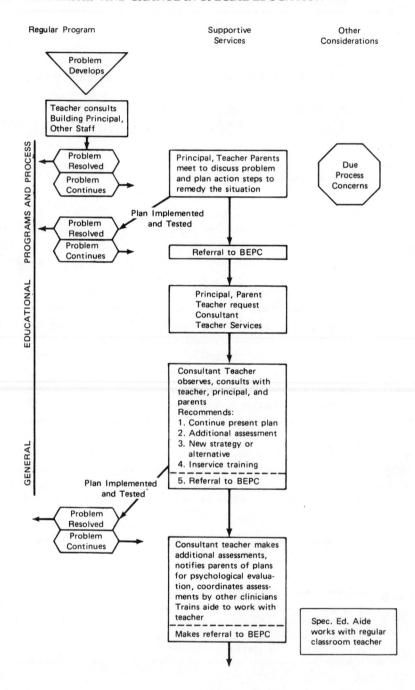

Figure 9-1. The Cooperative Educational Planning and Placement Process.

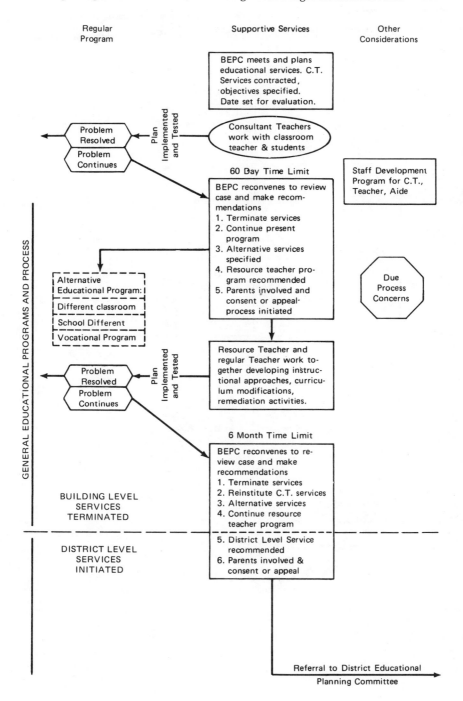

Regular
Program

Supportive Services

Other
Considerations

BEPC meets and plans
educational services. C.T.
Services contracted,
objectives specified.
Date set for evaluation.

Plan
Implemented
and Tested

Problem
Resolved

Problem
Continues

Consultant Teachers
work with classroom
teacher & students

60 Day Time Limit

Staff Development
Program for C.T.,
Teacher, Aide

BEPC reconvenes to review
case and make recom-
mendations
1. Terminate services
2. Continue present
   program
3. Alternative services
   specified
4. Resource teacher pro-
   gram recommended
5. Parents involved and
   consent or appeal
   process initiated

Alternative
Educational Program:

Different classroom

School Different

Vocational Program

Due
Process
Concerns

GENERAL EDUCATIONAL PROGRAMS AND PROCESS

Resource Teacher and
regular Teacher work to-
gether developing instructional approaches, curriculum modifications,
remediation activities.

Plan
Implemented
and Tested

Problem
Resolved

Problem
Continues

6 Month Time Limit

BEPC reconvenes to re-
view case and make
recommendations
1. Terminate services
2. Reinstitute C.T. services
3. Alternative services
4. Continue resource
   teacher program

BUILDING LEVEL
SERVICES
TERMINATED

DISTRICT LEVEL
SERVICES
INITIATED

5. District Level Service
   recommended
6. Parents involved &
   consent or appeal

Referral to District Educational
Planning Committee

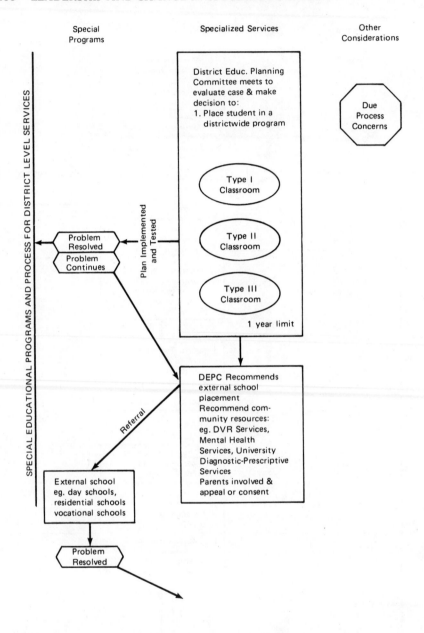

Special
Programs

Specialized Services

Other
Considerations

SPECIAL EDUCATIONAL PROGRAMS AND PROCESS FOR DISTRICT LEVEL SERVICES

District Educ. Planning
Committee meets to
evaluate case & make
decision to:
1. Place student in a
   districtwide program

Due
Process
Concerns

Type I
Classroom

Type II
Classroom

Type III
Classroom

1 year limit

Problem
Resolved

Problem
Continues

Plan Implemented
and Tested

DEPC Recommends
external school
placement
Recommend com-
munity resources:
eg. DVR Services,
Mental Health
Services, University
Diagnostic-Prescriptive
Services
Parents involved &
appeal or consent

Referral

External school
eg. day schools,
residential schools
vocational schools

Problem
Resolved

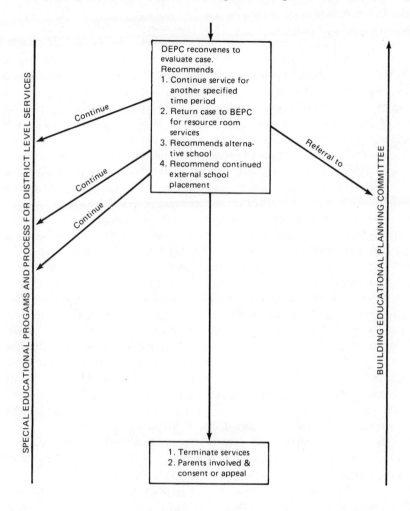

process begins when any participant in the teaching-learning situation is sufficiently concerned to involve others. The teacher with the parent, student, and/or principal begins determining the nature of the problem definition, generates alternative causes and potential solutions, and plans for the implementation and pilot testing of the solution. If the problem is not resolved at this time, then the second phase of the cooperative planning model continues with an escalating cycle of planning, pilot testing, and re-evaluation of a planned solution. The model utilizes the BEPC or DEPC as the decision mechanism for processing information that supports (1) continuation of the planned intervention; (2) modification of the present intervention; and (3) termination of the intervention. The termination decision can be either to return to the regular classroom program, or to refer to another level of supportive services and/or an alternative program.

A description of the program and services is provided next. It is important to note that decision-making for the movement of children to and from each side of these models' continuums requires explicit criteria applied during the BEPC and DEPC planning activity. Specific time frames should be rigorously adhered to for continuous reevaluation.

The authors believe each school system needs to chart the individual planning process. This illustration should serve as a guide for the reader's development of a similar process. The utilization of such a process for internal and external uses are plentiful. Internally, it can be used for job orientation, training, and in formal group planning of individual programs in the least restrictive environment at the building or district levels. It can also serve as a vehicle for identifying the full range of program options and their interrelationship. Externally, it should provide external agency personnel with a frame of reference and depict how those agencies "fit" with the school district's program continuum.

The process illustrated in Figure 9–1 applies to elementary and secondary programs. The secondary level may, however, take on different forms depending upon the particular structure of the district. For instance, secondary school structures might plan a forum based upon a block or departmental team rather than a building wide team concept. Team chairpersons might also be different than at the elementary level. Secondary team chairpersons might be drawn from the ranks of department chairpersons, assistant principals, or grade level team leaders. However, a monthly review of team functioning in the individual educational planning process should be initiated and chaired by the building administrator.

DESCRIPTIONS OF
BUILDING AND DISTRICT LEVEL MODEL SERVICES

Consultant Teacher Services

This consultant is a highly trained educator who is skilled in diagnosis, remediation and behavior management, and is able to work with teachers and administrators. This person maintains a key role in coordinating services, scheduling and implementing a cooperatively determined plan. He/she is housed in and operates from an individual building. A primary responsibility of the consultant's role is to assist regular classroom teachers in the individualizing of educational programs for children. In this area, the consultant confers with teachers, students, parents, and administrators and other members of the BEPC in order to prevent problem situations in the teaching-learning process from becoming problem regularities as described by Sarason. The attention of the consultant teacher might be directed at these broad areas:

1. *Consultation*—listening, observing, gathering factual information, counseling and assisting the teacher, student or parent.
2. *Assessment*—assessing the discrepancy between the teacher's expectation and the student's performance. This might necessitate academic testing of a formal or informal nature, data collection of frequencies of behavioral responses, interviews that are problem-identifying in nature, and/or diagnostic-prescriptive teaching.
3. *Crisis management*—as recommended by Morse[10] the consultant would be capable of on-the-spot interviewing and arbitrating skills to resolve critical events that occur in students' lives in school.
4. *Prescription*—recommending instructional programs, behavior management strategies, curriculum materials, and so forth that will facilitate the student's performance.
5. *Inservice training*—instructing other educational personnel in the improvement of such areas as instructional strategies, curriculum modification, behavior management or other topics that are concerns of the staff within the building. The consulting teacher also serves a systems maintenance function in liaison role with the professional staff development center in order to facilitate the transfer of training from the center to his/her own classroom situation.
6. *Referral*—referring to the Building Educational Planning Committee or the District Educational Planning Committee for more direct intervention services. The consultant could become involved with any student in the building who is in need of any of the services listed above. The consultant teacher services would be by the BEPC or to any teacher and student relationship requested.[11]

At a more intensive level of service, the consultant would deliver the first phase of intervention services to teachers who have identified students in need of specialized educational support. These services would be delivered within the regular classroom. Although the student might leave the room for diagnostic testing or prescriptive teaching, it would be infrequent and only for short periods of time. This service would be provided on a contractual basis with the regular and consultant teacher specifying what outcomes are desired, what plans will be followed, and what materials or resources will be utilized. This initial contract would be for a maximum of sixty school days. The consultant teacher would

[10]William C. Morse, "The Helping Teacher–Crises Teacher Concept." *Focus on Exceptional Children*, Vol. 8, No. 4 (Sept. 1976), pp. 1–10.

[11]S. Sarason, *The Culture of the School and the Problem of Change* (Boston: Allyn and Bacon, 1971).

conduct an intensive educational assessment of the student to determine actual level of functioning, potential of setting and conditions, and learning strengths and weaknesses. A motivation system utilizing contingency contracting might be derived and instituted as well as a behavior management plan, if the student is presenting behavioral problems. The consultant would also be responsible for coordinating other assessments if BEPC recommends it after the teacher's initial referral.

At this level of intervention, a teacher's aide or volunteer would be utilized to provide release time for the teachers to confer, to assist in teaching the students, and to help in preparation of materials. Referral to the district's professional development opportunities center would be a necessary step if teachers fail to meet mutually determined criteria. The consultant teacher and regular teacher should decide on the nature of the aide's activity and the training process the aide will need. It should be a joint effort, with the regular educator training the aide in classroom organization, daily activities, class activities, class rules and limits, and so forth. The consultant teacher should train the aide in working with the student's problems. Special attention should be given to relationship building, setting and enforcing limits, reinforcing programs and contingencies, managing of behavioral excesses or deficits, observing behavior, and so on. The special education teacher-aide should be utilized on a case-by-case level and should not be permanently assigned to one teacher. This person should be able to assist several teachers on any given day. During difficult periods in a student's adjustment, however, the aide might be assigned to work with only one teacher until the problem is overcome. The decision, however, should remain with the BEPC.

At the end of the contractual time period an evaluation would be done by the teacher and consultant to determine what objectives were met, what plans could not be implemented, what prevented the successful completion of the contract, and the like. At this time, a new contract might be negotiated or the present contract continued for another specified period, or referral might be made to the BEPC for more intensive services.

The responsibility for the student's instruction is still maintained by the regular classroom teacher. The consultant teacher does not "take over" in the classroom but observes, assists, and infrequently demonstrates an instructional strategy in the regular teacher's classroom. It is important for the child to feel that he/she is a member of a regular class, and that his/her teacher is the same teacher that all the other children have. If special attention is given by someone other than his/her teacher or teacher's aide, it is infrequent and used only for demonstration purposes. There should be no question in the student's mind as to whom he/she is responsible, who will give directions, and who will make decisions with him/her, and evaluate his/her work to the parents.

Other aspects of the consultant's job will reflect the unique needs of the classroom teacher and the school structure. Each teacher, classroom and school presents a different field of forces which must be appraised before the consultant implements consultation activities. Falik and Sichel[12] suggest that the professional posture of the consultant is perhaps less important than the interpersonal skills, knowledge of the systemic characteristics of the setting in which the consultant works, and the ability to utilize information gathered from many services for assisting the teacher in generating an operational plan to solve classroom-based behavioral problems. Examples of important qualities that are necessary for a consultant are:

I.   Interpersonal Characteristics
1. ability to build feelings of trust and understanding
2. patience in dealing with frustration experienced by the teacher and student
3. insight into dynamics of self and others
4. ability to adjust to the environment, to the teacher's needs and student's needs
5. ability to listen, to hear the teacher's problems, attitudes and feelings without pre-evaluating or prejudging them.

II.   Knowledges
1. understanding of the nature of the school, the teachers in that building, and the school system
2. awareness of the scope and sequence of the curriculum at each grade level
3. comprehension of the incidents and events that have affected the teacher prior to your involvement
4. awareness of the teacher's expectations for the student's academic and social growth
5. awareness of motivational strategies for the teacher as well as the student.

III.   Skills
1. ability to give and receive feedback
2. capability of analyzing the problem in terms of environmental conditions, teacher's instructional style and curriculum
3. capacity to observe and report on what the teacher and the student do in their interaction
4. ability to communicate effectively, so that the teacher has a clear understanding of the nature of the contractual relationship
5. aptitude for interacting as a member of the school team, accepting responsibilities given to other personnel and making and honoring commitments.

Resource Teacher Program

The next level of service for handicapped children, or those with special needs, utilizes a resource program approach. The decision to place a student in this service is made by the BEPC after a complete evaluation of the student's performance and reevaluation of his potential alternatives indicate that the stu-

---

[12]L. Falik and J. Sichel, "Classroom Consultation as an Intervention Strategy," *The Reading Teacher* (November 1972).

dent is not adapting to the educational program. Although in rare instances it would be possible for a student to be referred into the resource program directly (without receiving consultant teacher services), most students will be placed in the resource programs only after consultant services have been deemed ineffective or inappropriate. The student's problem might be an excess or deficit of behavioral responses that interfere with the educational alternatives available and the education of others; it might be an unsuitable learning environment, or other conditions that preclude achieving or adapting to a regular or alternative program.

The placement of the student into the resource program is limited to a maximum of six months, or 120 school days, at which time a decision must be made to return the student to full-time regular class placement, to utilize consultant teacher services, to provide more intensive intervention techniques in a self-contained classroom, or to maintain the resource program for another 60 day period. The student's instruction and supervision is still the responsibility of the regular class teacher. This accountability is supported by the fact that at least 50 percent of the student's daily school schedule is made up of regular classroom activities.

The decision to place the student into the resource teacher program is made by the BEPC with parental participation in the decision-making process and consent to the decisions made. It is critical to underscore the need for continuous cooperation with the parents and clear specification of parental responsibilities in fulfilling the contractual objectives set out by the BEPC. The parents could be asked to assist the school in the child's education by serving as a monitor and recorder of the child's behavioral responses outside of school, by implementing the same behavioral management strategies used in school, by providing opportunities for students to practice academic skills taught in school by informal evaluation of the child's achievement, and by reporting to the child's teacher his/her expectations and opinions as to the child's performance.

The focus of the intervention in the resource program is diagnosis and development. The diagnosis would involve identifying the child's learning strengths, locating materials that facilitate the student's developmental learning, and evaluating the environmental conditions that assist the student in accomplishing learning tasks. Developmental aspects require that the resource teacher work with the regular classroom teacher in evaluating student needs and planning individualized programs. The regular classroom teacher is the coordinator of the student's academic program; the resource teacher plans activities around the regular class work. Resource teachers would provide materials to assist the regular classroom teacher when necessary. The regular class teacher and student should understand that the resource program is designed to facilitate the student's learning of skills and regular classroom material. It is not intended to be an exclusionary measure for the collection of special-need children. The instructional strategy that best accomplishes successful experiences should be utilized. A task-analysis approach such as that recommended by Brown[13] and Frank[14] offers promise as a most efficient and economic instructional model, but the teacher needs expertise in other instructional models and should be encouraged to be flexible and innovative in educational approaches. Regardless of the approach used, documentation and communication should be carefully recorded so that the teacher can provide a clear description of what was done, and how it worked so that specific objectives can be evaluated and revised periodically. The ultimate proof of the success or failure of the delivered service is in the student's performance on academic tasks specified in the instructional objectives and his/her behavioral responses in the regular classroom.

Specific target behaviors for students placed in resource programs can be determined during the BEPC process and prior to the actual placement. This enables the establishment of a baseline of occurrence. The regular classroom teacher may need help in making a careful behavior observation and collecting data on the frequency of occurrence; either the consultant teacher or resource teacher should assist in this activity. The target behaviors must be described in specific, operationally defined, performance terms, with criteria stated to ensure agreement among all persons observing the student. There are many excellent books, articles, and other resources on behavioral observations and recording, and the resource teacher should have several for use in training regular class teachers and parents to record the frequency of target behaviors.

One of the most important elements in the decision to place the student in the resource program will be the student's behavioral responses. The resource teacher must be skillful in the application of behavioral principles to enable the student to develop a repertoire of adaptive behavioral responses. Reinforcement schedules should be established that can be maintained in the regular classroom. Motivation systems such as those described by Homme and Tostl[15] should be instituted to create the positive attitude teachers deem necessary in their classrooms. In some cases the resource teacher may find it is necessary to train the student in ways to reinforce the regular teacher.[16]

An important decision must be faced by the regular and special educator in terms of the educational plans for the student who is seen by both. The issue faced is: what educational experiences are in the best interests of the student?

[13]L. Brown, "Instructional Programs for Trainable-Level Retarded Students," in *The First Review of Special Education*, eds. L. Mann and D. Sabatino (Philadelphia, Pa.: Buttonwood Farms, Inc., 1973), pp. 103–36.

[14]A. Frank, "Breaking Down Learning Tasks: A Sequence Approach," in *Teaching Exceptional Children*, 6 (1973) 1, pp. 16–19.

[15]L. Homme and others, *How to Use Contingency Contracting in the Classrooms* (Champaign, Illinois: Research Press, 1970).

[16]P. Graubard, ed., *Children Against Schools: Education of the Disruptive* (Chicago: Follett Publishers, 1969).

Particularly with junior high school and high school age youngsters, a decision must be reached as to the academic needs of the student such as reading, writing, and arithmetic skills, versus the social and economic skills necessary for survival in the world outside of school. Prevocational and vocational training should be offered as early in the student's educational program as possible, and the academic program should be modified to arrange for work-related skills such as measurement for industrial activities, filling out job application forms, reading charts, graphs, and other technical subject areas, banking activities, and the like. These are only a sample of skills that need attention in the student's school program.

After the sixty day period is concluded, the BEPC should reconsider return to the regular classroom with or without the consultant and/or aide supports or it should reconsider referral to district level DEPC and/or other alternative programs and services.

Applied Experimental Classrooms

Any model for the delivery of educational services to children and teachers must account for the severely handicapped and multi-handicapped as well as for the mildly handicapped or children with other special needs. It is recognized that there are some youngsters whose handicapping condition initially precludes them from receiving their education in the regular classrooms. Autistic children, the severely and profoundly retarded, and the sensory impaired children with multiple handicaps present challenges to educational programming. Leaders in special education and related disciplines are slowly accumulating evidence as to how to program for these students. Quite clearly the predominating instructional strategy being employed with severely handicapped children is an applied behavioral strategy.

Our model recognizes this notion and considers that what educators are doing is experimenting in educational programming and searching for management strategies that facilitate adaptive behavioral responses. With this as our conceptual framework, the authors propose that at the district or intermediate unit level, experimental services should be established that serve the low incidence population of handicapped students and others who have exhausted the services offered at the building level. The intent here is to develop new techniques that can move students to a higher level of functioning, at the same time achieving as close a relationship to the mainstream as possible. These classrooms reflect some of the assumptions proposed by Hewett[17] in his discussion of a hierarchy of educational tasks and the engineered classroom. A second assumption is that there

---

[17]F. Hewett, *The Emotionally Disturbed Child in the Classroom: A Developmental Strategy for Educating Children with Maladaptive Behavior* (Boston: Allyn and Bacon, 1968).

are different levels of behavioral adjustment and learning skills and a student's ability to achieve success in school is dependent upon these skills and tasks. The process that encourages development of these skills shapes the student's responses to meet the objectives presented to him/her by the teacher. As indicated in Figure 9–1, placement in these programs can continue up to one year with re-evaluation annually. Children can move when they have met the criterion specified at the District Education Planning Committee (DEPC) meeting. All youngsters can enter and exit from these settings only after the DEPC meeting has been held.

The experimental classrooms would be of three types. The Type I classrooms would serve students with learning and/or behavioral problems that are beyond the capabilities of the resource program and consultant teacher programs. This type of classroom would be highly structured. The teacher's attention and planning would focus on shaping the student's behavior so that he could be returned to the regular education classroom through the assistance and support of the resource teacher program. Academic instruction would parallel as nearly as possible what is offered by the program. Attention would also be given to socialization processes and developmental learning needs unique to each student. Scheduling techniques would be instituted in the manner recommended earlier by Gallagher[18] which allows many opportunities for appropriate behaviors and personal success. The major objectives of this classroom, however, would be to identify reinforcers that control responses and arrange contingencies so that the teacher is able to manage the student's behavior. Once these objectives are met the student should be able to function partially in the regular classroom.

The Type II classrooms are designed for the more severely disorganized students whose behavioral excesses or deficits are so serious that they are unable to attend to task, are uninvolved, or cannot control their responses sufficiently to benefit from the instructional program offered in the Type I classroom. It is felt, however, that they have potential for the acquisition of adaptive behaviors and can be returned to the regular school based Type I program. The goal is for students in Type II classrooms to be moved into Type I classrooms by shaping their behaviors towards participation in the instructional program offered in the Type I program. In many cases, automatic decisions to make regular annual placements should be resisted. Periodic rotation within and between programs may provide alternative perspectives for forestalling total resignation to a set of expectations that fail to foster growth. Instruction offered in the Type II classrooms would be highly individualized and structured to facilitate the acquisition of specific skills and compensatory behaviors that promote active involvement in the teaching-learning process.

The Type III programs are designed for the most severely handicapped

[18]J. Gallagher, "The Special Education Contract for Mildly Handicapped Children," *Exceptional Children*, 38, (March 1972), pp. 527–36.

youngsters with disabilities that impair their learning to the extent that they need independently implemented individualized instruction. In these settings attention would be given to shaping early developmental behaviors necessary for higher levels of performance. Attention to stimulus of a person, manipulation of objects, sequence of responses to a direct command, and eventually a language and other forms of communication (manual sign language, for instance) would be developed.

This type of classroom would service the low incidence population of handicapped students who may also be in need of medical and related health intervention management in any type of setting. Students referred to as part of the "zero reject" population would be served here. The intent should not be to provide a custodial program in the public schools; it should be to offer an educational setting where techniques can be developed and applied in helping the student move to a higher level of functioning. The students' educational experiences should focus on their developmental needs and should provide skills for dealing with problems associated with their handicapping conditions. These experiences should not emphasize the differences between the students and others, but they should provide as normal an educational experience as possible. Students in the Type III classroom should be exposed to all the conditions and experiences of everyday school life that are available to non-handicapped students and should be a part of other activities provided in the school and community. Regular school based facilities following the affirmative school within a school concept should be fostered.

District educational planning committee meetings would be held annually to consider the reevaluation of the students in the experimental classroom programs. Decisions would be reached concerning the appropriate objectives for each student's instructional program, behavioral development, and socialization needs. Alternative placements with external school programs, such as public and private hospitals, community sponsored workshops, or a combination of these programs and settings, would offer a more appropriate educational placement for students than one in a singular service with limited provisions.

District EPC meetings would also be called to reprogram students back through the experimental classrooms or directly to resource teachers or the regular classroom if so indicated. This would be monitored and coordinated by the program administrator and staff. Both the BEPC and DEPC meetings would negotiate the parent's role in the management of a student's total program. Parent training programs would be provided as long as the child was in the Type III program and any one of the experimental classroom programs. The district's professional staff development personnel would be available to any teacher receiving these youngsters. Before a child had been programmed back into a resource room or a regular classroom, a short intensive experience, including observation in both settings, would be undertaken by the professional staff development center personnel assigned to work with both parents and teachers.

ALTERNATIVE EDUCATIONAL PROGRAMS

These programs represent a modification of the organization and structure of the regular grade approach. Popular applications, such as the Parkway School in Philadelphia, have generally been alternatives to junior and senior high school structures. These programs, also referred to as community schools, involve the use of community resource, retail business, and commercial–industrial organizations to provide an extended work-study approach.

"Schools within schools" or "mini-schools" are another modification. Here students and staff are encouraged to cooperatively modify curriculum within designated space in existing facilities. The major attraction of this program is the appeal to students who have been disenfranchised by the college prep program orientation in the schools. Staff are attracted by the opportunity to create with students alternative experiences leading to broader life experience or career orientation.

Street academies first became popular in the late 1960s. These programs were established for junior and senior high students who were considered disruptive youth. Programs were established in urban neighborhoods where students generally attended classes in modified store fronts, unused school buildings, and large houses. Schools in New York, Harlem and White Plains have had some success in programming for the difficult-to-reach students for some years.[19]

Each of these programs can program for students with learning and emotional problems. While the latter programs were often established to maintain suspended or excluded youth, they have been successful in providing educational programs for identified handicapped youth. They represent alternative settings that depend on a student's initiative, responsibility, and commitment towards establishing and participating in educational experiences that are more closely aligned with what he/she perceives as significant. The setting should be a flexible structure that is more facilitative than hindering.

Special education can play a role in establishing similar programs. Work study models and experience with disruptive and disturbed youth have caused special educators to cooperate with general education administrators and mental health and social service personnel in designing alternatives to the public school structure. Programs for disturbed youngsters in junior and senior high schools continue to be a major challenge to educators nationally.

PROFESSIONAL DEVELOPMENT OPPORTUNITIES

The concept of staff development is a critical component in this model. The increase in enrollment of handicapped students in public schools, the hesitancy to remove or exclude students from the regular classroom, and the push to

[19]G. Dennison, *The Lives of Children* (New York: Random House, 1969).

mainstream handicapped students should continue to force regular education personnel to assume responsibility for the instruction and management of exceptional children.

Regular classroom teachers have responded by pleading for inservice training assistance in the daily programming for these children. Teachers unions and educational associations have been asked to assist the teacher in the management and instruction of the disruptive students in their classes. Existing teacher contracts have provisions that restrict the number of handicapped students that can be placed in a teacher's classroom. With these thoughts in mind, we propose that special education must assume responsibility for some of the staff development needs of regular education personnel.

Legislation and litigation has fostered the placement of exceptional children in regular classrooms without consideration for regular teacher's knowledges, competencies, and understanding of the problems and procedures inherent in the special student's education. Unplanned integration of exceptional students into regular classrooms has resulted in the missed opportunity to encourage regular educators to develop attitudes and action toward prevention of learning problems and behavioral disorders.

Educational renewal suggests a continuous examination of "how we do" and "what we do" in the teaching-learning process. Process evaluation and feedback with professionals that emphasizes personal and social life adjustment, as well as vocational preparation for children and youth, is needed.

The creation of such personal professional growth will require more administration involvement than the mere acquisition of the resources to launch such a program. Consequently, active participation in professional staff development will also be required. Consultation in and training for group facilitation, team building, coordination of educational planning, designing alternative educational settings and the like should be part of such a center's activities. Berry[20] and Burrello, Guarino, and Poinsett[21] and Kuik and Burrello[22] have been developing prototypic models for assisting districts in developing leadership skills with outside consultation and support. Meisgeier has provided a detailed description of activities for a district-wide staff training program in Texas. Some high need areas are:

1. Individual assessment and diagnostic teaching.
2. Behavior management (individual and group).

[20]K. Berry, *Models for Mainstreaming* (San Rafael, Calif.: Dimensions Publishing Co., 1972).

[21]L. Burrello, R. Guarino and S. Poinsett, "Research and Practice: Its Implications for the Changing Role of Special Education Administrators," *The Second Review of Special Education*, eds., L. Mann and D. Sabatino (Philadelphia, Pa.: Buttonwood Farms, Inc., 1974).

[22]D. Kuik and L. Burrello, *Training General Education Personnel as Mainstreaming Change Agents* (Final Report to Saginaw, Michigan Public Schools, 1976).

3. Task analysis.
4. Material selection and development.
5. Contract learning.
6. School-home management.
7. Individualized instruction.
8. Use of volunteer or instructional aides.[23]

This district service and other intermediate units could be extended to all instructional personnel. The initial focus would be on the cycling of teachers and administrators who need assistance for implementation of educational plans developed cooperatively with building supportive resources, that is, teacher–consultants, resource teachers, psychologists, or others.

Major training vehicles would include demonstration teaching, simulation, and clinical and classroom observation. Follow-up assistance would be coordinated by the teacher consultants within the individual schools. Both in-service credit and university courses could be arranged in conjunction with colleges and universities. Fox, and McKenzie[24] and Deno and Gross[25] have described such cooperative agreements. Reger[26] and Burrello[27] have argued for a clearer relationship between the schools and universities in preservice as well as in-service training of special and regular education personnel. The current focus on competency models with a behavioral objective framework should facilitate the requisition of a common frame of reference for guiding communication and practice within an accountable process. The designation and assignment of responsibilities between public school consultants and trainers and university personnel would depend upon each group's expertise in fulfilling the agreed upon competencies.

In larger school systems (those with an average daily attendance of at least 15 to 20,000) special educators could play a significant role in providing such service. In small districts, intermediate units should offer an educational and skill training service for administrators, parents, and instructional personnel within local school districts. State department leadership will also be necessary to support special projects in intermediate units and configurations of intermediate units providing comprehensive personnel development contracts.

[23]C. Meisgeier, 1973 "The Houston Plan."

[24]W. Fox and H. McKenzie, "An Introduction to A Regular Classroom Approach to Special Education," *Instructional Alternatives for Exceptional Children*, ed. E. Deno (Minneapolis: Leadership Training Institute, 1973).

[25]Stanley Deno, and Jerry Gross "The Seward University Project: A Cooperative Effort to Improve School Services and University Training," *Instructional Alternatives for Exceptional Children*, ed. E. Deno (Minneapolis: Leadership Training Institute, 1973).

[26]R. Reger, "How Can We Influence Teacher Training Programs," *The Journal of Special Education* (1974), pp. 7–15.

[27]L. Burrello, "A Reexamination of Assumptions of University Teacher-Training Programs Within a Social Systems Model," *The Journal of Special Education* (1974), pp. 15–21.

PARENT INVOLVEMENT

Clearly a major effect of the litigation that has occurred is the new role that parents have been playing in the planning and placement process for their children. Each process in almost every state under P.L. 94–142 contains a set of due process safeguards, including an appeal process when the school district and parent cannot agree on the placement decision. Here, we would categorize the parent involvement at three levels.

1. Input is solicited from parents by professionals at the building level, principally through the regular classroom teacher and building principal. This could be considered a building educational planning meeting, involving three parties.
2. Next, an official building educational planning meeting might involve a change in the child's educational status from a full-time regular class pupil to a resource room pupil. At this point the parents would participate by assisting in the development of a home–school program. They would work in conjunction with the school to provide a consistent management program for the child. A role identification for parents would be specified, including some statements of activities and criteria of success. As part of an appeal process, the director of supportive services would also be available to parents if they are having difficulty working through a set of alternatives available at the building level.
3. At the district educational planning and placement committee meeting parents would again have an involvement in the planning and placement process and would identify appeals at each process stage.

Parents are involved in the planning, placement and the appeal process at the initial problem identification stage and during any subsequent change in the student's program. From the initiation of the teacher consultant program to district experimental programs or external school programs, parents would be asked to give their consent to the service and placement. If parents did not agree with the educational planning committees recommendations or had problems in accepting or believing this was most appropriate for their youngster, an appeal process could be initiated through each level of school administration (from the appropriate intermediate office to the state superintendent, if necessary).

Parents should also be involved in the contract notion that is noted in Gallagher's work.[28] A key point is that parents assume responsibility as parents in the educational treatment and management planning for their youngster. They too may need additional training to rearrange interaction patterns with their youngsters; this is critical. Behavior treatment programs developed in conjunction with teacher consultant personnel, school psychologists, social workers, and other supportive staff would be made available to the parents. Techniques that are implemented by the professional personnel should be explained to the parent and the opportunity to receive training in the staff development center should also be

[28]J. Gallagher, "The Special Education Contract," pp. 527–36.

encouraged. The primary focus should bring a level of awareness to the parent's expectations for the youngster, to their expectations for the school program, and to an analysis of these expectations in reference to the child's accomplishments. Then the facilitating and hindering behaviors seen in others in the child's environment, which can affect the child's ability to perform, should be investigated. It is critical that a behavior management program be available to parents when it is deemed appropriate and when they are willing to participate. The fact that this service is available should be emphasized. The service should be made available certainly at the district experimental program level as well as earlier in the educational planning if deemed mutually acceptable and appropriate.

SUMMARY

The major highlights involved in leading and administering special education as a supportive and specialized experimental service are summarized below and in Figure 9–2:

1. Building level teams can develop services at that level for all children with special needs as opposed to district teams developing experimental programs for lower incidence youngsters.
2. A specified time contract can be made for placements into an educational alternative process that ties supportive services to the regular education program.
3. An educational planning and placement process which might affect and prevent the labeling of children as deviant can be offered.
4. Both general and special education personnel can share in the joint problem-solving measures that relate to the handicapped youngsters and others with special needs.
5. A supportive service staff can cooperatively work together to develop a continuum service. Services within a variety of environments and settings and conditions can provide for the wide range of youngsters, and professionals and parents can hopefully work together for the best interests of children.
6. The public schools can assume, along with universities, a responsibility for professional development after graduation and certification has been achieved, for the facilitation of a climate for process evaluation and experimentation to further develop special instructional technologies and empirical curriculums.
7. Deliberate efforts can be made not only to involve parents in decision-making, but to train them to be more effective partners with professionals in the education of their children who have complex and often confounding problems.
8. Data can be generated within an action research model, with intervention and evaluation into an evolutionary process, through a feedback cycle, leading to a more efficient planning and instructional process.

We have resisted the unplanned and fragmented response of leadership personnel to the delivery of all services to handicapped and special-need children. The push for free and appropriate education for *all* children in the least restrictive environment implies the development and acceptance of an innovation within the

Regular Education		Inter-relationship Process	Supportive & Specialized Services	
Settings	Problem		Settings	Services
Regular Classroom	Reading Prob. Speech Prob. Behavioral Prob.	Conference with teachers, student, parents, principal		
	Learning Prob. Behavioral Prob.	Conference between teachers, parent, principal, consultant teachers		Consultation
	Problems continue	BEPC C.T. services contracted for 60 days	Regular Classroom	Consultation, assessment, in service training for parents, teachers and spec. ed. aide
	Problems continue — Alternative educational program (new class alternative sch.)	BEPC reviews case and makes recommendations 1. Terminates services 2. Continue present program 3. Alternative program arranged 4. Placement in resource teacher program for 6 months	Resource Program	Spec. ed. Supervisor consults with building principal and parents
	Problems continue — Alternative school	BEPC reviews case and makes recommendations 1. Terminate services 2. Reinstitute C.T. services 3. Alternative school 4. Continue resource teacher program 5. District level services	Resource Program	Consultant teacher services Resource Room teacher services
		DEPC called to evaluate case and recommendations 1. Continue placement with resource teacher with additional support to regular teacher 2. Continue alternative school program 3. Recommend placement in District level program for 1 year	Resource Program Type I, II, III Classrooms	Regular teacher receives training in staff development center Aide provided C.T. assists regular teacher and resource room teacher
		DEPC reviews and recommends 1. Return student to resource teacher 2. Continue placement for 1 additional year 3. Placement in alternative school 4. Placement in external school	Type I, II, III Classrooms	District office annual review and case conferencing to determine appropriate placement

Figure 9-2. Summary of Relationships between Regular Education and Supportive and Specialized Services.

public schools. In order to increase the capacity of teachers to provide for these children, a reorganization of special education and other supportive services is necessary. We have proposed that the special education leadership role initially become a linking role between special education and other central office services. Eventually all supportive services will be rearranged into one division in the schools that will coordinate all supportive services at the building level. The specific organization design to use in the implementation of the plan is shown as using two strategies with a matrix and self-contained task unit.

10

New Roles
for Leadership
of Special Education

If the analysis the authors have made regarding the field of forces impinging on special education is accurate, and if our projections regarding the development of new organizational models are realized, the special education leadership roles will have to change to conform to these requirements and expectations.

The overarching need for leadership in the field involves the competency for dealing with change. This includes reacting effectively to the products of change and proacting effectively with the process. Some specific areas of maximum change, both those which have been thrust upon special educators from outside sources and those which need to be initiated or fostered by leadership persons, can be identified.

The special education administrator must be concerned with a changing definition of the scope and processes of the field and the roles to be exercised. A stretching of the boundaries of inclusiveness has come about largely from forces outside the education establishment. Inclusion of extreme ends of deviance within special education (the severely handicapped) has introduced new roles and new facility needs, as well as expanded curriculum philosophy and instruction. This new territory requires management, but, more importantly, it requires exploration, creative development, and interpretation to the larger educational system and community. The average educator (as well as the average citizen) holds a concept of education that does not extend to such behavioral objectives as toilet training, maintenance of eye contact, or extinction of self mutilative behavior. The organization of curriculum and the development of technical skills for achieving instructional objectives for the severely handicapped place critical demands on the specialist administrator, but more crucial is the task of attaining the acceptance of such concepts in the political–social context in which all education services are perceived. In the competitive market for scarce resources, questions of efficacy must be confronted that will require responses drawing on both values and cost-benefit data. Performance criteria must take on a different framework of assumptions than has been the case in typical educational endeavors, both for the recipients and the providers of services. Past demands on special education administrators have not required such a diverse array of management skills, and past practices have rarely demonstrated them. This added portion of the special educator's responsibility not only requires more intensive involvement, but also incurs more per-capita expenditure than any previous population. It constitutes a major shift of emphasis within the administrator's role as well.

There is a subtle but significant transfer of certain responsibilities for students occupying the nearly normal range of the continuum. As the ideal of providing service in the least restrictive alternative environment increasingly "catches hold," the portion of the mainstreaming concept that applies to the mildly deviant (in which resource and consultative services gain ascendance where self-contained special classes had formerly held sway) should be increasingly made the responsibility of the generalist administrator. Certain aspects of services to children, while still the concern of the special educator, are no longer the exclusive, or even *primary* property of the specialist. This constitutes an additional shift in the definition of the field. The field is not merely picking up more children on the severely deviant end, and relinquishing those who are mildly deviant, to general education. That is only part of the issue. The more significant issue is the change in *relationship* between the specialist and the generalist, as it concerns the mildly deviant, who have always constituted the *numerical* bulk, though probably not the most technically demanding portion of the clientele.

Inherent in this change of definition is the change of roles, which requires interpretation, training, and adoption by the educators and the community at large. The establishment of the consulting teacher concept, the resource teacher concept, the educational diagnostician, and any number of other possible combinations and variations on those themes, makes a significant demand on the administrator as a trainer, facilitator, translator and transmitter of change. The challenge of change does not end with new teaching roles, but also includes new administrative roles, for both the special educator and the generalists with whom they interact. Recognition of this requirement is manifested in the provisions of federal law (P.L. 94–142) regarding delivery of inservice personnel development for all types of educators, both specialist and generalist. While this requirement has implications for higher education institutions, it has even greater significance for practitioners who can best identify training needs and who can best determine the viability of possible training approaches (providing the administrator–practitioner can expand his/her self concept to include that function).

A number of distinctly identifiable dimensions to the special education administrator's role can be described. These will be outlined as follows: (1) the advocate role, (2) the facilitator–trainer role, (3) the policy planner role, (4) the monitor-evaluator role, and (5) the program manager role.

TYPES OF ROLES

The Advocate Role

With increasing attention to the guarantee of service rights for children who may have their rights abridged, and with public concern for the implementation of what the court and/or the legislature promises, the special education administrator may increasingly become the agent through which service is guaranteed. It is argued that an employee inside the system cannot function as an advocate for the system's clients. This is true when the relationship between the system and the client is totally adversarial, which is sometimes the case. However, there are many decision points in the process of serving clients where advocacy is the appropriate behavior. It is still viable behavior for the special education administrator, even though he/she receives a paycheck from the system.

The P.L. 94–142 requirement, stating that due process hearings be administered by a person not employed by the organization involved, reflects a recognition of the need to separate the individual interests from the organizational interests. With the guarantee of impartiality at the hearing officer level, there is greater assurance that client advocacy can be exercised from persons within the system as well. Knowing that an appealed decision will be given impartial hearing should encourage the organization administrator to adopt a direct advocacy posture in reacting to client need. The administrator will need to focus more on the guaranteeing of rights and due process in the attainment of such services, rather than focusing exclusively on the technical aspects of service delivery. The challenge of exercising the client advocate role is the inherent duality in representing both the client and the organization. Role conflict must be accepted as a basic, inevitable aspect of the job. Tolerance for ambiguity, whether an inborn or acquired characteristic, becomes a crucial element in the special education leaders' profile, if the client advocate role is to be assumed.

The Facilitator-Trainer Role

In view of the change agentry emphasis in the needs for leadership in the field, and in view of the new roles to be established, the administrator must be more heavily involved in staff development than he/she has been in the past. Exclusive dependence on training institutions for work in this area is out of the question.

Both regular and special education personnel must receive orientation, technical assistance, and training for new roles and functions. While a general level of personnel preparation can be expected to occur at the institutions of higher education, most key personnel will already be employed. The optimal program application at the local level will occur when the program administrator is actively involved in the entire team development. Obviously, a single administrator cannot be a technical expert in all aspects of the special education needs of the students coming under his jurisdiction. Certain staff development activities will require specific technical assistance from other sources. However, the responsibility for such development, and the interpretation of necessary role changes that affect most of the school personnel (regular classroom teachers, school principals, as well as special education personnel) should rest on the shoulders of the special education leader. Formal and informal training activities, staff development workshops, and such functions that have been traditionally associated with academic professorial roles, should belong to the field administrator as well.

The requisite skills for exercising such responsibility may come from a number of different sources. The facilitator function primarily makes use of consultative behaviors. These may utilize the "helping relationship" concept, as elaborated by Argyris,[1] Rogers,[2] Combs[3] and many others. The characteristics of the helping relationship outlined in Gibb's[4] brief classic, which sets forth a paired list of orientations that help or hinder an individual in being of service to another, may provide an attitudinal framework for the consultation process.

The concepts of reciprocal trust, cooperative learning, mutual growth, reciprocal openness, shared problem solving, autonomy, and experimentation as facilitators of growth are more easily idealized than operationalized. Specific skills related to these orientations may well require exact selection and training of those who expect to function in consultative roles.

A sourcebook for the development of consultation skills by Morris and Sashkin[5] presents a step process, including skill building experiences concerned with

1. Surfacing problems: helping people learn to generate information
2. Feedback: helping others learn to share information
3. Group process: assisting people with working effectively in groups
4. Diagnosing problems: aiding people in understanding problems and developing action alternatives

[1]Chris Argyris, "Explorations in Consulting-client Relationships," *Human Organization*, 20 (1961), pp. 121–33.

[2]Carl R. Rogers, "The Characteristics of a Helping Relationship," *Personnel and Guidance Journal*, 37 (1958), pp. 6–16.

[3]Arthur Combs, D.L. Avila, and W.W. Purkey, *Helping Relationships: Basic Concepts for the Helping Professions* (Boston, Mass.: Allyn & Bacon, 1971).

[4]Jack R. Gibb, "Is Help Helpful," *Forum* (February 1964), pp. 22–27.

[5]William C. Morris and Marshall Sashkin, *Organizational Behavior in Action: Skill Building Experiences* (New York: West Publishing Co., 1976).

5. Goal setting: helping people learn how to determine where they want to go
6. Conflict management: helping people learn to deal with conflict
7. Evaluation: helping people learn how to determine the effects of actions

This analysis of the process of facilitating the consulting relationship represents a major portion of the facilitator-trainer role. An additional aspect of the role concerns the execution of inservice training, drawing on the more general training methodologies.

A review of literature[6] compiled by the Inservice Teacher Education Project, under sponsorship of the National Center for Education Statistics and the National Teacher Corps, points out a number of forces driving various interest groups toward collaboration. The movement toward shared control of inservice education has both educational and political aspects. It is recognized that input from broad constituencies would enhance the quality of teacher education, while at the same time there is a goal of decentralizing the governance of teacher education.

New York State is cited as an example where, since 1972, the Regents have mandated that higher education institutions affiliate with school districts, teachers' organizations, and communities in order to apply for certification of their teacher education programs. The force of teacher militancy is cited as having significant impact toward inclusion of teacher organizations as members in consortia concerned with teacher education and certification. The general disenchantment of the public with the educational establishment has led legislators to require collaboration, since "to much of the public, the 'establishment' of higher education personnel concerned with the preparation of teachers has resisted change and will continue to do so unless there are counterbalancing forces created which require it to pay more attention to the needs of communities and of teachers in the field".[7]

The influence of the federal government in this respect has been very evident in the collaboration procedures required by the Teacher Corps and the Urban/Rural Program. In spite of this requirement, there are important limitations in local school districts that constrain the local administrator's role as a collaborator in inservice education programs.[8] While the LEA is clearly in the best position to define needs and has a supply of both clients and potential trainers, it is the board of education that must be responsive to political pressures emphasizing local service delivery. Collaboration with inservice training activities not restricted to local boundaries (particularly when little slack exists in operating

---

[6]Alexander M. Nicholson, Bruce R. Joyce, Donald W. Parker and Floyd T. Waterman, *The Literature on Inservice Teacher Education: An Analytical Review* (ISTE Project, Stanford Center for Research and Development in Teaching, 1976), pp. 33–35.

[7]Nicholson et al., *Inservice Teacher Education*, p. 35.

[8]Roy Edelfelt and Margo Johnson, eds., *Rethinking In-Service Education* (Washington, D.C. National Education Association, 1975).

budgets) is likely to be viewed as a dispensible frill, not sufficiently central to daily operations.

In responding to expressed needs for personnel development, the local administrator will be expected to provide leadership in negotiating and executing such activities. However, precedent and support for organizational involvement in personnel development is at best uncertain. Since the administrator must reside within the local organization, his/her position will be uncomfortably "in the middle."

The Policy-Planner Role

Somewhat related to the aforementioned roles, but differing by being more closely related to traditional expectations of the leadership process, is the role dimension that deals with policy development and specifically calls for planning activity. While planning can and should be a part of every activity—however small, specific, and limited in scope—the impact of planning (and particularly the lack of planning) is felt most when broad policy issues are involved.

Historically, the issues in which special educators have been involved have been sufficiently circumscribed so that the presence or absence of planning has been of little notice. In the current complex of forces this is not the case. The special educators' policies have significant impact on the actions of systems as a whole. The existing forces that drive toward change in special education, such as the influence of new federal laws, have broad implications for total public and private education, as well as for related domains of human service delivery.

The passage of P.L. 93–380 in 1974 firmly established the importance of the planning function in the repertoire of skills of the special education leader. By requiring that each state provide a full educational opportunity for all handicapped children, and develop a comprehensive blueprint and timetable for exactly how this goal should be achieved, the special education leadership at the state level was clearly faced with the development of a new skill.

In a paper prepared for a conference of state leaders sponsored by the National Association of State Directors of Special Education in early 1975, Hartman acknowledged the many problems that a legislative mandate for planning imposed. However, the benefits to be eventually accrued from the process were also evident. "From a programmatic-standpoint, planning can offer an opportunity to rethink existing programs and approaches, to try new ideas and incorporate recent improvements and innovations into special education programs."[9] The desire for quickly rectifying long standing inadequacies in services, brought on by court orders and advocacy pressures, could cause an attempt at, or at least an

---

[9]William T. Hartman, *Notes on Developing a State Plan for Special Education*, Washington: National Association of State Directors of Special Education, 1975.

expectation of, immediate implementation. The reality, however, is that overnight implementation is impossible, and the far more prudent course is the development of steady, incremental progress toward the desired objective. Such incremental change is primarily dependent on the validity of the planning process.

Hartman has emphasized that the type of comprehensive planning that has challenged special educators in the past has largely called for the orchestration of the interests of a number of diverse groups. Calling for major attention to group leadership are: (1) the necessity of consensus building through the satisfaction of each group's agenda, (2) the reconciliation of opposing views between such varying interests as those of teachers, principals, support personnel, superintendents, boards of education, advisory councils, parents (whether as individuals or as groups) and local, state, and federal agencies representing health, welfare, and education (including personnel preparation interests in higher education). Comprehensive planning, according to this view, is an exercise in political give and take, seeing that major concerns of each constituency are considered, that input on solutions is solicited, and that information feedback is faithfully supplied. In special education, planning cannot be accomplished unilaterally, and the acceptability and utility of the final plans is dependent on the success of constituent involvement. Burrello, Kaye, and Peelle[10] have illustrated the nature of the involvement of these significant legitimizer and consumer groups in the planning process. Figure 10–1 indicates what steps management personnel should consider in the pursuit of broad-based participation in the planning effort.

In steps one and two, state and federal legislatures, as well as the state board, intermediate education agency (IEA) and local school board personnel, are involved in establishing the parameters for what would occur in a school for an individual child. These groups have to be involved in an annual needs assessment and they must also approve an annual action plan at the end of the planning process. Note that the next two steps of the planning process, three and four, indicate the need for analyzing past practices and the need for setting priorities (which should involve processes, activities, and events) in order to potentially include everyone who chooses to be involved. The responsibility of the management personnel, at all three levels, state, IEA, and local, is to establish a planning process that maximizes the number and variety of potential members of the state community. As noted in the state planning process, two vehicles are suggested: (1) The state staff, along with IEA personnel, should develop the progress reports, develop needs assessments, determine annual priorities, and develop a process by which these can be shared with others within and without the management system. (2) As established by law, the needs assessments and annual priority generation (which grow out of these assessments) must be in-

[10]Leonard Burrello, Nancy Kaye and Evan Peelle, eds., *S.T.A.N.S.E. Initial Report*, State of Michigan, Department of Education Grant #0655–37 and U.S. Department of Health, Education and Welfare, Office of Education, Bureau of Education for the Handicapped Grant #OEG-007-507294, August 1976.

PLANNING STAGES FOR MANAGEMENT PERSONNEL	Citizens of a state are represented by:	State/Federal Legislators	St. Board of Education	SEA Management	IEA/LEA/Bds. of Education	IEA/LEA Management	Professional Associates and Individual's Prof.	Parent Advisory Committees SEA/IEA/LEA's	Parent Associations and Individual Parents
1. Established parameters, laws, rules fiscal policy	✓	✓			✓				
2. Review past practice	✓	✓	✓	✓	✓	✓	✓	✓	✓
3. Needs assessment	✓	✓	✓	✓	✓	✓	✓	✓	✓
4. Annual priorities, goals	✓	✓	✓	✓	✓	✓	✓	✓	✓
5. Activities: What to be done; How; When; by Whom?				✓		✓			
6. Resources needed: Fiscal/human				✓		✓			
7. Evaluation methods/criteria				✓		✓			
8. Proposed annual plan and accountability					✓		✓	✓	✓
9. Negotiated plan and accountability established	✓	✓[1]			✓[2]				

1. State Negotiated Plan;
2. IEA/LEA Plan negotiated after State Plan has been negotiated.

Figure 10-1. Participants' Role in the Planning Process.

itiated formally by the U.S. State Department, but not necessarily independently of the IEA or LEA level personnel.

Steps five, six, and seven in the state planning process indicate that program management personnel at the three levels will come together and determine which activities and resources are needed for the implementation of the year's plan. They will also identify evaluation methods and criteria. Once this is accomplished by the management personnel, these decisions are returned to and reviewed by parent advisory committees and other consumer groups before the presentation to local and intermediate boards and superintendents. It is then passed upward to the state board and legislature who indicate support and allocate resources for the projected plan. Obviously, resources and support will always be scarce. Therefore, a clear consensus of what should happen within the given resources must be carefully evaluated and reported in each planning level's annual progress reports to allow for (1) continuation of program and services in the future; (2) termination; or (3) modification.

Requirements for state-wide planning by the state government branch concerned with education of the handicapped include a responsibility for coordination of information with all agencies involved in any way with service to the handicapped, such as Departments of Mental Hygiene, Corrections, Institutions, and so on. This fixing of responsibility across boundaries, traditionally separated by agency roles, places an unprecedented demand on the planning function at the state level.

Similarly, the federally imposed requirement on states for planning is transferred downward to intermediate and local agencies in ways that affect not only the direct services for the handicapped, but also the organizational structure of the entire system. This can be seen in the issue of family rights and privacy and the provisions for procedural safeguards. Although these provisions of federal law deal with pupils who are considered handicapped, the effects carry over to a broader population. The thrust for serving the handicapped in the least restrictive alternative environment also has direct bearing on the total school program. Therefore, the special education leader, in planning for the narrow domain of the handicapped, is involved with policy development for the larger system as well. Participation in matters of total school curriculum, general pupil assessment, classification, placement, and instructional systems are the legitimate concern of the special education administrator as a member of the total policy determining staff.

The fundamental and most generic unit of planning established under Public Law 94–142 and in most states' mandatory laws is the individualized educational planning by interdisciplinary teams of professionals and parents. Beginning with individualized education plans, all programs and services needed for handicapped children are organized. This information (gathered during case conferencing) forms the basis of planning at the building level, total district level, intermediate level, and, ultimately, at the state level.

As planning accrues in each level, it should be noted that the information on needs, objectives, and resources is not merely cumulative. The responsibilities, organizational structure, and organizational climate at each level affects the forces and breadth of planning efforts. Figure 10–2 illustrates how each planning level target, and type of program and service might be organized in relation to one another. The components are described as follows:

1. Service Types:
   a. Direct programs or services, that focus on the direct impact on children, the parents of handicapped children, the direct implementors of programs and services to children and/or their parents, and administrators, supervisors and supportive personnel.
   b. Indirect programs or services, that are not intended to impact directly upon the program or service target, but to impact on the providers or trainers of the service to still another client.

2. Impact Targets:
   These include children, parents, instructional personnel, supportive personnel, and supervisory and administrative personnel.

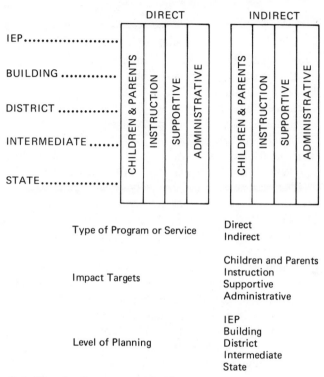

Figure 10-2. Planning Programs and Services.

3. Program or Service Planning Levels. These are as follows:

a. Individual educational planning, that is, plans developed during and after individual educational planning and placement by committees (IEPPC) within local and/or intermediate school districts, the state school for the blind, and the state school for the deaf.

b. Building planning, which involves building-based planning committees, that plan for specific individual children, as well as groups of children, within the local school district building unit.

c. District planning, which refers to district-wide planning for local schools, as opposed to individual educational planning and building unit planning. These are the programs and services that permeate two levels and a variety of impact targets. They differentiate between direct and indirect services within a local school district.

d. Intermediate educational unit level of planning, which relates to the programs and services that cut across local school districts within its constituent groups. It plans for county- and intermediate-wide services and programs that are directly operated or contracted out of the IEA office. Multiple educational units or regional planning would be reflected in individual educational unit planning statements.

e. State planning, which involves the collaborative determination of statewide priorities, resource needs, and projected programs and services. It is designed to implement those programs and services with individual educational units and regional configurations of educational unit groups.

After the annual plan of operation, when resources and responsibilities of management personnel at each level have been designated, the actual planning effort's effects should impact on individual educational planning back through each level of the system. Thus, the state planning process reflects the cumulative effect of the state's facilitation of direct and indirect service delivery to individual children and other significant target groups. It also describes projected programs and services that will be responsive to the changing organizational climate and conditions at each level. The diamond figure illustrates individual educational planning as the beginning and the end of the State Special Education Services Delivery System of planning (See Figure 10–3). The State Plan is the fulcrum in the planning process. The hourglass overlay on the diamond figure illustrates the progressive needs assessments across the responsible planning level. It also illustrates the translation of those needs into an annual action plan, which describes programs and services designed to meet those quality and full service mandates, to the extent that the state appropriates the necessary resources both separately and cooperatively through combinations of funding formulas.

The conceptual skill necessary to deal with the complex interrelationships among various programs, for foreseeing and considering the multiple effects of changes in any one component, is an essential ingredient of the policy planning role. Whenever change is accelerated, the need for planning becomes accentuated as well. If the issues surrounding change are sufficiently broad to affect general policy, in school and other social agencies, then planning becomes even more crucial. The requirements for change that generate from the special educator advocacy role tend to lead to policy development that places an especially high demand on planning.

Planning techniques draw upon major problem-solving activities such as definition of problem, identification of information needs and sources, collection and analysis of information, generation of solution possibilities, identification of alternatives, selection of a trial alternative, outlining of action steps, identification of resources, determination of action responsibilities, and development of evaluation measures. Skillful exercise of these techniques will require a background of training and experience that goes considerably beyond the traditional expectations for administrative preparation.

The Monitor-Evaluator Role

As an outgrowth of the functions associated with the three previously described roles, the special education administrator may frequently be found in the position of checking on the degree to which others are carrying out the program. The program may have been made initially possible through advocacy action, may have become reality through planning and policy development, and may have been implemented through facilitation and training. All of these have involved the special education administrator in key ways. Yet the actual operational

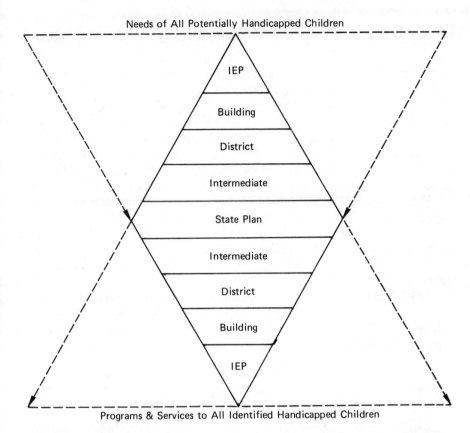

Figure 10-3. Role of State Planning in the Identification and Delivery of Services to Handicapped Children.

management of the program may be entirely in the hands of the general administrator and other personnel in the mainstream of the system. The bulk of the population needing some level of service will be enrolled in such generalist-managed programs. With this enrollment, the role of the specialist administrator becomes one of monitoring, evaluating, and guaranteeing to the clients that the operating programs are truly meeting the needs. In some instances this function occurs by the court's appointment of a *Master*, where the operational situation evolves out of a court order. In these cases the function is performed by persons outside the system. However, a parallel role by persons inside the system, following the model of the *Inspector General* is also possible. Given the evolving status of special education services, this is the role that the administrator often turns out to be playing.

In each of the four roles described, note that the functions approximate those that might also be carried out by persons outside the organization, or if not outside, by persons in a staff rather than in a line role inside the organization. If the special education administrator is playing these roles, it is a staff position. Stating it in another way, special education is changing to the extent that the majority of special services are delivered under the general education administration; the special educator then becomes increasingly a staff officer. The type of "inside-outside" relationship that such a role implies to the management of the service delivery system is an unfamiliar one to typical organizations. For optimal fulfillment of the monitor-evaluator function, specific training in evaluation methodology will be required. Even more crucial is the development of relationship management skills that permit the special education leader to impose the compliance monitoring "inspectorial" authority that new federal and state laws and regulations require. He/she should do this without completely losing the capacity to lead in advocating, facilitating, and planning.

In a number of states a system for executing this function from the state agency level has been developed and is being implemented. Some examples will illustrate the manner in which SEA staff relate to the LEA as compliance monitors.

Florida, in 1975–76, began a Program Audit procedure whereby SEA personnel who had previously functioned almost exclusively as consultants to the local systems, began to take on auditor's responsibilities in certain interactions with the field. There were six areas of audit examination, which are defined as:

1. Program coordination—dealing with the process of local program leadership.
2. Personnel—dealing with compliance with required qualifications of personnel.
3. Program organizational structure—dealing with compliance with approved program structure.
4. Instructional program—dealing with verification of approved instructional programs.
5. Facilities—dealing with compliance with approved facility requirements.
6. Individual student profiles—dealing with compliance with eligibility criteria, procedures for screening, referral, identification, placement and dismissal of students.

With the institution of this audit procedure, it was recognized that personnel conducting the audits would also be those who had a major advising and assisting function in the development of programs. This posed unavoidable threats to auditor independence. Recognizing this, the Florida manual dealing with audits points out:

> Circumstances which *may* impair the auditor's ability to be independent and impartial include:
> *Relationships* of an official, professional, and/or personal nature that might cause the auditor to limit the extent or character of his inquiry, to limit disclosure, or to weaken his findings in any way.

Preconceived ideas about the objectives or quality of a particular program or personal likes or dislikes of individuals, groups, or objectives of a local educational agency.

Previous involvement in a decision-making or management capacity in the operations of the local educational agency or program being audited.

Biases and prejudices, including those induced by political or social convictions, which result from employment in or loyalty to a particular group, institution, or level of government.

Financial interest, direct or indirect, in an organization or firm which is benefiting from the audited program.

Based upon these recognized threats to auditor independence, the Program Auditor *must* (1) describe in a specified prominent place within the audit report his/her relationship with the district and programs being audited; (2) participate in a Pre-Audit Orientation Session which will stress:

 a) recognition of threats to auditor independence
 b) exercise of due professional care in conducting the audit report
 c) utilization of written audit procedures
 d) utilization of the audit report format

These requirements should minimize the recognized threats to auditor independence and thus increase the impartiality of the auditor's conclusions, judgments, and recommendations.[11]

In recognition of the difficulty of dual, sometimes conflicting role expectations, the state department organization has been modified in some instances so that one part of the state office takes over a program development function while another assumes supervisory, compliance monitoring functions. New York State is an example where two such divisions within the Office for Education of Children with Handicapping Conditions have recently been established. The division of supervision in this case is responsible for two bureaus: the Bureau for Regional Programs and the Bureau for Special School Supervision.

The job description of this division indicates responsibility for providing, through subordinate supervisory personnel, technical assistance to all local districts of the state (to state supported schools and to private contract schools) for the evaluation of programs and allocation of funds. This division also ensures that all programs are in compliance with regulations of the commissioner.

A formalization of such procedure has also been undertaken in Massachusetts as a part of the implementation of that state's dramatic legislative reform, Chapter 766. During 1976 the Bureau of Program Audit and Assistance established a three-level system for enforcing compliance. The first level was concerned with individual complaints and involved the development of a systematic way of handling such complaints. The plan called for recording and analyzing individual complaints so that when patterns of noncompliance were

---

[11]Bureau of Education for Exceptional Students, *Exceptional Student Program Audit* (Florida Department of Education, Division of Public Schools, 1976), p. 6.

discerned, a regional office team could conduct an investigation in the local system. This investigation would constitute the second level and would still be limited in focus to the area in which the non-compliance pattern had been evidenced, and would be executed by regular Bureau staff. The resulting report to the school system from this level would mandate a response from the LEA, indicating the steps to be taken to rectify the problem.

Finally, a third level of audit was designed to provide a comprehensive assessment of all the law-required components within any one local system. This level would draw upon expertise outside the regional offices, and would provide opportunities for those conducting the audits to become "effective brokers of good practices and good ideas".[12] It was the intent of the SEA to develop a schedule that would permit periodic audits at the third level of comprehensiveness on a cycle of perhaps every four years. The format for such comprehensive assessment has called for certain tasks to be fulfilled by the LEA being audited while other tasks will be carried out by the auditing SEA. An audit process time line, indicating each task and time allocation is displayed in Figure 10–4.[13]

This audit procedure is designed to focus on nine general areas, which are indicated below, with a statement of the overall goal of the audit in each area.

Staff Development	Determine the qualifications, supervision, and professional development of special education staff.
Public Communication	Define the scope and effectiveness of communication with the public concerning Chapter 766.
Services for Three and Four Year Olds	Establish the extent to which required services for three- and four-year-olds are provided.
Kindergarten Screening	Find out whether the required screening procedures and follow-up are provided for Kindergarten children.
Core Evaluation	Determine the structure and effectiveness of the process for referral and evaluation of students in need of special services.
Program Delivery	Specify the extent to which student's needs are being met by school district's special education programs.
Physical Facilities	Establish whether the facilities used for delivering special services are appropriate.

[12]Division of Special Education, *Proposed Three Year Plan* (Commonwealth of Massachusetts, Department of Education, 1975), p. 23.

[13]Division of Special Education, *Chapter 766 Program Audit* (Commonwealth of Massachusetts, Department of Education, 1976).

Transportation   Find out whether appropriate transportation is provided for students with special needs.

Finance   Determine adequacy and appropriateness of special education funding and budgetary processes.

Perhaps a differentiation between the monitor-evaluator role and the others described above can be drawn on the basis of proximity to the point of service delivery. While the other roles seem to require regular, close involvement with the service delivery action, the monitor–evaluator role may be relatively feasible on a more intermittent, periodic basis. Leadership at the SEA level, as opposed to the LEA level, may be expected to successfully execute the monitor–evaluator role. By the same rationale, the magnitude of an LEA may also determine the degree to which certain leadership personnel play the monitor–evaluator role. In very large organizations, with dual level decentralized administrative structures, the role of the central leadership persons may be heavily devoted to monitor–evaluator functions while the decentralized (area) personnel might be appropriately divorced from that process.

The Program Manager Role

A significant aspect of the changes taking place (and needing to take place) is the development of service programs for the small population of the severely deviant, where operations must largely differ from those of regular education and quite possibly be separate from it. The programs of direct service in these instances require line administration from some source, and that source needs expertise in the technical aspects of the specific conditions of the pupils and the curricula, instructional methods, facilities, and the like, associated with their needs. Since this is the case, the development of new programs for severely handicapped would suggest a quite different role from the other four; one that is in the conventional sense a line officer. This role might possibly overlap simultaneously with the other four, and be executed by the same individual, but in some cases it might require a distinctly separate encumbent. Given what has been said about the other four roles, the program management functions would obviously be constrained to the rather narrow territory of the severely deviant. Where and how to determine the territory of direct program management and that of staff role relationship will be a difficult and arbitrary choice at best, but there are at least some fairly obvious dimensions on which to focus the dividing line. Level of incidence may be as good as any other dividing basis since it tends to correlate strongly with whatever other dimensions are being used, such as the need for sharply different total program goals, curriculum, facilities, instructional mate-

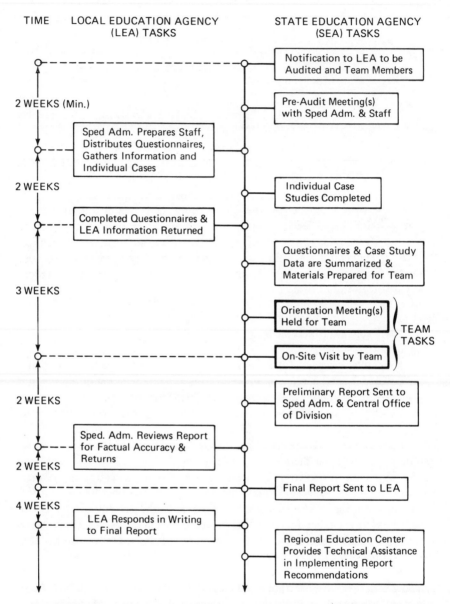

Figure 10-4. Audit Process Time Line. *Adapted from* Program Audit, *Division of Special Education, Department of Education, The Commonwealth of Massachusetts, 1976.*

rials and/or approaches that are totally divorced from anything in mainstream education. The clinical category of disability, while a factor in each of the other dimensions, is probably the least significant indicator of whether a program needs direct management by a specialist administrator, or whether it falls in the much larger domain of needing only staff leadership support by the specialist and management by the generalist. Mental retardation, for example, does not create needs that call for programs requiring direct management by a specialist. Neither do programs for speech impaired pupils involve only staff support. Rather, the determining factors deal with the *type* of service delivery, which tends to be a function of *intensity* of service need. This, in turn, is likely to be a matter of *severity* of handicap, cutting across many clinical categories. Services for the mildly handicapped among the mentally retarded, the emotionally disturbed, the speech impaired, among others, call primarily for staff leadership. On the other hand, services for the profoundly retarded, the severely autistic, or the severely aphasic, may well involve a kind of delivery system that requires a direct program manager.

SUMMARY

The effects of many changes in the field, as well as the pressing need for still more changes, places a high demand on leadership from those persons who hold administrative positions in special education. The demand is most manifest in the new roles and modifications of existing roles that special educators are beginning to play. While the relatively familiar role of program manager remains important, its focus is changing. The policy planner role and the monitor–evaluator role are both expanding in prominence, though based on established principles of administrative behavior. In contrast, the roles of advocate and facilitator–trainer make demands for which there is little precedent in established practice or administrative theory.

However the distinction between roles is drawn, and however roles are fulfilled by individual encumbents, preparation for the roles should call for training models that are more appropriate than either the general or special education training programs have been in the past.

11

Implications for
Leadership Training

The preparation of personnel for leadership roles would seem to call for new training approaches, given the current status of the field, the forces which have been described, and the evolution of new models. If the multiple roles described in the previous chapter have validity, a calculated design for the acquisition of appropriate knowledge, attitudes and skills essential to those roles must be accessible to the systems and to the individuals desiring to lead them.

BEGINNINGS OF TRAINING PROGRAMS

Personnel preparation programs having a clear special education administration identity date from approximately 1965. The funding of some developmental projects within special education departments in higher education institutions from 1965 to 1970 by federal grants, marks the beginning of the field as a training entity. The whole process was initiated by an article by Milazzo and Blessing[1] citing the need for specific training programs and the subsequent awarding of program development grants from the U.S. Office of Education. Such awards were distributed to approximately twenty institutions over a short time, and training was launched. Institutions receiving grants for the development of a categori-

[1]Tony C. Milazzo and Kenneth R. Blessing "The Training of Directors and Supervisors of Special Education Programs," *Exceptional Children*, 31 (1964), pp. 129–41.

cal program of special education administration in the initial years of the effort were:

University of Arizona
University of Cincinnati
Colorado State College
University of Connecticut
Columbia University, Teachers' College
University of Georgia
University of Illinois
Indiana University
University of Iowa
University of Kansas
Michigan State University
University of Michigan
University of Minnesota
University of Oregon
Pennsylvania State University
University of Pittsburgh
Syracuse University
Temple University
University of Texas at Austin

The vigor of the programs varied over the decade since initial funding, with a few programs fading from view entirely and additional programs being established later with federal support at such institutions as Georgia State University, University of Florida, University of Alabama, Ball State University, California State at Los Angeles, Southern Illinois University and University of Kentucky.

It would be easy to say the activity in those few institutions has constituted the entire special education leadership training in the United States. In one sense this has been true. Prior to that time, and nowhere outside that small group of institutional training programs had there been anything like the concerted, goal directed effort at particular administrative personnel preparation. In another sense, we must recognize that the persons filling the bulk of the leadership positions have not come from those earmarked programs, but from elsewhere, and this situation is likely to continue for some time. Data from the Kohl and Marro study,[2] the earlier data from Mackie and Engel,[3] and much informal observation makes it clear that persons occupying leadership positions in special education have, for the most part, come from other than "official" training programs.

Casual observation suggests that in the past such persons in small systems

---

[2]John W. Kohl and Thomas D. Marro, *A Normative Study of the Administrative Position in Special Education*. (Grant No. OEG-O-70-2467 [607], U.S. Office of Education), Pennsylvania State University, 1971.

[3]Romaine P. Mackie, and Anna M. Engel, "Directors and Supervisors of Special Education in Local School Systems," *U.S. Office of Education Bulletin, 1955*, No. 13 (Washington, D.C.: USGPO, 1956).

tend to have come into the job from a background of special education teaching, with little administrative experience or training, and certainly none emphasizing the specific field. In larger organizations, particularly at the higher levels, the role is often filled by someone with a background in general educational administration, with little, if any, experience or training in special education. It is not surprising for this to have been true in the 1950s and 60s. To the degree that it may still be true in 1980 may be a reasonable measure of the viability of the concept or the effectiveness of the efforts of the past decade.

THE MARKET FOR TRAINING PROGRAMS

Note that we are dealing with a relatively thin market. The number of positions to be filled is relatively small, compared with teaching or other general administrative roles. The supply of "appropriately" prepared persons is even smaller. While this makes for an attractive employment situation for graduates of recognized, well established programs, it also means that most positions will be filled, by necessity, by persons who are not so prepared. This reflects the bias that, other things being equal, training program graduates will make better candidates for existing positions than persons from other sources. This bias is not universally shared, and many employing agencies place considerably more importance on other factors, so that the selection of other than specifically prepared persons is often by choice, rather than by necessity.

To reiterate, there are two sides to the problem we have posed: relatively small output of prepared personnel and a relatively low premium placed on such preparation by most employers.

To elaborate on the first point, the investment and commitment for administrative training programs has been modest. At the peak year of BEH investment in such programs, barely one hundred full-time students in post-masters degree programs in administration, distributed across some twenty institutions, were supported by federal funds. The rather feeble commitment of the universities is also reflected by the observation that when categorical funding of administrative and all other training programs gave way to block grant funding to each institution for all special education training activities, the number of students enrolled in administrative programs dropped off sharply. While the greater flexibility of trainee support alternatives makes precise accounting more difficult, it would appear that in recent years the total number of federally supported full-time administration students nationally is not much over fifty. A number of universities that had made a concerted effort in this area between 1965 and 1970 have since reduced or abandoned the programs, even though retaining a fairly consistent effort and output at other levels and within other categories of special education personnel preparation.

Another aspect of the low output problem was demonstrated by Vance and Howe[4] in a study of the graduates of BEH supported administrative training programs. Covering the years from 1965 to 1971, the study revealed that a rather significant proportion of the 208 program graduates, (28.9 percent) had gone into university teaching positions. Some had diverted into other positions, leaving only 120 (57.7 percent) serving in a variety of administrative leadership positions. Though the authors have maintained that these figures were evidence of relative success and realization of the training programs' intent, one could take the other view that the diversion of even eighty-eight out of the short supply of 208 is too much of a loss. Something is amiss within and between the training programs and the field of practice when prospective field administrators defect to academia, without even first serving their time as practitioners. Obviously, we cannot extract a guarantee from students as to future career paths, but there may be specific actions in the area of student selection, training program charateristics, and the field of practice that would increase the utilization of program output.

To return to the problem posed earlier, the relatively little attention paid to academic preparation of prospective special education administrators by employment agencies, we must recognize that this idea of specific training has not had sufficient time to achieve a solid place in the array of professional preparation sequences known by most informed persons. Only a few states have established certification requirements for special education leadership roles, and even fewer have recognized a role specific training requirement.

One national study by Kern and Mayer,[5] reported that twelve of thirty-eight responding states had specific certification requirements for the director of special education position. Forgnone and Collings[6] reporting on data collected in 1973 for all fifty states, found that twenty-three states required no administrative certification or endorsement for special education leadership positions. Another eighteen states required only the general administrative certificate. According to that interpretation, only nine states had any type of special administrative requirement. Of these nine, three had approved university training programs, while the other six had established specific courses and/or field experiences, as well as teaching experience requirements for the awarding of credentials by the state education department.

Considerable misinterpretation of facts probably occurs between the developers of survey instruments and the agencies responding, but it is safe to say

[4]Vernon L. Vance and Clifford E. Howe, "Status of Special Education Administration Students Who Received USOE/BEH Training Grants," *Exceptional Children*, 41 (1974), p. 120.

[5]W.H. Kern and J.F. Mayer, "Certification of Directors of Special Education Programs: The Results of a National Survey," *Contemporary Education*, 42 (1970), pp. 126–28.

[6]Charles Forgnone and Gary D. Collings, "State Certification–Endorsement in Special Education Administration," *Journal of Special Education*, 9 (1975), p. 5.

that credentialing standards reflect a fairly low level of concern about the preparation of persons for the leadership of public school special education programs.

Given the thin market (a low level of both supply and demand), employing agencies have been more prone than in other administrative recruitment efforts to fill positions on the basis of satisfactory experience inside the system, with minimal regard for specific academic training. There have been notable exceptions, but it appears that a vast majority of positions are filled from within, even after a broad-scale search of training programs and an elaborate interview procedure of applicants from a nationwide pool. It cannot be assumed that such searches are only window-dressing for the fulfillment of affirmative action requirements. In most cases the choices probably reflect the clear preferences of the decision makers for system maintenance rather than change—for the "safe" familiar person rather than the unknown risk. Possibly training program graduates represent too much of a threat to administrators employing in all but the most progressive, change-oriented organizations. It is also possible that training program graduates do not display the competence that is found in persons who are "home grown" within the system. Administrative trainers and trainees must constantly consider the match between program characteristics and the "buying" market, even though it may be considered crucial to bring about change in that market. As in the frequently quoted admonition of Al Smith, "If you want to lead a parade, don't get more than two blocks ahead."

THE STRUCTURE OF TRAINING PROGRAMS

As indicated earlier, the sources of personnel for filling special education administrative positions include much more than the federally funded, or otherwise specifically developed training programs. It should not be implied that candidates from these other sources, inside or outside the systems in which they become employed, are always completely without appropriate training. Many persons with upward professional mobility are able to secure academic courses and other experiences, on a random, informal basis, without enrollment in a designated degree program. Since much of the relevant preparation of designated programs is also open to anyone else, and since approximately equivalent courses exist at many institutions, individuals may prepare themselves through other special education degree programs, through other general administration degree programs, or through no degree program at all. The absence of a specific certification requirement in most states further facilitates that option. External degree programs of the Nova University variety may be involved. More courses in special education administration and related content are offered at universities than are established designated degree programs. Even more short-term institutes, summer session workshops and similar activities sponsored by institutions of higher education and by state education agencies provide additional vehicles by which inservice personnel can prepare for new roles.

We must remember that most of the preparation, formal or informal, in this area, is not going on in the "official" places. This fact may suggest a particular function for those institutions featuring designated degree programs, perhaps a model generating function. But those institutions must first focus on their product output in order to have a means of evaluating the program and any models that may be a part of it.

Trainers must look to the needs of the field in order to determine how to improve the student selection process, how to make training programs both relevant and effective, and how to maximally market the products. As implied earlier, the definition of those needs may vary among viewers. The need for leadership in special education, as viewed by the representatives of the community power structure, the chief administrative officers of the school system, and the special interest group concerned with exceptional children, will be different among each group. Although there will be certain areas in common, even those may exist for different reasons, and it is the differences that must be kept in mind in attempting to describe the current needs of the field.

The Content Focus of Training

If we consider the multiple roles described in the previous chapter, some of the needs for training to accommodate to the changes and required flexibility become evident. A primary problem in the development and implementation of training programs directed toward these multiple ends may be an inherent conflict between the program management functions and some other role functions. This is particularly true in the case of the advocacy role, to a lesser degree in the facilitator–trainer role, and to an even lesser degree in the policy–planner role and the monitor–evaluation role. While it is generally understood that everyone plays a variety of roles simultaneously, direct conflict among roles can be expected to seriously reduce the facility with which any role is played. Accordingly, training for a variety of roles would be possible, though adversely affected by whatever role conflict exists.

Evidently the most well established training programs out of which special education administration training has grown, are those that focus on the program management end of the continuum. These would include something of the monitor–evaluator role and probably the policy–planner role as well. Probably the idea of the administrator as a trainer–facilitator is very recent; and the advocacy concept in training is found more often in rhetoric than in fact, and only recently even there.

Advocacy, and such similar concepts generating out of civil/human rights interests have generally been in direct conflict with the organizational maintenance functions of management since they have tended to challenge establishment structures. While the facilitation of change is professed as a major goal of educational leadership, the implementation is characteristically a matter of controlled and regulated change rather than immediate change as proposed by advocates. The image associated with advocacy is clearly one of radical, more than incremental change. The standard image of the administrator is a person ensuring continuity and conservative maintenance of status quo. Furthermore, personnel training functions have been typically associated with more change-agentry than has been feasible in program management functions. In certain situations these differences may be more a matter of image than fact, reflecting the stereotype that is popularly held by observers of the various leadership roles. But the image is held with sufficient consistency to have an effect on the way the trainees, as well as the trainers, approach their leadership preparation task.

In special education, personnel training has been firmly established in the preparation of teachers and other persons who can deliver direct service to students or clients. One assumes that the special services to which such teachers are committed will be carried out in spite of, or with little support from, an uncaring public. This lack of support is blamed on an uncaring school system, specifically represented by an administrator who is expected to attend to majority preferences more than minority needs and rights. An unwritten aspect of the teacher training curriculum has been that of coping with an underdog status and securing for their clients the things that administrators (the personification of establishment rigidity) resist granting.

In a similar vein, the preparation of trainers of teachers, researchers, and other academic types has tended to reflect many of the same assumptions. The adversarial relationship between academia and the field of practice is still another variation of this problem, which contributes to the expectation that the school administrator will be the person against whom the special educator will have to pit his strength and skill in advocating for the exceptional pupil. Whether planned for or not, the curriculum for special education teachers has included an advocacy orientation. To a certain extent, this has approximated an anti-administration orientation.

The Roots of Training Programs

Note that the initial development of training programs for special education administration, in 1965–1970, took place almost exclusively within departments of special education, rather than in departments of educational administration. Given the nature of professional relationships in the field and the existing vehicles for funding special education training from the federal level, this is not surprising. It also reflects the normative primary identification of the role, and predicts the philosophic slant likely to be found in the programs.

To the extent that training programs for administrators of special education have had their roots in these existing special education preparation programs, a specialist–activist orientation, whether subtle or overtly expressed, is probably present. With the increased emphasis on rights, due process, and advocacy in the field in recent years, training programs have in many instances formalized such advocacy training, written down the unwritten curriculum, and become more open in promoting activism in the preparation of personnel. For example, some of the course titles that are recent additions to university catalogs include "Human Service Planning and Change Agentry," "Open Education for the Handicapped," "Radical Special Education," and "Alternatives in Special Education." While these titles may promise more challenge to existing systems than they deliver, they reflect an attitude that is consistent with the thesis regarding special education preparation: values promoted in the special education foundation, which constitutes one major part (perhaps half) of a special education administration training program, are those that confront and challenge the larger segment of established systems by advocating for individuals and for change.

However, special education administration training programs have a dual lineage. They have as a parent, the general educational administration training programs that have been designed to prepare superintendents, principals, school business managers, and, in more recent times, educational planners, personnel directors, contract negotiators, and so on. It has been well understood by developers of special education administration programs that unless the products of such programs can hold their own among other administrative personnel, they will not be able to carry out their mission. They have to show the same credentials, talk the same language, and sometimes bid for the same positions as those vying for superintendencies. Therefore, the curriculum tends to draw on the same courses and other training activities, as well as on the same foundations as the general administration training programs.

In a study of the status of special education administration training programs affiliated with the University Council for Educational Administration (UCEA), Goodman and Sage[7] attempted to assess the degree of interaction between the two departments (special education and educational administration) in which the programs found their dual parentage. The study was undertaken to provide baseline data for an evaluation of the results of a special project, the General–Special Education Administration Consortium, whose mission was to facilitate such interdepartmental communication and cooperation. Among the twenty-eight institutional training programs on which data were obtained, there was a wide variation in the amount of interaction shown by the particular measures utilized.

This study tapped the perceptions of professors and department chairpersons from both special education and educational administration departments, in regard to the importance and observed occurrence of thirty-six possible indicators

[7]Thomas J. Goodman and Daniel D. Sage, *The Status of Relationships Between Departments of Special Education and Educational Administration* (Columbus, Ohio: UCEA, 1973).

of interdepartmental communication and cooperation. The thirty-six indicators were grouped into seven general categories, designated (1) professional interactions, (2) collegial relationships, (3) joint curricula, (4) joint programs, (5) joint internship, (6) joint research, and (7) joint recruitment.

Summary observations drawn from the data indicated that the greatest realization of the consortium mission was taking place in the area of curriculum. While professional interaction was viewed as a very relevant factor, it was acknowledged as being almost nonexistent. A similar gap between perceived importance and actual occurrence was found in joint internships. The factors of collegial relationships, joint program, joint research, and joint recruitment were more optimistically perceived, but on almost every item the special education respondents saw significantly greater importance in the indicators of interaction and more evidence of its occurrence, than did the generalist counterpart. The specialists saw considerably more inclusion of curriculum content relevant to both specialists and generalists than did the educational administration professors. This would seem to indicate that the flow of interaction is largely one-way. That is, the specialists are drawing upon the generalists more than the generalists are drawing upon the specialists. This has been reinforced by the degree to which major–minor combinations between special and general administration students have been reported.

In an attempt to illuminate the observed data on interdepartmental communication and cooperation in these training programs, Goodman[8] collected data on the status of special education administration professors and the relationship between a number of status factors and the level of interaction within the institution. It was noted that most professors tended to identify much more strongly with the field of special education than with educational administration. However, no discernable relationship appeared to exist between any of the status measures of the professors or the departments and the degree of interdepartmental communication and cooperation.

Institutions having joint appointments of professors between the two departments, extremely rare in the early years, are becoming more common. In recent years, the establishment of "hard money" line positions for special education within departments of educational administration has been noted at the University of Texas, Indiana University, and the University of Wisconsin.

Inherent Conflicts

It has been observed that educational administration programs are much more apt to be concerned with the majority, the large group, and organizational maintenance. This does not accuse the general field of educational administration

---

[8]Thomas J. Goodman, *A Study of Some Characteristics of the Professor of Special Education Administration Relating to Communication and Cooperation with Professors of General Educational Administration* (Doctoral Dissertation, Syracuse University, 1978).

of being callous to individual needs, or of being interested only in perpetuation of bureaucratic structures. However, it is accurate to describe the issues foremost in the minds of educational administrators as being different from and sometimes in conflict with those of special educators.

These differences in value orientation may be specifically manifested in instances where training programs are focusing on preparation for the advocacy role. This preparation necessarily involves subversion of change resistant, established systems; the decentralization of power by sharing it with consumers; and the guaranteeing to parents of the opportunity to participate in decisions about their child's program or educational plan.

It is easy to paint everything black or white in this respect, and to present the conflict as "champions of the handicapped against rigid bureaucrats" or "guardians of established order and responsibility against wild-eyed welfare radicals." However, neither of these characterizations is valid. It is reasonable to expect a set of opposing roles. A dynamic equilibrium is not only unavoidable but probably the best we can hope to have between the existing forces.

Whether it is desirable, or even possible for a single person to resolve the internal conflict and be both the manager and the advocate becomes the question. If it is possible and desirable, how can training be organized to facilitate it? Can we expect a mix of training approaches and content from existing special education and educational administration programs to provide what is needed? Perhaps the most appropriate kind of preparation would be dealing with one's own intrapersonal conflict, that which must grow out of the ambiguity of the multiple roles of the present-day special education administrator.

ADAPTATIONS TO TRAINING PROGRAMS

A significant extension of the interactive process in the UCEA managed General–Special Education Administration Consortium (GSEAC), is another project developed by the same organization with funding from the federal Bureau of Education for the Handicapped. This project proposes a mechanism for promoting innovations in staff development for both special and general leadership personnel in local school systems. The major mechanism is the creation of a "Partnership" involving universities having special education administration training programs, and a few selected school systems and state education departments. In the proposal, a statement regarding goals and objectives is as follows:

GOAL I: To implement a national university–school system–state department partnership to facilitate the design, testing, and diffusion of staff development innovations for general and special education administrators.
Objective 1. To create a new "Partnership" involving the GSEAC universities, selected school systems, and a few state departments of education.

Objective 2. To create a special linkage and facilitating agency external to but spanning "partnership" universities, school systems, and state departments.

Objective 3. To establish and activate national communication channels for use in implementing and interpreting partnership activities and in diffusing produced outcomes.

GOAL II: To develop more explicit and systematic ways of assessing the staff development needs of general and special education administrators.

Objective 1. To articulate and logically evaluate different strategies of needs assessment.

Objective 2. To develop and test techniques related to selected strategies for those interested in assessing training needs.

Objective 3. To facilitate needs assessment by those interested in improving staff development.

Objective 4. To develop a resource capability to aid interested partnership members in planning and implementing training activities following needs assessment.

GOAL III: To design, implement, and evaluate a series of integrative staff development experiences for general and special education administrators.

Objective 1. To use identified problems in given school systems as a basis for designing and evaluating staff development experiences.

Objective 2. To promote linkage arrangements and staff exchange between universities and school systems to facilitate staff development.

Objective 3. To design staff development experiences for groups of leaders representing different school systems and universities.

GOAL IV: To design training materials for those interested in improved staff development of general and special education administrators.

Objective 1. To assemble from already developed training materials modules for staff development purposes.

Objective 2. To develop new training materials to meet needs not being met through existing materials.

Objective 3. To disseminate information about newly assembled and developed materials to interested users.[9]

The central office of UCEA is seen as the facilitating and linking agency through which exchange could take place for the improvement of both field and academic members of the partnership. The UCEA also facilitates the increased integration of the separate fields of leadership training and practice.

Differentiation of training on the basis of role functions of administration versus supervision has been attempted in a few instances. The need for such distinction has been highlighted by Johnson, Gross and Weatherman[10] in their suggestion that special education leadership should be redistributed in noncategorical ways that support the special/regular education interface. They draw a distinction between the general, policy making, total program evaluation functions and the special, individual program development and implementation. The more general func-

[9]University Council for Educational Administration, *A Proposal for the Improvement of Staff Development for General and Special Education Administrators Through a New Partnership* (Columbus, Ohio: UCEA, 1975).

[10]Richard A. Johnson, Jerry C. Gross, and Richard F. Weatherman, *Decategorization and Performance Based Systems—Special Education in Court* (Minneapolis, Minn.: University of Minnesota, 1973).

FUNCTION CLUSTERS FOR SPECIAL EDUCATION LEADERSHIP SYSTEMS

GENERALIST
(Manager/Administrator)

Personnel Recruitment
Expeditor and Facilitation
Program Advocate
State Reporting Systems
Public Relations
Budget Development/Monitoring
Various Administrative Duties
Information Clearing House

} Level-Specific Responsibility

SHARED*

Program Planning
Program Evaluation
Staff Development
Agency Liaison

SPECIALIST
(Program Supervisor)

Personnel Evaluation
Personnel Supervision
Student Placement
Case Management
Curriculum Development
Materials Evaluation
Parent Education

} Within Level, Program-Specific Responsibility

*Other functions may also represent "shared" functions, contingent on negotiations between the generalist-manager and the specialist supervisor. Typical examples are "personnel evaluation" and "personnel supervision."

Figure 11-1. Function Clusters for Special Education Leadership Systems. *Adapted from Richard A. Johnson, Jerry C. Gross, and Richard F. Weatherman,* Decategorization and Performance Based Systems—Special Education in Court, *University of Minnesota, 1973, p. 267.*

tions would be those that would call for skills acquired in general administrative training programs, with relatively little need for the technical training associated with special education. On the other hand, the functions listed for the supervisor level would draw heavily on the more technical specialist training. Figure 11–1, illustrates the classification of functions, as Johnson and Gross have seen them.

Attention to the training of supervisors in special education has been the mission of another BEH funded special training project at the University of Texas at Austin. The Special Education Supervisor Training (SEST) Project, from 1972–1975 focused on the identification of competencies needed for the improvement of instructional leadership in special education.

Approaching the task of training with the idea of developing a competency guided program of activities, the SEST project identified three domains of behaviors in which all professional leaders engage. The first domain, problem solving, and the second domain, human relations, were seen as generic to all leadership positions. However, the third, job task domain represented the job specific, interchangeable portion of the model. The competencies identified as specific to supervisory instructional leadership were:

1. developing curriculum
2. developing learning resources
3. staffing for instruction
4. organizing for instruction
5. utilizing supporting services
6. providing inservice education
7. relating to public

From these seven broad areas a listing of more specific critical competencies (statements of behavior patterns to be demonstrated in actual job situations) were developed. They formed the behavioral targets toward which supervisor training could be directed. It was determined that, "The critical competency concept is one of professional performance specification which describes a fairly complex array of on-the-job behaviors which produce, when manifested at a reasonably high quality level, a product or a service which would be highly valued by school officials under most educational conditions. Furthermore, each critical competency is of such a nature that most professional personnel could not demonstrate it without special training."[11]

The SEST Project is one of the few leadership training activities that have limited the scope to the supervisor/specialist role. The more typical program, using an omnibus approach, must contend with the dual levels of functions.

If this duality is interposed within the broad scheme of skill specification provided by the familiar "Human–Conceptual–Technical" model, the competencies for which training should be organized might be classified as illustrated in Figure 11–2.

On the basis of what has been said about the kinds of skills needed, it would follow that training for administration in special education, while calling on a wide variety of resources, should attend to a number of high priority items. Whether this attention can be drawn from the existing curriculum in special education departments or from curriculum in general educational administration, or whether it must be developed entirely from the coupling of those two departmental curricula, probably cannot be generalized. It will vary from place to place. But the optimum development can be expected where trainees have the opportunity to study and practice processes such as:

1. Policy planning (needs assessment, advisory task force utilization, forecasting, long-range goal setting)
2. Change management (diffusion of innovation, utilization of knowledge, organization development)
3. Advocacy promotion (client involvement, assurance of due process, consumer rights)
4. Conflict accommodation (role differentiation, tolerance of ambiguity, personnel contract negotiation)

Citing these four general process areas does not deny the importance of more conventional competencies such as evaluation, financial and programmatic

[11]SEST Project, *Professional Supervisor Competencies* (The University of Texas at Austin, 1974), p. 13.

"GENERALISTS"

HUMAN	CONCEPTUAL	TECHNICAL
Inter-personal	Leadership Administration Theory Organizational Development	Employment of Different Leadership Styles Developing Shared Partici- pation in Leadership
Group Problem-Solving Building Consensus	Management School Organization System Analysis School Facilities	Developing and Allocating Resources
"	Learning Theory Curriculum	Long Range Planning Problem-Solving
Power and Influence	Analyzing Power and Influence in Groups Planned Change Organizational Climates Research and Evaluation	Conflict Utilization Communication
Group Facilitation	Child Variance Sociology of Education Philosophy of Education	Alternative Educational Models

"PROGRAM SPECIALISTS"

HUMAN	CONCEPTUAL	TECHNICAL
Team Building	Educational Philosophy	
Communications	Curriculum	Instruction
Group Facilitation	Child Variance Sociology of Education Planned Change Organizational Development	Identification Educational Alternative Settings Communication
Group Problem-Solving	Organizational of School as Social systems	Problem-Solving Strategies
"	Perception Learning Theory and Programming Instruction	Materials Resources
Power and Influence	Intervention Strategies	Consultation Supervision Evaluation
	Group Dynamics	Training

Figure 11-2. A Classification of Skills for Generalists and Specialists.

accountability, curriculum development, pupil personnel processing, and so forth. These first three are cited because they will be the crucial factors for productive administration at this time. Those skills, competencies, or attitudinal frames of reference will most likely be given insufficient attention in typical present day programs. Given the current state of the field, trainers may not know enough about these processes to provide an adequate focus on them. Trainers need to develop their own skills and program components to include and enrich what can be offered in those areas. Again, the issues are policy, change, advocacy, and conflict: How do we plan, promote, and manage them?

12

Roles and Responsibilities
of Regular Educators
In Service
to Handicapped Children

INTRODUCTION

Throughout the discussion of reorganizing special education, the implications for special education personnel have been noted. At this time, it is important to stress what it means for all other leadership personnel, from board members to teachers' union officials. It must be recognized that any major changes in school policy and operations must have both board and superintendent endorsement and support. Likewise, the participation of teacher organizations in providing input and feedback to new policy or program changes that will fundamentally affect teachers is necessary. There are three major topics that are significant for facilitating the reorganization of special education as supportive and specialized services. They are

1. values of key policy- and decision-makers in determining the course of the school system within the context of the larger state, national, and world community;
2. knowledge, requisite information about the nature of the client, vehicles of instruction, and management of resources;
3. skills to perform responsibilities and assume authority for which any leadership personnel must be held accountable.

Besides providing examples of each of these dimensions, the authors will draw specific implications of each for educational leadership personnel.

FACTORS FACILITATING REGULAR EDUCATOR SUPPORT

The Value Dimensions

In a recent national research association meeting, a congressional aide remarked that most congressional members base their decision-making on the personal values that they as committee members held; they regarded their staff's and trusted colleagues' values next. Another nine factors were then ranked in order from three to eleven. *Values* means the assumptions, attitudes or beliefs that board members and other decision-makers espouse. How do these values and assumptions get translated into decision-making criteria?

A set of values developed in part by a statewide task force is presented below. They illustrate personal assumptions that have affected this group's judgment of which goals and objectives they feel have maximized those values. They rank highest those goals that

1. *Improve Individualizing Services to All Children:* increase the service delivery to children by increasing the predictability and control of those behaviors that would improve those services.
2. *Develop Interdependency:* model and foster a climate of mutual needs, resources, and images of the future that will assure futures all desire.
3. *Encourage Innovation:* foster a climate where change (innovation) is seen as a process of growing rather than change for change's sake or that change implies what presently exists is bad.
4. *Encourage Individual Responsibility for Behavior:* identify individual responsibility, and the assignment of authority to allow decision-making to occur at the lowest level in the school system.
5. *Encourage Evaluation:* foster a climate where evaluation is seen as a process that provides information and feedback on both the product and process of an activity in order to make decisions concerning the alteration, continuation, or termination of the activity.
6. *Encourage Long-range Planning:* assess the impact of the forces that surround the school community and identify a set of desirable alternative futures for others in the community to consider.
7. *Encourage Educational Renewal:* support the continuous development of the human resources of the school system so that they can be responsive to societal change and the demands of participation in a world community.

These examples of school leadership personnel values are not complete. Values related to local control versus state or federal control of education and utilization of local resources could also be listed. Cost factors and community support for programs and services are also noticeably absent in this listing of values. They are not included here because they represent absolutes. They are not relative dimensions. They are unavoidable and will always affect decision-making. Once these values are surfaced and acknowledged, then other factors, such as cost and probability of support, should be considered.

Just surfacing and acknowledging that these values exist is necessary but not sufficient. After they are open for discussion and clarified, it is also necessary to determine the relative importance of these dimensions for the individual board member and administrator and to determine the mean for the group or groups. With weighted values and a consensus to use them for decision-making, they can become the primary basis for setting criteria and determining which programs or services should be supported within the resources available or which programs can be developed in time.

Implications for the Handicapped Child.   When a board member or a superintendent is called upon to define the responsibility of the school district to serve *all* children equally and appropriately, does he/she include handicapped children, too? Certainly under law, it is clear that the school district must provide for handicapped children. The law, however, does not guarantee or demand that either of the school systems' elected and legal representatives or its managers value the handicapped child equally. If past behavior of the school–community is any index of the future, it will take about twenty-five years before a significant majority of consumers and managers begin to equally value all handicapped children within the definition of their responsibility. Our history of dealing with the school segregation decision of the Supreme Court in 1954 and the subsequent latency in implementing that decision in the late 1970s is an illustrative example that basic values are affecting compliance.

Some specific suggestions to gradually move reluctant board members and administrative colleagues are presented below. In order to facilitate a more accepting attitude there is a need to emphasize the similarities among *all* children and staff. Finding ways to minimize differences in scheduling, transportation, lunch room, use of learning centers, libraries, and other special events will facilitate the inclusion of handicapped children and staff.

Special educators demonstrating the technology of instruction in regular classrooms to deal with children with special learning problems will increase the utility of specialized personnel as instructional resources to teachers. Finally, long-range futures planning, which emphasizes taking key policy makers into the distant future to project images of what they would like to see happening in schools, is an effective way of increasing appreciation for change and anticipatory planning. The futures planning scenario creates a different context for viewing today's problems. Alternative futures and definitions of today's problems create energy and a climate for changes in value, attitude, and knowledge.

The Knowledge and Skill Dimensions

In the initial statement of the knowledge dimension, three components were listed: (1) knowledge about the client and the client's needs; (2) knowledge about the technology used to maximize goals and objectives set in conjunction with the clients or their advocates; and (3) knowledge about the management of scarce resources. Each component operated in an interdependent fashion.

Much has been learned about children and their needs. Educators know that learning and schooling are not synonymous. We know that the environment of school and of the community can either facilitate or hinder learning. We know that the pathology or problem is not inherent in the child. Yet we still persist in making the child the primary target of our interventions. We continue to develop our technology of learning, but know that it is slowly being applied.

Special educators know that we cannot program handicapped children into regular classrooms without affecting all the children in the classroom in some way. We also know that our technology and experience with individualizing instruction is not only appropriate for children with learning problems but for other children as well. The focus of our interventions must include the regular classroom teacher.

We know that more than 10 to 12 percent of the children in schools need alternative individualized educational programming to meet their unique learning needs. Any systemic change will demand district support as well as building level personnel support and commitment to implement it.

Implications for Special Education Reorganization. The authors believe that special education, in any form, will not achieve the goal of individualized educational planning and placement in the least restrictive environment until all educators begin to share their concern for children who are failing in the public schools. The impetus for mainstreaming the exceptional children, while based in special education is, as Meisgeier suggests, designed to provide an impetus for educational renewal for the whole educational system. He defines this concept of mainstreaming in terms of "the development of an adaptive system of individualized instruction capable of continuous renewal."[1]

Many regular education leadership personnel have shown that increasing their awareness of handicapped children has increased their knowledge and concern for many other children who are in need of an alternative educational arrangement. Building administrators have become increasingly frustrated with the number and type of supportive services, each with a different child focus. Yet, closer examination reveals that many supportive services personnel are working with the same child. The fragmentation in many school districts has become the focal point for reorganization. Categorical rules, regulations, and funding formulas governing special education have hindered rather than facilitated the movement of handicapped children into regular classes. There is, however,

[1]Charles Meisgeier, "Mainstreaming in a Systems Context," *Shared Responsibility for Handicapped Students: Advocacy and Programming*, ed. Philip Mann (Miami, Fla.: Banyan Books, Inc., 1976), p. 179.

growing support and experimentation with alternative models of service delivery. There is even special education support that allows and encourages the mutual exchange and movement of children with special needs.

RESPONSIBILITIES AND AUTHORITY OF REGULAR EDUCATORS FOR HANDICAPPED CHILDREN

The reorganization of special education with other district supportive services involves specification of role responsibility and authority in the typical school district organization structure. To begin with, the responsibilities of the board and superintendent, then those of the central office or middle management personnel, and finally, those of the front-line manager (the building administrator) should be identified.

It must be stressed here, before further specification of responsibilities and authority is even attempted, that the responsibility of the public schools to service all children regardless of their handicapped condition is clear. To make this happen, special educators must work to increase the sense of responsibility of all regular education administration to handicapped children. It should be translated both affectively and in practice that *all* leadership personnel are responsible for *all* children in the schools. Special educators will be called upon in the future to assist all administrators and instructional staff in providing for all children in the least restrictive environment. The regular educator will need support and resources from special educators and others to meet his/her expanding responsibility. Unless the regular education administrator is held responsible for children in the school district and individual school building, we will *never* see the goal of equal educational opportunity for all children.

The superintendent and the district management team should set a five-year goal of assimulating special education with the board. This direction plan should specify their perception of the state of the district and the state of student achievement and adjustment within five years. Clearly measurable objectives and indicators of their predetermined success criteria should also be included. They should specify their own accountability for the success of the plan along with accountability of other leadership and supportive staff. Major objectives and other parameters should be prepared for feedback from the building administrators, the instructional staff, and the teacher organization in order to determine the estimates of need necessary for accomplishing the goals and objectives inherent in the plan. An annual review process should also be specified and assigned to a management group for the planning and conducting of the innovation. The impetus for this recommendation flows directly out of federal/state legislative mandates for annual program plans. LEAs must prepare annual program plans to receive 94–142 flow-through funds.

The superintendent and board should then direct the district management team to begin action planning after the initial statement of priorities has been reviewed and accepted by the community and staff. The task force leader of the district management group should be appointed by the superintendent. The superintendent should also be prepared to intervene when requested by the district management group to resolve conflicts and differences that the group is unable to resolve by itself. A monthly review of implementation planning reporting should also be initiated after the district task force is appointed.

Responsibilities of the District Management Team

The district management team should prepare its implementation plan based upon the data collected earlier. It should (1) produce a plan that maximizes existing resources and impacts upon each building level program in the district; (2) develop an annual need assessment device for assisting the allocation or development of resources; (3) plan for the distribution and organization of district level resources so that as many full-time personnel as possible can be assigned to the building; (4) begin to solicit external resources for the coordination of supportive programs and services; and (5) prepare a plan of district organization for the planning, organizing, stimulating, monitoring, and evaluating of special education and other district supportive service reorganization. This organization should also include a statement of accountability for ascertaining the role of the district level staff in the direct delivery of supportive services to the building administrator, instructional staff, and student.

The district special education administrator can facilitate building administrators' accountability for all children by direct negotiation of the competencies presented in Appendix B. The authors believe that building administrators will assume additional responsibilities if they believe they control their building operations. Special educators, however, must be readily available to provide consultation and training when needed. Special educators should also retain responsibility for district compliance with state regulations and should periodically monitor budget and program components.

Responsibilities of the Building Manager

Before discussing the role of the management team or educational planning and placement teams at the building administrator level, it is important to discuss the specific responsibilities and indicators for this role.

There has been more discussion of the building administrator role in facilitating the individualizing of instruction for special-need children than any other leadership role in the schools. Melcher[2], Burke[3], Dunn[4], Berry[5], Deno[6], Graeb[7], Mann[8], Burrello[9], and many others have dealt with that role. Berry's mainstreaming project in California has reported that the degree of success they achieved was directly proportionate "to the degree to which the building administrator was risk-taking and achieving personal growth."[10] Almonza[11] has observed that the greatest change in building administrators occurred in their planning skills. When they assumed responsibility for all children assigned to their building, they increased their planning of individualized programs, anticipated problems, and brought about changes in the change process itself.

McIntyre's[12] analysis of building principal responsibilities and competencies provides some initial research on the building administrator's relationship in the administering of programs for exceptional children in their buildings. Burrello and Betz[13] began to adapt McIntyre's analysis to include indicators of those responsibilities and additional competencies. They substituted model indicators of special education issues in administration of programs for the handicapped at the building level.

[2]John W. Melcher, "Some Questions from a School Administrator," *Proceedings: The Missouri Conference on the Categorical/Non-categorical Issue in Special Education*, ed. E.L. Meyen (Columbia, Mo.: The University of Missouri, 1971), pp. 33–39.

[3]Phillip Burke, "Simulation with General Education Administrators and Its Effect on Their Attitudes and General Information About Special Education," (Doctoral Dissertation, Syracuse University) Ann Arbor, Mich.: University Microfilms, 1970, No. 72–6561.

[4]Lloyd Dunn, "Special Education for the Mildly Retarded—Is Much of It Justifiable?" *Exceptional Children*. 35 (1968), pp. 5–22.

[5]Keith Berry, *Models for Mainstreaming* (San Rafael, Calif.: Dimensions Publishing Co., 1972).

[6]Evelyn Deno, ed., *Instructional Alternatives for Exceptional Children* (Minneapolis: Leadership Training Institute, 1973).

[7]Thelma Graeb, "The Behavior Changes of School Building Principals Following Participation in a Special Education Simulation and Consultation Project" (Unpublished Doctoral Dissertation, Syracuse University, 1974).

[8]Phillip H. Mann, ed., *Shared Responsibility for Handicapped Students: Advocacy and Programming* (Miami, Fla.: Banyan Books, Inc., 1976).

[9]Leonard Burrello, ed., *Special Education Simulation and Consultation Project* (Special Training Project OEG-072-4309, U.S. Department of Health, Education and Welfare, Office of Education, 1975).

[10]Keith Berry, *Project Catalyst* (Special Training Project OEG-0-71-0387. U.S. Department of Health Education and Welfare, Office of Education, 1975).

[11]Helen P. Almonza, "Where are We Going? Reflections on Mainstreaming," *Shared Responsibility for Handicapped Students: Advocacy and Programming*, ed. Philip H. Mann (Miami, Fla.: Banyan Books, Inc., 1976).

[12]Kenneth E. McIntyre, "Administering and Improving Instructional Programs," in *Performance Objectives for School Principals*, eds. Jack A. Culbertson, Curtis Henson, and R. Morrison (Berkley, Calif.: McCutchen, 1974).

[13]Leonard Burrello and Monte L. Betz, *The Development and Validation of Building Principal Competencies on Administration of Programs for Handicapped* (Grant proposal funded by Bureau for the Education of the Handicapped Innovation and Development—U.S. Office of Education, 1977).

Betz[14] validated these indicators with expert panels, building principals who had special education programs and services currently operating in their buildings, and their respective directors of special education.

The adapted listing of Burrello and Betz was reduced from fourteen competencies and thirty-one illustrative indicators to eleven competencies and twenty-four illustrative indicators by an expert panel of university professors of educational administration and special education. The new listing is presented in Appendix B.

This new listing was distributed to ten school systems in Indiana with average daily memberships of 9,000 to 25,000 students. Within these school systems, nine directors and forty-five elementary principals participated in the study. All forty-five principals had experience as administrators with special education programs in their buildings.

Participants were asked to:

1. rank the competencies in order of importance
2. assign weighted values of importance to the competencies, and
3. rate the illustrative indicators in order of importance.

Next, Betz conducted follow-up interviews with each of the participants relative to their responses to the competencies and indicators in order to:

1. identify the types of authority currently held and desired by principals to administer special education programs.
2. describe the ideal relationship between a director of special education and a principal.

Based on the results obtained with this sample, the following conclusions were presented. Generalizations beyond the sample under study cannot be made.

1. The principal has a definite role to play in the administration of special education regarding matters involving instructional staff.
2. A shared type of authority between the principal and the director of special education seems most appropriate, especially regarding the selection of special education instructional staff.
3. Principals feel that individually delegated authority should be theirs in matters of student discipline, school schedule, coordination of support services, teacher assignment, and reemployment of staff at the local building level.
4. The role of the principal in due process hearings is ambiguous and unclear to both principals and directors of special education.
5. The relationship between the building principal and the director of special education can be delineated as follows: the director deals with system-wide matters and the principal deals with day-to-day matters involving the operation of the special education programming at the local building level.

[14]Monte L. Betz, *The Development and Validation of Building Principal Competencies on Administration of Programs for Handicapped* (Unpublished Doctoral Dissertation, Indiana University August, 1977).

Before clear demonstration of these responsibilities and negotiated authority is appropriately assigned, organizational development supporting and rewarding middle management and their respective staff must be undertaken. A framework for guiding organizational development in schools is presented later in this chapter.

Responsibilities of the Building Management Team

This team composed of representatives from all aspects of building operations should begin an assessment of children with special needs. A data basis must be established to ascertain the nature of the problems of children. In Chapter 10, an hour-glass figure was presented that traced planning for the needs of handicapped children from individual education planning (I.E.P.) to state planning. The I.E.P. process is a significant organizational intervention that can provide the basis of building level and district wide planning. As the building instructional leader, the building administrator can use this planning process to assess and match learning needs of children to those building (and, if necessary, district level) resources. An annual review of accomplishments measured against individual educational plan evaluation can provide the basis for gauging next year's needs for district resources, and/or redeployment of existing building resources. Procedural reviews for determining methods of service delivery that were most effective should also be obtained through a careful analysis of the I.E.P. process. The building administrator who assumes these responsibilities clearly is asserting leadership through planning and coordinating building resources.

Identification of current resources within the buildings should be initiated. The development of procedures from teacher referral to the delivery program of services and evaluation should be undertaken to determine the potential number of children and teachers served.

Developing and encouraging the utilization of existing resources is often overlooked. In building team development, resource sharing and exchanges will increase team participation and services to children with special needs. Berry[15] explains that the basic value inherent in Project Catalyst was that, with support, the building principal and staff could create their own models of individualized approaches to education in general and to effective mainstreaming in particular. The project was designed to motivate the principal and staff in testing alternative means of utilizing the human resources already available in the building.

A survey of existing district and building level services assigned to the building should be undertaken to examine past practices and problems. These surveys will serve as the basis for alternative models of an integrated supportive service delivery system. They are based upon the unique resources of the build-

[15]Keith Berry, *Project Catalyst,* p. 20.

ing administrator and the instructional and supportive staff assigned to the building. Once the building management has articulated what it can do, it should then specify any additional resources it needs to meet its own annual plan of outcomes. The building goals and objectives should be derived from objectives established by the district management team and the board.

Once all buildings have completed their planning, the district management team should convene a district sample of building level personnel for the generation of a set of criteria to be used in the allocation of other district resources. Future allocations will be based upon changing district needs as well as the success of the buildings in meeting their stated outcomes.

These planning, allocating, and evaluating processes make known the project outcomes or improvement projects the building and the district intend to pursue. They also make known the district and building level needs for resources. Building and district personnel are rewarded for their respective performance on the basis of data collected by one another. District level performance will eventually be evaluated by building level personnel and consumers while building level performance will be evaluated by district personnel and consumers.

CLASSIFYING ORGANIZATIONAL DEVELOPMENT INTERVENTIONS IN SPECIAL EDUCATION REORGANIZATION

Thus far we have examined the implications of reorganizing special education for all educational leadership personnel by role and level of administration in either the central office or the building level. It should be emphasized that regularly planned inter–role and interlevel planning, evaluating, and confronting will be necessary. Organizational development assumes that a willingness to confront problems is a sign of organizational health rather than a sign of sickness. The development is an integral part of continued growth and renewal.

A most ambitious project plan designed to affect the reorganization of special education as supportive services is currently being studied and proposed by Birch[16]. Each organization unit from the superintendent's cabinet to the individual building management team will be interfaced with another unit. As these groups of managers model the confrontation of assumptions, values, and projected images of what they desire to see happening in schools, still other interactions between individuals throughout and external to the system will be set in motion.

Peelle has described the basic conceptual framework of organizational development as applied to the special general education leadership relationship. Organizational development is the application of behavioral sciences to a planned

---

[16]Edward Birch, "The Training and Design of Management Systems to Increase the Accountability of Educators to Serve *All* of the Children" (Grant Proposal Submitted to the Bureau for The Education of the Handicapped: Special Projects, U.S. Office of Education, 1976).

and systematic effort to increase organizational effectiveness. Its emphasis "is on improving the ability of a total system to cope with relationships within the system and with the environment."[17]

Lawrence and Lorsch[18] emphasis on organizational development is concerned with four basic interfaces:

1. *Organization–Environment:* Key problem—assessing and adapting to changes in the environment.
2. *Group–Group* (within organization): Key problem—integrating and coordinating.
3. *Individual–Organization:* Many problems—motivation, role expectations, commitments to goals, self-actualization, and so on.
4. *Person–Person* (Interpersonal relations with the organization): Key problem—people working together in groups or superordinate–subordinate interactions.

Schmuck and Miles[19] consider the four interfaces in terms of who and what will be the focus of attention in an organizational development activity. They also suggest two other dimensions: (1) types of problems and (2) modes of interaction. All three dimensions are then illustrated as a cube to demonstrate how to classify organizational development activities.

Similar organizational development interventions must accompany the effort being described here. The key interaction will occur in terms of Lawrence and Lorsch's levels. District-wide administrators and building administrators will have to confront one another with new responsibilities and decision-making in order to produce integrated supportive programs and services. Key person to person interfaces will also be needed between peers, assistant superintendents and directors, as well as between the supportive services chief and building administrators.

It should also be noted again that the matrix design presented in Chapter 8 will highlight priority differences between the operational personnel and supportive services staff. Therefore, other potential problem areas to be expected center around goals and plans and communication.

All the interventions described by Schmuck and Miles appear appropriate for the accomplishment of such a major organization design and structure change. They are presented below with their respective definitions in the order in which a district might typically implement such an innovation:

1. O.D. task force establishment: setting up ad hoc problem-solving groups or in-

[17]Evan Peele, *Statewide Technical Assistance Network in Special Education: Initial Report*, eds. Leonard Burrello, Nancy Kaye, and Evan Peele (State of Michigan, Department of Education Bureau for Education of Handicapped. Grant #OEG-G00-75-00361, December, 1975), p. 11.

[18]Paul Lawrence and Jay W. Lorsch, *Developing Organizations: Diagnosis and Action* (Reading, Mass.: Addison–Wesley Publishing Company, 1969).

[19]Robert Schmuck and Matthew Miles, *Organizational Development in the Schools* (La Jolla, Calif.: University Associates, Inc., 1971).

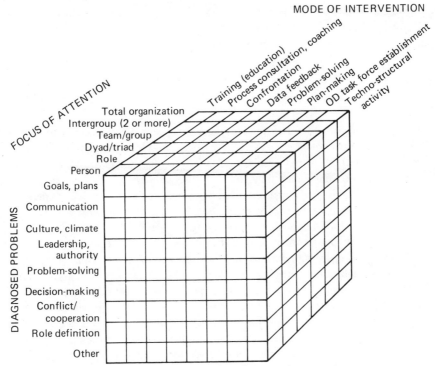

Figure 12-1. The O.D. Cube: A Scheme for Classifying O.D. Intervention[26]. *Reprinted with permission from R. Schmuck and M. Miles, eds.,* Organizational Development in the Schools *(La Jolla, Calif.: University Associates, 1971), p. 8.*

ternal teams of specialists to ensure that the organization solves problems and carries out plans continuously.

2. Plan-making: focusing primarily on planning and goal setting for the replotting of the organization's future.

3. Techno-structural activity: altering the organization's structure, work-flow, and means of accomplishing tasks.

4. Data feedback: systematically collecting information, which is then reported back to appropriate organizational units as a base for diagnosis, problem-solving, and planning.

5. Problem-solving: focusing on problem identification, diagnosis, and solution invention and implementation through meetings.

6. Training or education: directing teaching or experience-based learning. Such technologies as lectures, exercises, simulations, and T-groups are examples.

7. Process consultation: watching and aiding on-going processes and coaching to improve them.

8. Confrontation: bringing together units of the organization (persons, roles, or groups) that have previously been in poor communication; usually accompanied by supporting data.[21]

[20]Schmuck and Miles, *Organizational Development,* p. 8.
[21]Schmuck and Miles, *Organizational Development,* p. 9.

Most efforts of this nature would also employ the services of an organization development team. This team could serve as process consultants at all times and should also provide specific technical assistance in each of the remaining six areas.

SUMMARY

Once the basic parameters of the reorganization plan are established and receive approval, the superintendent may need to review previous descriptions of his/her own role and board responsibilities. This is important for two reasons: (1) any major district reorganization may cause a subsequent change in top management behavior, especially with regard to what decisions he/she may choose to delegate in office; and (2) periodic review of responsibilities and decision-making authority provides both parties with an opportunity to meet current demands, shift the personnel, or engage in other job or district changes. Once the superintendent has engaged in this process, he/she should then proceed to review each district manager's responsibilities, authority, and annual plan of activity. Finally, building administrators should then initiate their review with district administrators to whom they are responsible. In the description of the model proposed earlier, they would be responsible to a director of elementary or secondary curriculum and a director of supportive services. This dual authority structure or matrix organizational design has been recommended for the easy integration of district resources into the building level operations. The building administrator would be accountable to the district's administrator of supportive services, as well as to the district administrator of general school programming.

APPENDIX B

Adapted Instrument Building Principal Competencies[1]

by Monte L. Betz, (Ed.)[2]

PRINCIPALS' BEHAVIORS IN THE ADMINISTRATION OF PROGRAMS FOR
HANDICAPPED CHILDREN

Competency No. 1: The principal assists in the selection of personnel for instructional responsibilites.

Illustrative Indicators: (a) The principal interviewed three candidates for a resource teacher position and subsequently recommended priorities for hiring to the superintendent.

(b) The principal justified the recommendation for reemployment of each teacher (including all full-time special education staff) with written evidence of competence in the accomplishment of performance objectives.

Competency No. 2: The principal relates needs of students to school system goals and legal requirements.

Illustrative Indicators: (a) The principal established and chaired a weekly building planning meeting to discuss teacher referrals for supportive services.

[1] Adapted from Kenneth McIntyre.

[2] Reprinted with permission Monte L. Betz, (Ed.) Director of Special Education, Wauwatosa School District, Wauwatosa, Wisconsin 53213.

(b) The principal prepared a review schedule of all children coming up for annual review with the district psychologist and social worker.

Competency No. 3: The principal assigns or reassigns instructional staff to optimize conditions for learning.

Illustrative Indicators: (a) The principal provided tangible evidence of having matched individual teacher competencies with specific job requirements in the assignment of the special education learning resource teacher.

(b) The principal reassigned three regular class teachers on a rotating schedule to operate the learning resource program for two hours a day for one week on the basis of skills they had acquired in a summer institute. The learning resource teacher assumed the teaching responsibilities of the regular class teachers during the rotating schedule.

Competency No. 4: The principal defines goals and objectives that are unique to the school unit.

Illustrative Indicators: (a) The principal met each semester with supportive services staff assigned to his/her building to offer alternative plans to meet teacher requests for assistance.

(b) The principal analyzed a district level report on demographic data pertaining to the number of school children sent to other schools because programs and services could not be provided at this school unit.

Competency No. 5: The principal leads in-service training sessions for teachers.

Illustrative Indicators: (a) The principal organized and led a group of teachers in a visit to a demonstration school or a learning resource center.

(b) The principal conducted or participated in a laboratory training session for teachers on behavioral management of disruptive students.

Competency No. 6: The principal guides the development of instructional units to implement unique goals and objectives.

Illustrative Indicators: (a) The principal assigned the task of developing an instructional unit on mental health problems to a curriculum committee.

(b) The principal appointed the resource teacher to assume the responsibility for preparing an initial unit on remedial exercises for children with visual discrimination problems.

Competency No. 7: The principal explains school and school district instructional policies and procedures and reports instructional problems and achievements to the school constituency.

Illustrative Indicators: (a) During the first semester, the principal explained attempts by school personnel to individualize instruction for students to seven lay groups in the community.

(b) With the assistance of his special education staff, the principal wrote a column for the local newspaper each week dealing with various aspects of serving students with special needs (i.e., parent volunteer program, cross-age tutoring, mainstreaming, etc.)

(c) The principal is prepared to appear at a due process hearing, in compliance with state law, to report on the appropriateness of the school's recommended special education placement of a specific child.

Competency No. 8: The principal inventories the changing needs for time and space for various instructional purposes.

Illustrative Indicators: (a) The principal initiated the process of devising the school schedule with a faculty discussion of the time and space implications needed to permit more time for the development of individual educational plans for children identified as having special needs.

(b) The principal worked with a team of instructional and maintenance staff to make recommendations for the removal of architectural barriers.

Competency No. 9: The principal collects, organizes, analyzes, and interprets data concerning other-than-teacher influences on learning.

Illustrative Indicators: (a) The principal participates with a subcommittee to study the quality and quantity of this year's supportive services from the district's central office to children with special needs and teachers.

(b) The principal initiated a study of peer preferences among students and used the results for planning and scheduling purposes in order to facilitate mainstreaming of handicapped children.

(c) The principal organized a study of the school's report card and of individual educational plans developed for children with special needs which resulted in the addition of criterion-referenced measures.

Competency No. 10: The principal collects, organizes, analyzes, and interprets data concerning the performance of students.

Illustrative Indicators: (a) The principal made a systematic study of student discipline problems related to emotional problems, their causes, and the teachers involved; the results were used in planning constructive programs with teachers to deal with the causes.

(b) The principal and faculty developed a buddy system of student peers to provide help to potentially disruptive youngsters during lunch, during recess, and during assemblies.

Competency No. 11: The principal organizes and coordinates the non-instructional services to optimize the accomplishment of instructional goals.

Illustrative Indicators: (a) The principal worked with the director of transportation to change the bus schedule so that handicapped students could participate in late-afternoon activities.

(b) The principal rearranged the lunch schedule so that older student volunteers could provide assistance to handicapped students during their lunch period.

13

Leadership, Management,
and Research
in Special Education

INTRODUCTION

Research, development, and evaluation activities in the public schools are typically given scant attention and are largely unfunded. To any other business or industrial organization, such activities are fundamental to future growth and solvency. Unlike industrial and commercial enterprises, education and other public service organizations do not operate within a competitive context.

The lack of the competitive impetus places greater importance on systematic examination of educational practice if school systems are going to reduce the discrepancy between their goals and their current status, however defined. The impetus to reduce this discrepancy must become an integral part of the leadership's agenda in the public schools.

Research, development, and evaluation activities must be defined in the context of daily management. Miles[1] depicts organizational behavior in terms of organizational and people variables (see Figure 13–1). The overriding influence is the leadership's management philosophy. The philosophy affects the way in which managers use the integrative mechanisms to bring the organizational and people variables together for the production of high performance and satisfaction in staff.

[1]Raymond Miles, "An Overview of the Field," *Organizational Behavior-Research and Issues*, ed. G. Strauss, R. Miles, C. Snow and A. Tannenbaum, (Belmont, Calif.: Wadsworth Publishing Company, Inc.), p. 14.

233

Figure 13-1. An Overview of Organizational Behavior. *From* Organizational Behavior: Research and Issues *by George Strauss, Raymond T. Miles, Charles C. Snow, and Arnold S. Tannenbaum.© 1976 by Industrial Research Association, Reprinted by permission of the publisher. Wadsworth Publishing Co., Inc., Belmont, California.*

In schools, the organization's leadership should focus on the goal of maximizing student learning. The task involves defining curricular domains with the professional and lay communities. The technology becomes the instructional processes that derive from the curriculum; mostly, though, it evolves from the capabilities and attitudes of the instructional staff.

In Miles' diagram, three classes of people are found in education. They are managers, instructors, and supportive staff. Each group comes with unique sets of capabilities, attitudes, and needs. The management is subdivided into three levels: boards of education, district level managers, and building level managers. Supportive staff is further subdivided into district and building level, professional and non-professional personnel. Instructional staff are almost exclusively found at one level, the building level. These divisions increase the significance of establishing a management philosophy and coordinating management integrative efforts across levels.

Before research, development, and evaluation activities can be placed and discussed, it is necessary to differentiate research from evaluation. McIntyre[2] notes five major differences:

1. Evaluation does not demand making assumptions that will be generalized to other groups or settings whereas research aims at results that are generalizable to others;
2. Evaluation depends upon internal validity measures, whereas research requires external validity measures before considering other populations or settings;
3. Evaluation requires detailed descriptions of the educational intervention under study for ascertaining how the process has affected the outcomes, while such information is only briefly presented in research studies;
4. Evaluation does not attempt to control relevant parameters as in research, rather it attempts to observe and describe them;
5. Evaluation studies are more likely to use descriptive statistics rather than inferential statistics in research efforts.

Blackman differentiates researchers into two categories: theory builders and system developers. Each type of research is concerned with different questions. The theory builders ask questions concerning why and how the phenomena affects the learning in selected environments. This type of research has also been referred to as conclusion-oriented research. Systems development research is concerned with questions of what will work with large numbers of children. This type of research is referred to as decision-oriented research.

> In decision-oriented research, the intention is not to expand knowledge on how children learn or think but more pragmatically, to help make reasonable decisions about what techniques will work to teach what content to whom. . . Put it another way, the teacher is being helped to become a more intelligent selector of interventions to use with children.[3]

THEORY BUILDING OR SYSTEM DEVELOPMENT

While both types of research are necessary for growth-oriented organizations, leadership personnel have been increasingly more supportive and interested in questions concerning what's best for the majority of children. They continue to ask questions related to the evaluation of interventions rather than to the things that affect children's learning.

Following the need for decision-oriented research and evaluation of program effects on children, leadership and management personnel need to consider system engineering problems as well as behavioral engineering problems. Help-

[2]Robert McIntyre, "Evaluation of Instructional Materials and Programs: Application of a Systems Approach," in *Exceptional Children*, 37 (1970), pp. 213–20.

[3]Leonard S. Blackman, "Research and the Classroom: Mohomet and the Mountain Revisited," *Exceptional Children*, 39 (November, 1972), p. 184.

ing teachers to be better selectors of interventions is a behavioral engineering problem while determining a community consensus on goals and types of services for the schools is a systems engineering problem. The authors believe that leadership and management personnel should be concerned with both behavioral and systems engineering research. The personnel should also maintain and extend their efforts with regard to evaluation.

Top leadership cannot be involved to the same degree in each type of activity. For this reason, the authors have developed a conceptual model for identifying research that is related to issues that have as their primary responsibility management of special education and other supportive services for special-need children.

MODEL FOR RESEARCH ISSUES
IN MANAGING SUPPORTIVE SERVICES

The Bureau of Education for the Handicapped, through its Research Branch, sponsored four research conferences in 1974 and 1975.[4] Those research conferences covered four research tasks: (1) early childhood education of the handicapped; (2) education of the severely handicapped; (3) career education for the handicapped; and (4) personnel selection, training, and utilization. Each research conference was guided by a simple conceptual model which contained three components: settings, personnel, and programs. Each of the research tasks was presented along an actual versus an ideal continuum. This represented a discrepancy in terms of the three components leading to some desired effect on pupil outcomes.

This model illustrates how the specific types of research and evaluation affect the integrative mechanisms that managers must employ in maximizing student performance and satisfying personnel in educational settings.

RESEARCH TASKS

Three research tasks drawn from Reynolds and Balow[5], Lilly[6], Burlingame[7], and Kaye[8] can be identified. Each research task should be ultimately designed to af-

---

[4]Proceedings of the Conference on Research Needs Related to the Development of Personnel to Serve the Handicapped. Bureau of Education for the Handicapped (U.S. Office of Education, March, 1975), pp. 55–56.

[5]Maynard C. Reynolds and Bruce Balow, "Categories and Variables in Special Education," *Exceptional Children*, 38 (January, 1972), pp. 357–66.

[6]M. Stephen Lilly, "A Training Based Model for Special Education," *Exceptional Children*, 37 (Summer 1971), pp. 745–49.

[7]Martin Burlingame, "The Federal Role in the Preparation of Educational Leaders," *Training Educational Leaders–A Search for Alternatives*, eds. N. Drachler and G. Kaplan (George Washington University, Institute for Educational Leadership, 1976), pp. 40–56.

[8]Nancy L. Kaye, *Assessing Communication Patterns and Attitudes of Special Education Management Personnel in a Technical Assistance Network* (Doctoral Dissertation, University of Michigan, 1976).

fect decision-making in instruction or in the planning of new directions for the individual school system or state agency.

Research Task #1: Differential Instructional Systems

Reynolds and Balow are primarily concerned with educational decision-making that would require "attention to variables that produce interaction effects with educational treatments, that is, variables that help educators to make a difference rather than a prediction."[9] Their approach is based on variables rather than categories of disability. The variables selected for study are based upon those factors that enable parents, teachers, and building administrators serving as a case conference committee to determine which instructional systems will facilitate the child's development. An instructional system is defined by Reynolds and Balow as "integrated sets of procedures, curricula, and materials, that may be used to achieve certain major learning goals with children."[10]

Placed in Figure 13-2 is an example of decision-oriented research on differentiated instructional systems. It has implications for a series of integrative mechanisms for leadership personnel. First, this research task is a developmental activity. Once the specific schemes for language development have been identified and made available to the system in terms of any material or human resources, training staff will follow. This concept demands a different conceptual set in parents, in external agency personnel, and in school system staff. The development and training may also eventually affect job design and relationships between supportive and regular instructional personnel. Finally, this research task can also have implications for formal participation schemes. The vehicle that brings all participants together under most state and federal laws is the requirement for comprehensive planning for individual children referred to the building or to the district teams of professionals and parents. This group planning scheme will be fundamentally changed as this type of research is applied in determining which decision variables best match the educational alternatives to the needs of individual children with special learning problems. The list of potential areas of study are presented as discrepancies in the model. Once the ideal is accepted in each area, specific goals and objectives can then be determined. (The other dimensions in the cube will not be considered at this time.) Finally, selection of individual objectives with settings and personnel involved must be approved before work on the research task can begin.

Once the results of this development and training activity are reviewed, decisions to disseminate or replicate will be made. In these particular examples, some aspects of the research can be applied in planning almost immediately through continued training. Applications in implementation, however, would

[9]Reynolds and Balow, "Categories and Variables," p. 359.
[10]Reynolds and Balow, "Categories and Variables," p. 360.

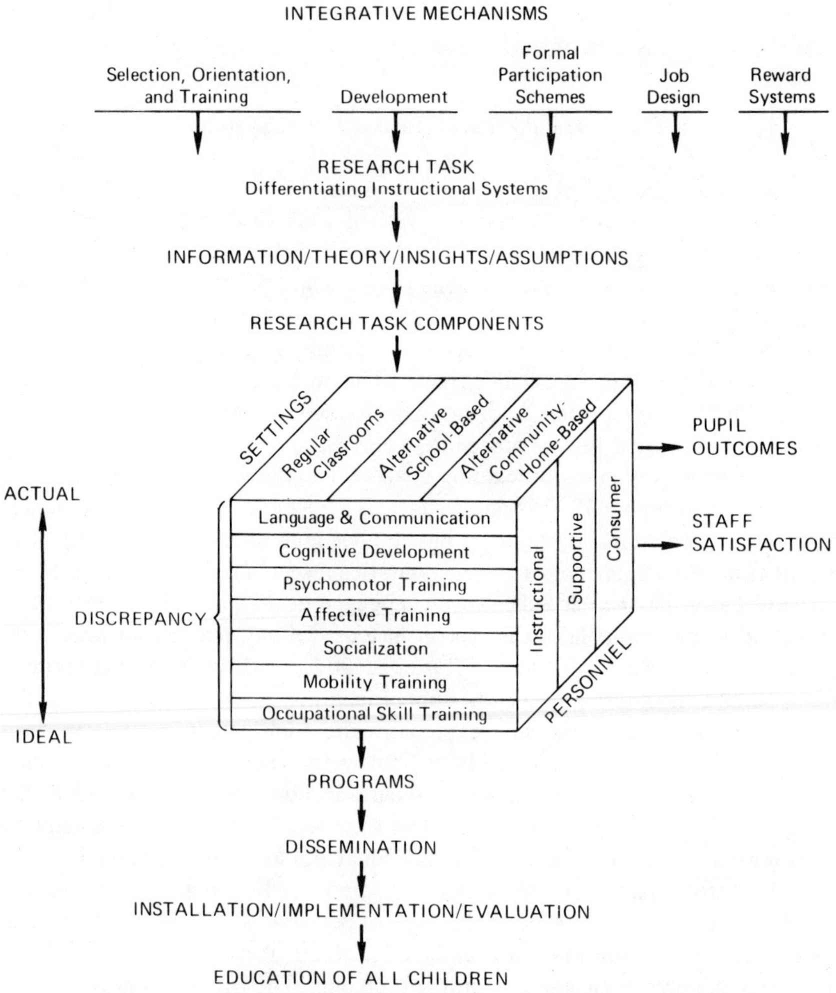

INTEGRATIVE MECHANISMS

Selection, Orientation, and Training	Development	Formal Participation Schemes	Job Design	Reward Systems
↓	↓	↓	↓	↓

RESEARCH TASK
Differentiating Instructional Systems

↓

INFORMATION/THEORY/INSIGHTS/ASSUMPTIONS

↓

RESEARCH TASK COMPONENTS

↓

PUPIL OUTCOMES

STAFF SATISFACTION

ACTUAL ↑

DISCREPANCY

IDEAL ↓

SETTINGS — Regular Classrooms — Alternative School-Based — Alternative Community-Home-Based

Language & Communication
Cognitive Development
Psychomotor Training
Affective Training
Socialization
Mobility Training
Occupational Skill Training

Instructional — Supportive — Consumer

PERSONNEL

↓

PROGRAMS

↓

DISSEMINATION

↓

INSTALLATION/IMPLEMENTATION/EVALUATION

↓

EDUCATION OF ALL CHILDREN

Figure 13-2. Research Task #1: Differentiating Instructional Systems. *Adapted from*: Proceedings of the Conference on Research Needs Related to the Development of Personnel to Serve the Handicapped; *Bureau of Education for the Handicapped, U.S. Office of Education, 1975.*

have implications for still other management mechanisms, such as for reward systems and supervision.

Research Task #2: Selection/Training/Utilization of Personnel

The second research task is derived from the work of Lilly. In his concept of special education as supportive services, he suggests that regular school instructional personnel should be recruited "who are competent as teachers and effective in interacting with their peers, without regard to present teaching assignment or program affiliation."[11]

The research conference on personnel utilization mentioned earlier provides additional rationale for a research task critical to the concept of special education as supportive services. The participants recommended that research on personnel utilization should focus on two priority needs. They were:

1. To determine the relationship of pupil outcomes to organizational atmosphere and alternative configurations of manpower utilization: The specific questions that were suggested were:
   What effect does the degree of openness in a school system and different staffing patterns have on student achievement?
   Do they affect teacher productivity?
   What are the relative cost-benefit ratios?
2. Develop and implement various teacher role models (such as the teacher as a program manager) and compare the efficacy of alternative models.[12]

In Figure 13–3 the research task is placed within the adapted model discussed earlier. Here all but three of the integrative mechanisms might be potentially affected. The first and most obvious management task is the recruitment, selection, and training of regular instructional staff as supportive service persons. Training can proceed only after clear competencies have been derived, and job design and reward systems have been devised. Both job design and reward systems should be a part of organizational development and formal participation schemes involving representatives of teacher associations or unions.

The training program should be based upon validated competencies. Certainly, part of this research task will involve assessing which combination of supportive service personnel functions affect higher levels of both teacher satisfaction and pupil achievement. Measures of the trainees' success and satisfaction will follow.

The other areas of management functioning will follow the implementation of the new services. They are communication and control, supervision, and management of conflict. Identifying and communicating responsibility and accountability will concern both students and parents alike. Supervision and negotiation of conflict is expected in most new programs where interpersonal contact is frequent and demanding of new behaviors.

Once results of new ways of utilization of personnel have been implemented and their effect on pupil and staff has been determined, decisions pertaining to dissemination and the remaining steps will follow. It should be noted that dissemination of innovations, especially one involving job design and re-

[11]Lilly, "A Training Based Model," p. 747.

[12]Proceedings of the Conference on Research Needs Related to the Development of Personnel to Serve the Handicapped. (Bureau of the Handicapped, U.S. Office of Education, March, 1975), pp. 55–56.

ward systems for teachers, will be watched closely for their "hidden agenda." Teacher bargaining officials and the participants in this research task will study dissemination and installation systemwide very carefully. The subsequent effects on the formal participation of teachers and organizational structure and design will be a major concern.

Research Task #3: Developing a Community Consensus on the Role of Special Education as Supportive Services

The need for establishing community support while setting new directions in education is a truism for educators today. Burlingame[13] and Kaye[14] have discussed both a rationale and a technology for assisting educational planners in ascertaining and influencing the community mood. Burlingame has noted that information was lacking for thwarting the critics of the 1960s. He indicates that they could not be refuted. We have little or no capacity to gather information that bore on their concerns "let alone point out any inaccuracies on what they thought they found in schools."[15] The change in leadership, he points out, is based upon societal issues: Who has the right to determine what constitutes legitimate social demands for educational services? Translating these unclear social mandates into technical proposals and extending rights of participation into educational decision-making is still unsettling. Unquestionably, an example is the issue of educational services versus treatment services which is under study by professionals and parents. It involves at least three human service systems: education, mental health, and public health.

Kaye's[16] research involves determining how a statewide problem-solving forum can be established and still can represent the total constituency of management personnel in the state. Using communication network analysis and multidimensional scaling of significant concepts identified by selected participants, she has been able to determine if a nominated sample of representatives are truly representative of the network of managers without the state. These procedures are still being replicated for the continued assessment of the perceptions of the entire network on key concepts that affect their own jobs, change, and service planning for handicapped children. This technology allows managers, through a large group and survey process, to assess professional or community awareness, position, and concerns. These, in turn, may affect reaching a consensus for guiding the management of the schools. This technology goes beyond community needs assessments, since it includes either endorsing a particular program or issue. Kaye's research provides a communication strategy for further analysis, for

---

[13]Burlingame, pp. 40–56.

[14]Kaye, "The Federal Role," *Assessing Communication Patterns*, 1976.

[15]Burlingame, pp. 43–56.

[16]Kaye, "The Federal Role," *Assessing Communication Patterns*, 1976.

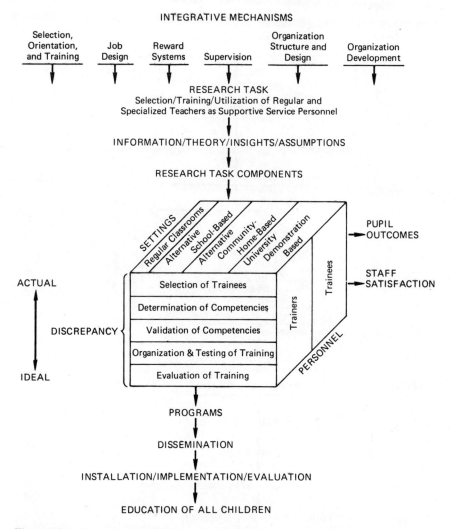

INTEGRATIVE MECHANISMS

Selection, Orientation, and Training | Job Design | Reward Systems | Supervision | Organization Structure and Design | Organization Development

RESEARCH TASK
Selection/Training/Utilization of Regular and
Specialized Teachers as Supportive Service Personnel

INFORMATION/THEORY/INSIGHTS/ASSUMPTIONS

RESEARCH TASK COMPONENTS

SETTINGS
Regular Classrooms
Alternative School-Based
Alternative Community-Based
Home-Based
University Based
Demonstration Based

PUPIL OUTCOMES

STAFF SATISFACTION

ACTUAL

DISCREPANCY

IDEAL

Trainees
Trainers
PERSONNEL

Selection of Trainees
Determination of Competencies
Validation of Competencies
Organization & Testing of Training
Evaluation of Training

PROGRAMS

DISSEMINATION

INSTALLATION/IMPLEMENTATION/EVALUATION

EDUCATION OF ALL CHILDREN

Figure 13-3. Research Task #2: Selection, Training, and Utilization of Personnel.

the validation of community sentiment and for the validation of a continuing communication channel that is manageable and organized for the study of its effectiveness. It also provides periodic checks for determining if subsequent programs or proposals are working, so that the management can adjust the program course without returning to the starting point.

In Figure 13–4, the third research task is presented. This task can be applied to an individual school building or to an entire state as it has already been described. Managers in and between each level of the school district will con-

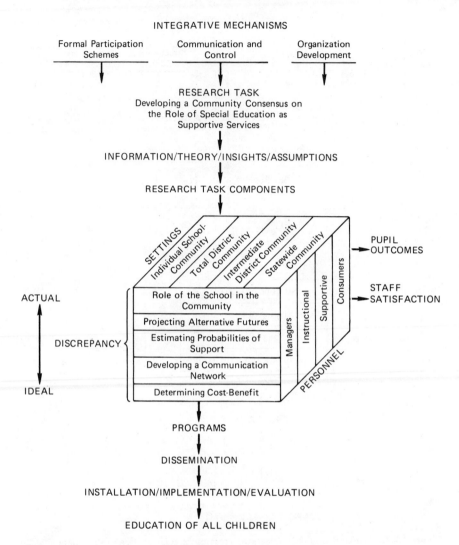

Figure 13-4. Research Task #3: Developing a Community Consensus.

sider the following integrative mechanisms: formal participation schemes, communications, and organizational development activities.

Determining a community consensus on the role of the school will be the concern of the research task presented here. Utilizing a futures perspective can provide the orientation for the consideration of the unknown as well as the known, and for the past as well as the present. This research task will not be complete without ascertaining support for the new direction and estimates of budget increases or decreases. All of the above will provide the major decision-making criteria for changing the structure and design of special education in the schools.

This research task could be described primarily as a formal joint professional and community problem-solving effort. It has been argued that specific technology has extended the process to affect other management activities designed for the maintenance and further development of the organization of the schools. Communication and organizational development are fundamental to organization growth. New communication channels with the consumers should hopefully increase the credibility and commitment of management and the instructional staff. Clearer mandates should also reduce the amount of guessing as to where and who supports the schools. They should also increase the efficiency of implementing the specific and desirable goals the community espouses. This research should also serve management in organizing their human resources in new ways to increase their capability to respond to new initiatives or deal with lingering problems. Hopefully, new alliances of teachers, managers, and consumers can restore a sense of community, of value, and of interdependency in the work toward common goals and projected annual targets.

SUMMARY

In this chapter, research was differentiated from evaluation. More importantly, the chapter was designed to emphasize the role of management in research and the effects of research on certain management functions. These management functions bring together the mission of schools with the needs and aspirations of the staff who work in schools. Three research tasks were presented that were representative of system development and applied research rather than of theory building and conclusion-oriented research.

The focus of research in education for management personnel has generally been on the teaching-learning process. Managers should continue to support research designed to increase the quality of instruction. Likewise, educators in leadership positions should examine their organizational structure, communication, and accountability measures as well as other integrative mechanisms for two major reasons:

First, leadership persons concerned with organizational development, organized audits, evaluation, and exploratory research need to identify inadequate performance and shed obsolete or, unproductive activities. Drucker[17] has noted that public service institutions in the absense of a market test are removed from the competitive context that forces private enterprise to abandon yesterday's activities or else suffer bankruptcy.

[17]Peter F. Drucker, "Managing the Public Service Institution," *The Public Interest* (1973), pp. 43–60.

Second, leadership persons need to examine their behavior in the changing, dynamic context of the American public school system. They will continue to be held accountable for the management of resources designed to increase the quality of school life for student and professional alike. Attention should be given to managing schools by managers lest others do it for them.

14

Financial Issues
in a Changing
Special Education
Service System

Considerations of the processes of leadership and change, which have been discussed in several previous chapters, cannot be complete without also recognizing the financial issues that interact in the process. Whatever happens by way of programmatic change, shifts in philosophy, or policies generating from legislation or the courts, regardless of the leadership processes that accompany such changes, the financial factors that may affect or be affected by the other changes need to be understood. The philosophical foundations behind the financial structures for all education, the alternative approaches for funding the delivery of special education services, and the implications of funding for the quantity or quality of programs should be considered.

THE SEARCH FOR EQUITY

An underlying principle of all educational finance that has particular bearing on the financial structure of special education is the perennially elusive concept of equity. The pursuit of equity must involve the recognition of two elements: (1) the fiscal resources from which education can be supported, and (2) the needs of any population of children. It is axiomatic that in attempting to finance education in general, neither the needs nor the resources can be expected to be evenly distributed throughout the populace[1]. Historically, we have been more active in confronting the inequality of *resources* than in addressing the problem of unequal *need*. The funding of education in general has been, by Constitutional establishment, the responsibility of each state. The states, to a greater or lesser degree, have, in turn, passed on the responsibility to the local community. However, each state has retained at least a portion of the financial obligation at the state, as opposed to the local, level. The opportunity is provided to compensate for differences in financial resources among local communities, by assuming varying proportions of the total costs to be paid from the state level, thereby enabling distribution of the differences across a broader base than if all funds were raised and spent locally. None of the specific formulas developed for implementing this equalization principle have succeeded in totally equalizing financial distribution, at least to the satisfaction of the various local interest groups who view their particular financial situation to be in need of adjustment.

A complex of factors, more political than economic, are responsible for the seemingly endless struggle for an acceptable equalization formula. The opposing political philosophies concerned with local autonomy versus centralization, working in interaction with factors of relative wealth and population to be educated, create a perennial tug-of-war over the issue of equity, resolved only in the case of full state funding. Only in Hawaii, where the entire state constitutes one single school district and taxing unit, has that aspect of the finance problem been settled.

In recent years the issue has been made prominent through court actions, both state and federal, although the particulars regarding specific cases in California[2], Texas[3], and New Jersey[4] have led to varying decisions in each case. The U.S. Supreme Court's ruling on the Rodriguez case has established that the right to education must remain a state concern, rather than a federal concern. Despite this, in each case there has been acknowledgement of the inequity of educational opportunity caused by support systems that have depended on local revenues. A final ruling of the California Supreme Court in late 1976 has upheld the 1971 decision that California's method of financing its schools, with major dependence on local property tax, is contrary to the state constitution.

The concept of inequity of *resources*, and the need to do something about it, then, has been well accepted, though not fully resolved. The concept of inequity of *need*, though, has only been partially confronted. Only recently have equalization formulas begun to reflect the fact that certain localities, that is, large urban centers, carry the burden of disproportionate numbers of children with

---

[1]Many of the concepts presented here have been published in an earlier draft, by Daniel D. Sage and David Riley, *The Bounty Hunters* (Syracuse, N.Y.: Human Policy Press, 1975).

[2]*Serrano v. Priest*, 483 P. 2d 1241, 1244 (Cal. 1971).

[3]*Rodriguez v. San Antonio Independent School District*, 337 F. Supp. 1280 (Wd. Tex. 1971).

[4]*Robinson v. Cahill*, 62 N.J. 473, 303 A. 2d (1973).

handicapping and educationally problematic conditions. Recent equalization formulas also reflect the fact that the cost of specialized programming in sparsely populated areas must be disproportionately high.

The gap between recognition of the problem and attempts at resolution has been even greater in dealing with inequity of need than in dealing with inequity of resources. Children with greater-than-average needs have been overlooked to such an extent that they have not received an *equal* share of the educational dollar, let alone their *fair* share as might be determined according to need. As pointed out by the National Legislative Conference Special Committee on School Finance:

> Equality does not mean identical treatment. The crucial value to be fostered by a system of public education is the opportunity to succeed, not the uniformity of success. While all are equal under the law, nature and other circumstances yield advantages to some, while handicapping others. Hence, as the President's Commission suggested: 'To offer children only equal education, disregarding differences in their circumstances is merely to maintain or perhaps even to magnify the relative effects of advantage and handicap. Equal treatment of unequals does not produce equality.' A concept of equal educational opportunity should reflect a sensitivity to the differences in costs and variations in interests and needs of those to be educated.[5]

In short, the only way to treat children equally is to disperse funds unequally to meet children's unequal needs. Most states have attempted to do just that. State laws and/or regulations have been designed to provide an additional amount of state aid funds to local school districts for services to special-need children above and beyond that provided for the general school population. While the specifics of the state funding methods are varied (each having certain advantages and disadvantages), all of the "distribution methods" concerned with special education funding are based on the assumption that such support must rest on a broader base than that used for general education. To elaborate, whatever combination of local, state, and federal financial support exists for the education of the mainstream of the population, that portion of the population defined as having special needs will require heavier support from the less localized levels of government. The rationale for this assumption is that

1. Children with special needs, by definition, are a minority group existing as a small but significant proportion of the whole population.
2. The exact proportion will vary significantly from one subcategory of special need to another, and from one location to another, without regard to local economic ability to provide support.
3. The cost of educational services to meet these needs, will be proportionately greater than the costs for children at large, based on an uncertain and varying ratio utilizing: (a) geographic locale, (b) subcategory of special need, and (c) the particular patterns of service delivery employed.

[5]Anthony Morley, et al., *A Legislator's Guide to School Finance* (Denver: Education Commission of the States, 1973).

COSTS OF SPECIAL EDUCATION SERVICES

Documentation of cost differentials has been provided by a number of studies, the most extensive "landmark" data being provided by Rossmiller, Hale, and Frohreich.[6] Their data, taken from actual expenditures in twenty-four school systems across five states, has demonstrated the degree to which per pupil expenditures in special education programs have exceeded those of regular school programs. They have revealed the exteme variability between systems in cost indices (ratio of special education per pupil expenditures to regular per pupil expenditures) within each disability category. These findings have pointed up the need for focusing on cost variance as a function of service delivery approach rather than focusing on disability category as the major determinant.

A number of more recent studies have attempted to address the issue of costs of varying service delivery approaches, but each has been somewhat limited. Clemmons[7] has examined direct and indirect costs across seven exceptional program categories in six delivery systems: regular classroom with consultant, regular classroom with itinerant teacher, regular classroom with resource room, part-time special classroom, self-contained special classroom, and homebound or hospital instruction. The sample includes only six Minnesota school districts and the indices generated by the data are limited in generalizability. Jones and Wilkerson[8] have reported a similar study involving only two Indiana systems. It primarily checks the index figures of the earlier Rossmiller data. The study has yielded confirming data regarding the extreme variability in program costs associated with differences in program approach.

Gaughan[9] utilized a different type of sample for examining the cost differentials between regular school programs and special education programs, it classified by type of handicap and type of service provided. This sample of 171 projects funded under Title VI-B of the Education for the Handicapped Act was drawn from a nationwide population of 1252 projects operating in 1972, and therefore constituted a sample of much more extensive scope than the studies previously mentioned. An additional rationale for using such a sample was the independent accounting of costs in such projects, as required by federal regula-

[6]Richard A. Rossmiller, J.A. Hale, and L.E. Frohreich, *Educational Programs for Exceptional Children: Resource Configuration and Cost* (Madison, Wisconsin: University of Wisconsin, Department of Educational Administration, 1970).

[7]A.L. Clemmons, "An Assessment of Cost Variation in Selected Exemplary Special Education Programs in Six Selected Minnesota School Districts" (Unpublished Doctoral Dissertation, University of New Mexico, 1974).

[8]Philip R. Jones and W.R. Wilkerson, *Special Education Program Cost Analysis* (Unpublished study conducted for Indiana Department of Public Instruction, Department of Educational Administration, Indiana University, 1972).

[9]Joseph P. Gaughan, "An Examination of Cost of Financing Special Education Services: A Comparison of Cost by Handicap and Educational Services" (Unpublished Doctoral Dissertation, Syracuse University, 1975).

tions, which could be expected to yield more definitive data than in locally funded programs. Nine disability categories and five service alternatives were examined with adequate data for analysis coming from 102 of the sampled projects. While certain categories were served by only one or two of the alternatives, examples were found of projects for the educable mentally retarded, learning disabled, and emotionally disturbed using all five alternatives. Results indicated that service costs increased as the service became more restrictive or segregated, and that among those handicapping conditions using more than three alternatives, the relationship between cost and service alternative was stronger than the relationship between cost and handicapping condition.

Mean cost indices, across all handicaps, expressed as a ratio to regular pupil costs at 1.00, were for diagnostic consultative service, 1.07; itinerant service, 1.48; resource service, 1.76; integrated special class, 1.95; and segregated special class, 2.49.

The major limitation in the applicability of these findings was the degree to which federal Part B projects were nonrepresentative of the programming status quo. There is reason to believe that such projects represent the cutting edge of innovation, or at least "best practice" as known by those operating them. They generally utilize extra resource inputs, since they are supported totally from outside dollars and are established for the purpose of extending existing services. While the expenditure profiles of these projects can then be expected to be relatively free of usual local budget constraints, and therefore atypical, they should provide an example of "what ought to be," given reasonable support availability.

Costs and Relation to Quality

Identification of the sources of excess costs and the quantitative magnitude of differences in the costs of special education services have been the major focus of studies to date.

Attempts to draw relationships between cost and quality have been few and limited in scope. However, as competition for scarce financial resources has increased, the accountability issue has begun to shift from expenditure levels to the quality of services provided. One of the major constraints keeping policy makers from being more responsive to high-cost educational needs has been the lack of sound data about the relationship between input and output where these services are provided. Although pressure is now mounting, requiring special educators to better evaluate program quality, commitment to such accounting has been low and appropriate tools for accounting have been nonexistent. Wolfensberger and Glenn have stated that

> Operating a service agency was often equated with rendering a service; and both were equated with rendering quality services. Concern with the cost of a service in

relation to its benefit was rarely expressed. One reason for this is probably the fact that human managers considered it inappropriate to put dollar price tags on human service benefits.[10]

An elementary effort at providing data on the relationship between cost and quality of special education programs is found in a study by Rice which examines a number of cost and program quality indicators in a sample of nine of the largest BOCES special education programs in New York. The cost factors include (1) actual per pupil expenditures, (2) a cost index derived by comparing special education expenditures to regular per pupil expenditures in the same systems, (3) a tax effort index, and (4) an adjusted special education cost index, taking into consideration the tax effort in the component districts of each BOCES.[11]

The quality indicators selected in this study are a departure from traditional measures, and reflect a contemporary view of one general indicator: the degree to which a system practices the doctrine of least restrictive alternative. Four specific indices have constituted this global concept, (1) an exclusion index, based on the proportion of children placed outside the local public programs, (2) an inclusion index, based on the proportion of *severely* handicapped to other handicapped children served, (3) a normalization index, based on a standardized assessment instrument[12], and (4) a mainstreaming index, based on the proportion of students attending integrated as opposed to segregated programs in the system.

Conclusions drawn from the relationship between these cost and quality factors suggest that systems having higher cost indices tend to also have higher exclusion rates, a lower rating on the presence of normalizing experiences for pupils, and less mainstreamed services. These observations lend support to the idea that services provided in least restrictive environments tend to be less expensive. The problem in interpreting this observation and using it as a basis for firm conclusions lies in the uncertainty of whether these expensive, segregative services can possibly be handled in any other way. In both the Gaughan and the Rice study we must assume that the severity of handicaps in the populations represented have been randomly distributed across the systems studied and that a choice of whether to utilize a more or less restrictive programming alternative has been an open one. If in fact the system using a more expensive, more restrictive alternative has done so because that system has had an unusual group of children with more severe needs, then the significance of the relationship between cost

[10]Wolf Wolfensberger and Linda Glenn, *PASS: Program Analysis of Service Systems; a Method for the Quantitative Evaluation of Human Services. Volume I: Handbook*. Second Edition. (Toronto: National Institute on Mental Retardation, 1973), p. 2.

[11]Russell G. Rice, Jr., *A Cost–Quality Analysis of Special Education Programs* (Unpublished Doctoral Dissertation, Syracuse University, 1975).

[12]Wolf Wolfensberger and Linda Glenn, *PASS: Program Analysis of Service Systems; a Method for the Quantitative Evaluation of Human Services. Volume 2: Field Manual*. Second Edition (Toronto: National Institute on Mental Retardation, 1973).

and quality and the relevance of the quality indicator is lost. Since the sample in these and similar studies is limited, the interpretation of the observations must be made with caution.

A broader examination of cost-quality issues has been reported by the Pennsylvania Department of Education. In this study quality was measured with (1) achievement tests, (2) a social maturity instrument, and (3) observation of practices rated by a specially developed list of quality indicators. The sample was a randomly selected group of classes identified by disability category listed as educable mentally retarded (148 classes), socially and emotionally disturbed (68 classes), trainable mentally retarded (65 classes), physically handicapped (44 classes), and brain injured (33 classes). The study sought to answer questions regarding (1) the relationship between costs and student progress with basic skills and social competence, (2) the relationship between cost and quality as measured by ratings based on classroom observation, interviews with teachers and supervisors, and screening of pupil records, and (3) costs of various delivery systems within each category of exceptionality.[13]

Results indicated that while students showed significant progress in both basic skills and social maturity, and while quality measures on programs were generally good, costs did not consistently correlate with either quality measures or output measures. The analysis of varying delivery system costs was hampered by the fact that full-time self-contained special classes constituted the bulk of programs studied in each of the five categories. It appeared that this model was also the most expensive for the socially and emotionally disturbed, and for the physically handicapped. For the educable mentally retarded, the work study special classes were more expensive, and for the brain injured the model using a special class with regular class placement for selected academic work was most expensive. For the trainable retarded, there were too few cases of other than conventional self-contained full-time classes to allow a meaningful analysis. The few cases using the resource or consulting teacher model showed that this approach had a lower average cost. However, the real meaning of these observations was again obscured by the fact that the unit of analysis was the class, rather than the pupil, with only rough approximations of the number of pupils actually enrolled in each class. While state guidelines have required certain minimums and maximums, the latitude allowed and the provision for exceeding limits when using paraprofessional aides has prevented any conclusive determination of actual per pupil cost from this study.

The per pupil costs for each category, with all types of service models aggregated, have been reported for each of the Intermediate Unit systems involved in the study. These have yielded the same extremely wide range of re-

[13]Robert B. Hayes, John G. Cober, and Robert N. Reynolds, *Special Education Quality Cost-Effectiveness Study* (Harrisburg, Pa.: Division of Research, Bureau of Information Systems, Pennsylvania Department of Education, 1976).

ported costs that have been found in other studies, with the most expensive system in most categories reporting a cost three to four times as great as the least expensive system. In EMR programs the range of per pupil costs was less dramatic (from $1041 to $2820), but in others (that is, TMR, with a range of $1429 to $5660) the variance between school systems was striking.

Additional studies concerned with cost determination have been reviewed by Bernstein and others, who point out many of the problems in the attempts that have been made. Particularly noted is the fact that most studies involve an accounting procedure applied to an historical data base, but with past school accounting practices that have not been designed to yield the kind of data needed. In suggesting directions for future research they have posed four questions:

1. What is the relationship between the mix of resources used, costs for special education programs, and educational outcomes of the students served?
2. What are the critical factors that affect costs?
3. What are the simplest and least expensive means of isolating, recording, and monitoring special education expenditures?
4. How can accounting systems that record past expenditures be used to estimate current and future costs?[14]

They have further suggested that the field has been preoccupied with collecting data that turns out to be of very limited use, since the process of cost determination has been inadequately developed. They state that future attempts to design a cost accounting system should include a clear understanding of the type of information needed and the feasibility of obtaining it.

The implications that can be drawn from all cost studies on special education to date are as follows:

1. A precise and systematic means of accounting for special education costs, to a degree that permits valid comparisons to be made, is yet to be developed.
2. The breadth of variance in costs necessitates a means of gaining some precision, in order to adequately account for that variance.
3. Various programming approaches yield varying costs and may carry related quality implications.
4. Leadership in promoting change in programming approaches must take into consideration cost and quality factors, making use of the tentative evidence now available, but placing high priority on the pursuit of better evidence.

FUNDING APPROACHES FOR SPECIAL EDUCATION SERVICES

The nature of educational finance in this country, as opposed to most other countries, depends to a very small degree on federal support sources. "In 1970–71 in the nation as a whole 52% of school revenue was provided by local sources, 41%

---

[14]Charles D. Bernstein, Michael W. Kirst, William T. Hartman, and Rudolph S. Marshall, *Financing Educational Services for the Handicapped* (Reston, Va.: The Council for Exceptional Children, 1976), p. 12.

came from state sources and 7% from the federal government.''[15] Even with the massive increases in federal funding of categorical programs in the last decade, the percentage of the total coming from that level remains small.

In reacting to the issue of federal support versus federal intervention, Cronin points out that in 1976, less than 10 percent came from the federal level.[16] However, it should be noted that among the states, the variance on the proportion of federal contribution is rather high, primarily due to categorical funding associated with economic disadvantagement and federal facilities impact aid. For example, according to data compiled by the Education Commission of the States[17] for 1972–73, a number of southern states received federal support for public elementary and secondary schools that amounted to 12 to 17 percent of their total revenues, with Mississippi showing 26.9 percent for a national high. Other states (for example, Connecticut, Iowa, Michigan, Wisconsin) claimed under 4 percent federal support.

The proportions of federal revenue supporting special education have also been, until recent years, of relatively minor magnitude. While the passage of P.L. 94-142 in 1975 was heralded with the expectation of significant increases in federal financial support, the actual impact has, thus far, been modest. The allocation of federal dollars to the states and local systems is based on a formula using an increasing percentage of the average per-pupil expenditures nationally for *non-handicapped* children. The five per cent figure for 1978 allocation is to gradually increase to a ceiling of 40 percent in 1982 and thereafter. It must be recognized, however, that since the per-pupil costs for the handicapped will average at least twice the costs for the non-handicapped, the potential for federal sharing of the costs will remain, on the average, not more than 20 percent of the total. There has been much argument for amendment of the law to bring the eventual 1982 figure into effect much earlier, based on the logic of greater need to meet "start-up" costs. There has also been the expectation that Congressional appropriations will fail to keep pace with even relatively modest statutory authorizations. It is the consensus of most observers that although the federal impact on policy through regulation may become significant, the financial impact will probably remain limited.

In special education, as with the total scope of public education, the major consideration has been the manner in which the state has distributed funds for partially or totally equalizing the cost differentials between regular and special education services for local school systems. The various models for state support

[15]National Educational Finance Project, *Future Directions for School Financing* (Gainesville, Florida: NEFP, 1971), p. 9.

[16]Joseph M. Cronin, "The Federal Takeover: Should the Junior Partner Run the Firm?," *Phi Delta Kappan*, 57 (1976), p. 499.

[17]Handicapped Children's Education Project, *Financing Education Programs for Handicapped Children* (Denver: Education Commission of the States, 1973).

have been described by Bernstein and others,[18] Thomas,[19] Marinelli,[20] and by Sage and Riley,[21] and the issues relative to each approach have been debated. In an effort to focus on the implications for leadership and change in the field, the major points will be reviewed here.

Three general models for the distribution of extra funds for special-need children can be identified among the many varieties of plans throughout the fifty states. These can be best classified as (1) teacher unit reimbursement, (2) pupil unit reimbursement, and (3) special program reimbursement. Variations within each of these general classifications are in use, and will be described.

Funding by the Teacher Unit

Formulas for disbursement of state financial aid to local school districts are in some states entirely a function of approved teacher (or other personnel) units. In such a method, the state makes certain assumptions regarding the "reasonable" number of specialized personnel needed, given the size and characteristics of the local community, and, upon evidence that such personnel are engaged in approved programs, it reimburses districts with a certain amount per employee unit. The amount may be a flat rate per unit or a percentage of salary (up to an established maximum).

The teacher unit formula has the advantageous characteristic of closely associating financial support with the service provided. Since in most education budgets instructional personnel costs constitute the major proportion of all costs (60–80 percent), it is not difficult to calculate a formula that will cause the local system to be financially aided at a rate which "reduces the pain" of employing personnel who, in terms of pupil–teacher ratio, would be regarded as expensive. States using a teacher unit basis for all general support can easily adapt the same concept for special education.

The teacher unit system requires considerable regulatory activity by the state to determine the quantity of appropriate units, the parameters of permissible teacher–pupil ratio, and all other aspects of service delivery which are constituents of both costs and benefits. To the extent that state regulatory activity may be desirable (that is, to reinforce selected programmatic alternatives) the teacher unit support formula can be quite effective. It can, however, constrain local innovation. Given the variety of current and newly developing program-

---

[18]Bernstein, et al., *Financing Educational Services for the Handicapped*, pp. 25–26.

[19]Sister Marie Angele Thomas, "Finance: Without Which There Is No Special Education," *Exceptional Children*, 39 (1973), pp. 475–80.

[20]Joseph J. Marinelli, "Financing the Education of Exceptional Children," in *Public Policy and the Education of Exceptional Children*, eds., Frederick J. Weintraub, et al. (Reston, Va.: The Council for Exceptional Children, 1975), pp. 151–94.

[21]Sage and Riley, *The Bounty Hunters*, pp. 11–13.

ming alternatives, the increasing variety of possible staffing approaches, and the wide geographically based range of salaries and other cost factors, a unit system providing a flat rate for each employed person falls far short of equitably compensating excess costs.

Funding by the Pupil Unit

The more commonly employed mechanism for supporting excess costs is based on the pupil unit—either average daily attendance or average daily membership (enrollment). Typically, states using the pupil unit approach have established a series of maximum costs associated with each of the disabling conditions, for which reimbursement takes place upon verification that such expenditures have been incurred. The varying ceiling rate normally reflects the assumed differential in pupil–teacher ratio between the regular school program and the adequate instructional programming for the "condition" in question. Unfortunately, such ceilings, established as absolute dollar amounts, require frequent revision as general costs fluctuate. In addition, at no time do such ceilings approach an accurate representation of real cost figures for the wide range of possible service approaches for a given type of disabled child.

Funding by the Weighted Pupil Unit

One attempt to partially deal with these inadequacies is the variation on the pupil unit approach which uses a weighting formula for the average daily attendance (ADA) computation of the child with disabilities. This system has been in existence in some states for some time (for example, in Idaho where the ADA of children with disabilities is multiplied by 300 percent) and it was adopted in New York in 1974 through amendment of the education law. The New York version provides for a weighting of 1.25 for students defined as having "special needs" by virtue of academic underachievement, a larger weighting (2.0) for students defined as having "handicapping conditions," and an entirely different approach to funding for children defined as having "severely handicapping conditions."

The choice of the 2.0 index for most of the children who would be classified as handicapped reflects the data reported by Rossmiller, Hale, and Frohreich. Cost indices reported by the twenty-four representative school systems (high quality systems) varied widely across the ten "exceptional" categories for which data were collected, but an average of these indices, weighted in accordance with anticipated prevalence rates, approximates the 2.0 figure.

Any such system of weighting ADA has the merit of returning to local school systems the financial incentive for at least identifying those pupils in need of special education services. The assumption is made that identification will lead to service delivery, especially if regulatory mechanisms are employed so that "credit" for identified pupils is earned only when service, meeting some standard of acceptability, is provided. The flaw in the equitable operation of such accounting is that the complexity and intensity (and therefore the cost) of service judged appropriate for a given handicapped pupil can vary dramatically.

This variation is demonstrated in the Rossmiller data, which shows considerable variation among categories of handicap even when averaged across the twenty-four school systems. For example, costs ranged from a speech handicapped index of 1.18, an educable mentally retarded index of 1.87, to a physically handicapped index of 3.64. To the extent that this variation is uncontrolled, a single index (that is, 2.0) becomes dysfunctional. School systems could vigorously identify and provide minimally acceptable programs for all those pupils requiring a relatively low cost (less than 2.0) and give little attention to the relatively expensive services, while chalking up ADA funds on the basis of the established index.

Funding by Differentiated Index

The aforementioned discrepancy suggests that a differentiated index, based on available data relating to realistic costs for different categories of handicapped pupils, might provide an equitable means of supporting services. The differentiated index would be more or less equivalent to the formula used in many states that differentiates among special education "labels" in setting ceiling excess cost reimbursements. However, experience has shown that such differentiation, given the looseness of some of our categories, allows manipulation by school systems. Children can be easily classified into the label that offers the most advantageous financial return, with insufficient regard for the most advantageous program of services.

The differentiations in cost indices among disability categories revealed in the Rossmiller study are presumed to be based on differences in intensity of service need. The Rossmiller data also demonstrate wide variations within each category. Among the twenty-four systems reporting, programs for the visually handicapped showed indices ranging from a low of 1.05 to a high of 11.45. Programs for the emotionally disturbed ranged from 1.58 to 11.64, and for the auditorily handicapped from 1.05 to 5.88. It should be noted that the extremes in each program category, that is, the high cost programs, were not a matter of a particular school system tending to provide heavily supported programs across the board. Rather, the reporting of any given cost index for a category of program was largely a function of the level or intensity of the program provided. The school system reporting a cost index of 11.64 for emotionally disturbed and the other system reporting only 1.58 for the same category should not be considered to be referring to samples from the same population of pupils nor to comparable definitions of service. While the range is much less pronounced in other categories (for instance, in the speech handicapped), the problem, to a lesser degree, still exists there.

Funding by Special Program Reimbursement

The problems previously discussed emphasize the need for a financial system more directly related to actual needs and appropriate practices. Such a system would focus support on specific services provided. The principle of support for specific services has been implemented in a few states, usually as an extension of the pupil unit concept.

California law recognizes that in the case of at least one classification of pupil, the educationally handicapped, a great variety of possible services might be appropriate, each incurring quite different levels of cost. California law defines the educationally handicapped as those pupils who, though neither mentally retarded nor physically handicapped, have learning disabilities as a result of neurological impairments and/or emotional disturbances which render them unable to profit from regular classroom instruction. A differential excess cost reimbursement ceiling has been established to provide equitably for the variety of possible services that local districts might wish to offer these pupils. The services include special self-contained classrooms, learning disability group instruction supplementing regular classroom attendance, and home instruction.

Florida has attached a similar addition to the weighted pupil unit, first assigning various weights to clinical disability categories, but drawing distinctions between applicable weights for a given category on the basis of whether the service provided is a full-time special class or a part-time itinerant resource service. This is an attempt to reflect the relative intensity of service need and service cost, recognizing that children bearing the same "label" may still have different needs, in terms of intensity of service.

This procedure has led to the establishment of fifteen different approved programs with cost factors ranging from 2.3 to 15.0, using the full-time equivalency (FTE) of student time in each program as the basis for revenue allocation. If the weights assigned to the various programs accurately reflect actual cost differentials, such a system has the potential of providing the most precise and fair means of balancing revenue generation with cost expenditures, thereby achieving maximum equity. However, the realization of this potential depends on conscientious assignment of pupils to proper programs and on scheduling time in programs according to true needs and careful accounting of the resulting schedules.

Observers of the implementation of the Florida FTE system have expressed concern that a number of problems have ensued.

Marinelli[22] has indicated that since revenue generated is so directly connected to time pupils spend in various programs, the procedure may entice school administrators to make decisions about placements and schedules with more attention to the cost weighting of the program than to the most appropriate service for the individual child. Furthermore, since the system pays only for direct teacher to pupil instructional time, and does not provide for other supportive services, it fails to adequately encourage the use of the consultative model, to provide for supervision services, or to cover the actual costs of itinerant services where travel and preparation time are a significant part of the teacher's responsibility. While many of these criticisms can be rectified by adjustments to the regulations governing the FTE accounting procedure, there is good reason to question whether the system is so administratively cumbersome that it yields diminishing returns.

PROBLEMS INHERENT IN SPECIAL FUNDING

It is axiomatic that any procedure, regardless of its intent to provide fair and equitable distribution of funds, will be manipulated toward garnering the greatest possible share of the available dollars. Since the adoption of the FTE funding procedure, instances have arisen in Florida where state audits of local systems have led to charges of improper classification and placement of children and to charges of unauthorized accrual of state support funds. This is not inconsistent with other observations of legislative and policy changes in recent years which have shown that the introduction of an incentive or requirement for identifying individual handicapped persons (to procure funds or to meet a quota) has usually led to rather reckless labeling. The process, sometimes characterized as "bounty hunting," has caused inappropriate and unnecessary stigmatization of persons who, under other circumstances, would not be viewed as "special." This points up the persistent dilemma of opposing benefits: identification as a means of securing service versus nonidentification as a means of maintaining status as a "normal" citizen. This has been particularly noticeable in the case of a recent Congressional mandate ensuring that handicapped preschool children would have an opportunity to participate in Head Start programs operated under federal funds in local communities. The establishment of a 10 percent "quota," as an administrative means of implementing that mandate, apparently led to a situation in which many children, who otherwise would not have been identified as handicapped, were officially "listed" and perceived primarily as a function of the quota.

---

[22]Marinelli, "Financing Education of Exceptional Children," p. 178.

Bernstein, and others[23] have outlined a number of important decision criteria to be considered when planning for optimal programming and fiscal support. They point out that tradeoffs among the criteria will invariably be necessary, but to the extent possible:

1. A special education delivery system should be equitable. To accomplish this, adjustments are necessary to compensate between rich and poor districts, and between children with greater and lesser need for extra resources. The gross level of funding must be sufficient to permit these adjustments.
2. A special education delivery system should be comprehensive. It must provide financially not only for all kinds of exceptional conditions, but for all aspects of instructional and supporting functions, such as for personnel of all types, for materials, for equipment, and for transportation. If a system fails to provide for all personnel components (that is, educational, psychological, medical, and social services), and if it fails to provide for all instructional activities (that is, academics, vocational activities, work study, work experiences), the benefits to be expected will be severely constrained.
3. A special education delivery system should be flexible. The funding mechanism should allow for fluctuations in costs and for the introduction of innovation without suffering financially. In this respect, funding formulas tied to actual expenditures will tend to be more flexible than straight sum or unit allocation systems.
4. A special education delivery system should promote accountability. The chief issue is to fix the responsibility for the proper use of funds and provide a means of monitoring whether the responsibility is being fulfilled, by tracing the allocations and expenditures.
5. A special education delivery system should strive to be cost-effective. Cost-effectiveness depends on many other criteria, particularly flexibility and the capability of responding dynamically when need for change or encouragement of new programs is indicated.
6. A special education delivery system should be compatible with the total educational finance system. While noncategorical funding provides built in compatibility, categorical funding does not in itself imply that the systems cannot be compatible. The compatibility of the special and general finance systems is most crucial where attainment of least restrictive alternative programming is the goal. On the other hand, while such compatibility cannot guarantee quality in programming, it must be considered a prerequisite.
7. A special education delivery system should not be in conflict with the educational policies of the state. That is, consistency between programming goals and funding goals is crucial. To assure such consistency, overall coordinated planning must occur so that curriculum policies, organizational approaches, and funding structures are developed together.
8. A special education delivery system should avoid needless complexity. While the solution to balanced and equitable funding is an extremely complex issue, it should be possible to develop an accounting system which, in its everyday operation, is relatively manageable. The problem lies in the need for a system that has sufficient control to assure that planned intentions regarding service and fiscal support are carried out, yet which does not cause the controls to over-

[23]Bernstein, et al., *Finanacing Educational Services,* pp. 34–38.

whelm the system. The compromise between desirable simplicity and necessary regulation, as with all the other criteria mentioned above, will require careful planning and sound judgment to strike an optimal balance.

AN OPTIMAL SOLUTION TO SPECIAL EDUCATION SERVICE FUNDING

At the present state, finance of programs for the handicapped has been tied primarily to either the individual client (the pupil) or to the professional (the teacher). Attempts to tie funds to the program have been primitive, at best. The lack of definitive research on the costs associated with specific aspects of service delivery leaves policy makers with an insufficient data base for connecting funding to actual services. Yet, if such connections could be made, the benefits would be significant. The Florida FTE approach probably comes closer than any other approach to the optimal solution. However, it still is connected too much to disability categories and it is too limited in its connection to possible alternatives of instructional and supportive services. To improve upon that system, it would be necessary to

1. determine, through a study of a cross section of exemplary, comprehensive services, the actual costs of providing optimal services to meet any handicapped child's needs.

    This would entail a study across not only the identifiable clinical categories of children (as done in the Rossmiller study) but, more importantly, across each type of service provision deemed most appropriate within and among the clinical categories.

    As an example, an analysis is needed which examines the cost factors in providing a) consultant service to regular teachers, b) a resource teacher for delivery of both direct instruction (part time) for children with disabilities, and also a consultant service, c) a part-time special class structure, d) a full-time self-contained special class and so on. Such a study might be concerned with each of the alternatives as applicable to hearing impaired children, but also as applicable to emotionally disturbed children, to mentally retarded children, and probably to every other identifiable category. It is anticipated that the results of such an analysis would demonstrate the importance of associating cost to the particular service, and the minimal relevance of the clinical category.

2. establish a schedule, in accordance with the previous data, which would set forth average costs per child for each alternative service. Such a schedule could also reflect the range of costs which might be within reasonable, though broad, limits. It would be necessary to employ an adjustment index to allow for cost differentiation that operates strictly as a function of geographic region.

3. apply the cost schedule as a means of determining the total appropriation for a school system or other major population catchment unit, computed as a function of projected numbers of children and types of services to be delivered. The purpose of this procedure is to set a ceiling on imprudent expenditure while providing a pool of financial resources that would provide the most appropriate service to suit particular individual need.

4. distribute appropriated funds on the basis of documented actual services that have been provided. This would not require identification of specific children, but rather, the identification of each specific service designed to aid handicapped children in general. Usually this service would be manifested as personnel employed, but it would also include materials, contracts, and transportation. Administration and audit of the reimbursement claims would require the implementation of certain regulatory standards regarding types and design of approvable services, but these standards could permit flexibility in choice of the intensity (and therefore cost) of the service any individual child is to receive. The major objective of the procedure would be to tie financial support more directly to units of service, after delivery has been documented, with limits imposed only by a total allocation based on population and a projected cost schedule.

CONCLUSION

In order for a special education programming structure that fully embraces the concepts advanced throughout the book to be developed, it would be necessary to move to a total funding system that incorporates a recognition of varying need along an entire continuum of service alternatives for *all* children, not just the handicapped. Such a change would move away from the traditional categorical funding that has been the mainstay of special education service development. It has been generally conceded that categorical funding has promoted the isolation of exceptional children. Isolation, stigmatization, and all the attendant drawbacks have been tolerated because services have typically not been instituted unless earmarking of funds has come first. However, if the categorization of funding is attached to *services delivered*, not *children identified*, the benefits would be maximized and the negative consequences diminished. Likewise, the risks inherent in a move to entirely noncategorical funding, where school systems would be free to "short change" exceptional children, can be minimized by a strict accounting of the use of funds.

Marinelli has pointed out that the "purpose of any educational funding system should be its concern for providing economic resources to back up the assessed individual needs of each child."[24] This suggests that the kinds of resources which, through earmarking, have made possible appropriate services for the handicapped, should also be available to non-handicapped children who, from time to time, will also benefit from special services. As the ideology of services for the handicapped in least restrictive environments becomes realized, the continuum of services for all children, with appropriate financial resources, should also become possible. The minimizing of distinction between the normal and the handicapped, in terms of program, should be coincident with the minimizing of distinction between resources supporting the programs. It may be

[24]Marinelli, "Financing Education of Exceptional Children," p. 181.

argued that decategorization of programs must precede the decategorization of funds, since until a full service guarantee is available to all, the handicapped are vulnerable. On the other hand, it may be argued that until funds are decategorized a full continuum of services for every child in accordance with need will not be realized. The task for the leadership of the field is to bring about this dual evolution by sequencing the policy changes so that needs are identified, resources are committed, and programs are implemented more or less simultaneously, and with least possible emphasis on compartmentalized classification.

Index